"This compact volume contains a weal
sion of the characteristics of narrative
in which the narratives are set and canonical connections that include connections to
the Gospels. Thoughtful interactive questions and study resources could be used in
classroom and assignment work, making the volume valuable for professors as well.
It is accessible and well prepared. Beginning and more advanced students will benefit
from Schnittjer's work."

—**Lissa M. Wray Beal**, professor of Old Testament, Wycliffe College, Toronto

"Gary Schnittjer has written a concise, informative study of the Old Testament narrative literature that will serve as an ideal text for courses covering these books. In addition to its clear and engaging style, the volume is enhanced by numerous reader-friendly outlines, charts, tables, maps, and sketches. The 'Ancient Connections' sections are another helpful feature of the book, for they place the literature in its historical-cultural context and help the narratives come alive. In this way the author reminds us that God revealed timeless truths in the real world of ancient Israel. I highly recommend this book for those who want to know more about the true stories of the Old Testament."

—**Robert B. Chisholm Jr.**, chair and senior professor of
Old Testament studies, Dallas Theological Seminary

"*Old Testament Narrative Books* offers a penetrating and engaging entrée into this challenging corpus of biblical literature. With the carefulness of a seasoned scholar, Schnittjer situates each of the Historical Books in their ancient Near Eastern context without compromising their unique voice and character as biblical revelation."

—**Stephen Coleman**, dean of biblical and theological studies and associate professor
of Old Testament and biblical languages, Westminster Theological Seminary

"By focusing on the ancient context and biblical connections each book has with the overarching narrative of the Bible, this book situates each Old Testament narrative book in its context in an understandable way. Schnittjer successfully paints with a broad brush to provide engaging overviews of each book, while also demonstrating the payoff of careful reading and attention to detail. The connections Schnittjer makes to the gospel of Jesus and to life today, as well as the thoughtful questions he poses, are sure to engage readers who desire to bring their knowledge of Scripture to bear on modern life."

—**Denise Flanders**, assistant professor of biblical studies, Taylor University

"Schnittjer's *Old Testament Narrative Books* is an exceptionally readable, enjoyable, and helpful introduction to what English Bibles generally call the Historical Books. Schnittjer brings literary sophistication and canonical sensitivity to the task of explaining each text so that readers learn to read each book as a narrative whole."

—**Michelle Knight**, assistant professor of Old Testament and Semitic languages, Trinity Evangelical Divinity School

"Gary Schnittjer's *Old Testament Narrative Books* is a great addition to any catalog of works examining Israel's conquest through the restoration period. Explained within the theological story of redemption, it is extremely user-friendly, being filled with sketches of the author's making, relevant insights on ancient Near Eastern culture, and considerations toward practical Christian formation. Students of the Scriptures in both the church and the classroom will deepen their understanding of OT history, individual historical books, and love of God through this work."

—**Eric C. Redmond**, professor of Bible, Moody Bible Institute

"Gary Schnittjer once again guides readers through the Old Testament story in this trustworthy textbook. *Old Testament Narrative Books* chronologically introduces nine biblical books from the conquest to the restoration. With his signature literary approach, Professor Schnittjer delightfully highlights dischronological narratives, extended echo effects, and the narrative shaping of each book. Every chapter offers insightful connections—to the Bible, the gospel, and life—accompanied by substantial interpretive overviews and closed with interactive questions for students."

—**Kenneth C. Way**, professor of Old Testament and Semitics, Talbot School of Theology, Biola University

"Schnittjer's *Old Testament Narrative Books* is much more than a survey of the historical literature of the Old Testament. Combining literary, historical, cultural, intertextual, and theological insights, this work offers a deep and rich reading of these books. The church needs a fresh reminder of the theological and practical relevance of the story of the Old Testament, and Schnittjer has provided a valuable resource for moving us in that direction."

—**Gary Yates**, professor of Old Testament, Liberty University School of Divinity

OLD TESTAMENT
NARRATIVE BOOKS

Gary Edward Schnittjer AND *Mark L. Strauss*

SERIES EDITORS

OLD TESTAMENT NARRATIVE BOOKS

— THE ISRAEL STORY —

Gary Edward Schnittjer

SCRIPTURE CONNECTIONS

ACADEMIC
BRENTWOOD, TENNESSEE

To V & J

אשרי העם שיהוה אלהיו

CONTENTS

LIST OF ABBREVIATIONS

AB   Anchor Bible

ABC   Albert K. Grayson. *Assyrian and Babylonian Chronicles*. Texts from Cuneiform Sources 5. Reprint. Winona Lake, IN: Eisenbrauns, 2000. First published 1975 by J. J. Augustin (Locust Valley, NY).

ABD   David Noel Freedman, et al., eds. *Anchor Bible Dictionary*. 6 vols. New York: Doubleday, 1992.

AL   William L. Moran. *The Amarna Letters*. Baltimore: Johns Hopkins University Press, 1992.

ANE   Amélie Kuhrt. *Ancient Near East, c. 3000–330 BC*. 2 vols. New York: Routledge, 1995.

ANET   James B. Pritchard, ed. *Ancient Near Eastern Texts Relating to the Old Testament*. 2nd ed. Princeton: Princeton University Press, 1969.

AOTC   Apollos Old Testament Commentary

ARAB   Daniel David Luckenbill. *Ancient Records of Assyria and Babylonia*. 2 vols. Reprint. London: Histories & Mysteries of Man, 1989. First published 1926–27 by University of Chicago Press (Chicago).

ARI   Albert Kirk Grayson. *Assyrian Royal Inscriptions*. 2 vols. Weisbaden: Otto Harrassowitz, 1972–76.

AT   Author's translation

BBR   *Bulletin for Biblical Research*

BDB   Francis Brown, S. R. Driver, and Charles A Briggs. *A Hebrew Lexicon of the Old Testament*. Reprint with corrections. Oxford: Clarendon, 1951. First published by Oxford: Clarendon, 1906.

BFE   Mordechai Cogan. *Bound for Exile: Israelites and Judeans Under Imperial Yoke*. Jerusalem: Carta, 2013.

BOTCHB   Baker Old Testament Commentary: Historical Books

BSac   *Bibliotheca Sacra*

CAD   *The Assyrian Dictionary of the Oriental Institute of the University of Chicago*. Chicago: The Oriental Institute of the University of Chicago, 1956–2006.

CBQ   *Catholic Biblical Quarterly*

CC   Concordia Commentary

CLLBH   Avi Hurvitz et al. *A Concise Lexicon of Late Biblical Hebrew*. Leiden: Brill, 2014.

COS   William W. Hallo and K. Lawson Younger Jr., eds. *Context of Scripture*. 4 vols. Leiden: Brill, 2003, 2017. Vol. 1, *Canonical Compositions from the Biblical World*; Vol. 2, *Monumental Inscriptions from the Biblical World*; Vol. 3, *Archival Documents from the Biblical World*; Vol. 4, *Supplements*.

CSB   Christian Standard Bible

EBC   Expositor's Bible Commentary

ESV   English Standard Version

Even-Shoshan Abraham Even-Shoshan, ed. *A New Concordance of the Bible*. Jerusalem: Kiryat Sefer, 1990 [Hebrew].

FT   John Goldingay. *First Testament: A New Translation*. Downers Grove, IL: IVP Academic, 2018. Some proper names have been anglicized by permission.

GKC   Wilhelm Gesenius. *Gesenius' Hebrew Grammar*. Edited by Emil Kautzsch. Translated by Arthur E. Cowley. 2nd ed. Oxford: Clarendon, 1910.

HALOT   Ludwig Koehler, Walter Baumgartner, and Johann J. Stamm. *The Hebrew and Aramaic Lexicon of the Old Testament*. 2 vols. Leiden: Brill, 2001.

HDT   Gary Beckman. *Hittite Diplomatic Texts*. 2nd ed. Atlanta: Scholars Press, 1999.

IBHS   Bruce K. Waltke and M. O'Connor. *An Introduction to Biblical Hebrew Syntax*. Winona Lake, IN: Eisenbrauns, 1990.

IDB	George A. Buttrick, ed. *The Interpreter's Dictionary of the Bible*. 4 vols. New York: Abingdon, 1962.
JBTS	*Journal of Biblical and Theological Studies*
JETS	*Journal of the Evangelical Theological Society*
Joüon	Paul Joüon. *A Grammar of Biblical Hebrew*. Translated and revised by T. Muraoka. 2nd ed. with corrections. Rome: Pontifical Biblical Institute, 2011.
JPSBC	Jewish Publication Society Bible Commentary
JSNTSup	Journal for the Study of the New Testament Supplement Series
JSOT	*Journal for the Study of the Old Testament*
JSOTSup	Journal for the Study of the Old Testament Supplement Series
KEL	Kregel Exegetical Library
KJV	King James Version
LBH	Late Biblical Hebrew
LCL	Loeb Classical Library
LHBOTS	Library of the Hebrew Bible/Old Testament Studies
NAC	New American Commentary
NET	New English Translation
NICOT	New International Commentary on the Old Testament
NIV	New International Version
NIVAC	NIV Application Commentary
NJPS	*Tanakh: The Holy Scriptures: The New JPS Translation according to the Traditional Hebrew Text*. Philadelphia: Jewish Publication Society, 1985.
NRSVue	New Revised Standard Version Updated Edition
OTE	*Old Testament Essays*
OTP	James H. Charlesworth, ed. *Old Testament Pseudepigrapha*. 2 vols. New York: Doubleday, 1983, 1985.
OTUOT	Gary Edward Schnittjer. *Old Testament Use of Old Testament*. Grand Rapids: Zondervan Academic, 2021.
PE	Amélie Kuhrt. *The Persian Empire: A Corpus of Sources from the Achaemenid Period*. New York: Routledge, 2007.
REB	Revised English Bible
RINAP	Grant Frame, ed. The Royal Inscriptions of the Neo-Assyrian Period. Hayim Tadmor and Shigeo Yamada. Vol. 1, *The Royal Inscriptions of Tiglath-pileser III (744–727 BC) and Shalmaneser V (726–722 BC)*,

	Kings of Assyria. Winona Lake, IN: Eisenbrauns, 2011. A. Kirk Grayson and Jamie Novotny. Vol. 3.1, *The Royal Inscriptions of Sennacherib, King of Assyria (704–681 BC), Part 1*. Winona Lake, IN: Eisenbrauns, 2012. Grayson and Novotny. Vol. 3.2. *The Royal Inscriptions of Sennacherib, King of Assyria (704–681 BC), Part 2*. Winona Lake, IN: Eisenbrauns, 2014.
Roth	Martha T. Roth. *Law Collections from Mesopotamia and Asia Minor*. 2nd ed. Atlanta: Society of Biblical Literature, 1997.
RT	Mordechai Cogan. *The Raging Torrent: Historical Inscriptions from Assyria and Babylonia Relating to Ancient Israel*. Jerusalem: Carta, 2008.
SFAC	*Stories from Ancient Canaan*. Edited and translated by Michael D. Coogan and Mark S. Smith. 2nd ed. Louisville: WJK, 2012.
SGBC	Story of God Bible Commentary
TOTC	Tyndale Old Testament Commentaries
TT	Teach the Text
VT	*Vetus Testamentum*
WBC	Word Biblical Commentary

A NOTE TO PROFESSORS
FROM THE EDITORS

The textbooks in the Connections series feature somewhat shorter page counts than many traditional survey texts. Professors in traditional courses can use these textbooks to provide room in their courses for other targeted readings. Professors teaching courses in more concise formats can assign the entire textbook. In sum, the short page count is meant to offer maximal flexibility in course design.

Professors who adopt this book as a required text are welcome to access its supplemental professor's materials at no cost. Please go to bhacademic.com/requests.

Gary Edward Schnittjer, editor of Old Testament
Mark Strauss, editor of New Testament

INTRODUCTION TO
OLD TESTAMENT NARRATIVES

The narratives of Israel's Scriptures set forth the framework for the teaching, death, and resurrection of the Messiah—the gospel or good news. The gospel of Messiah makes sense based on the story of the kingdom, exile, and return presented in these narratives. This book is designed to help readers benefit from reading and studying the Israel story as told by the narratives of Israel's Scriptures.

Getting Started

This book introduces the narratives of Israel's Scriptures with an emphasis on ancient connections, biblical connections, gospel connections, and life connections. Here are the sections housed in the present introductory chapter:

Getting Started
Connections
How Biblical Narratives Work
Ancient Context of Old Testament Narratives

In this section a few key terms need to be defined and the narratives of Israel's Scriptures introduced. The terms *narrative* and *story* are used identically. **Narrative** refers to characters within a setting who overcome obstacles toward resolution.

Ancient **covenants** were formal agreements that operated on the analogy of two people who are not kin becoming kin.[1] In marriage and adoption covenants, unrelated people became kin—part of the same family—with inheritance rights being granted to the spouse or child. On the same analogy, suzerain-vassal treaties (covenants) between the **suzerain** (sovereign god or king) and **vassal** (slave, subject, client) likewise brought two persons into a kinship-like bond, wherein the vassal could be referred to as "son" or "slave" and the suzerain as "father" or "master" (cf. 2 Kgs 16:7). The major biblical covenants expressed kinship between the deity and his people. This kinship was epitomized by an oft-repeated covenant formula. For example, Yahweh said, "I will be their God, and they will be my people" (Jer 31:33).[2] Three of the covenants between Yahweh and Israel play a pivotal role in Old Testament narratives: the Abrahamic, Mosaic, and Davidic covenants. The Abrahamic and Davidic covenants were both irrevocable and permanent, and both were conjoined to the obligations of the Mosaic covenant.[3] The Mosaic covenant remained in effect for the worshiping community, even after exile. The people lived under the empire's civil law as well as the Mosaic covenant, until it was upgraded by the new covenant in the teaching, death, and resurrection of the Messiah (vv. 31–34).

Israel's Scriptures use two different terms for those who are not citizens of Israel. In this book **residing foreigner** refers to one who sought refuge in Israel and who submitted to the covenant of Israel such as through circumcision.[4] Residing foreigners were expected to submit to Yahweh's teaching like anyone else in Israel.[5] The term **foreigner** refers to ethnic others who did not seek to assimilate into Israel.[6] They did not take covenantal circumcision and did not submit to Yahweh's teachings. Foreigners may have been hostile, indifferent, or friendly toward Israel.

Much of Protestant Christian theology has been troubled by thinking too narrowly about "law" in the Old Testament. But the Hebrew term *torah* has an educational sense that means "teaching." For this reason, the term **Torah** with a capital *T* will be used as an English loan word to refer to the Five Books of Moses (Genesis,

---

[1] Discussion here indebted to Seock-Tae Sohn, "'I Will Be Your God and You Will Be My People': The Origin and Background of the Covenant Formula," in *Ki Baruch Hu: Ancient Near Eastern, Biblical, and Judaic Studies in Honor of Baruch A. Levine*, ed. Robert Chazan, William W. Hallo, and Lawrence H. Schiffman (Winona Lake, IN: Eisenbrauns, 1999), 355–72.

[2] For the locations of covenant formula in Scripture, see *OTUOT*, 282.

[3] See Gary Edward Schnittjer, "Your House Is My House: Exegetical Intersection within the Davidic Promise," *BSac*, forthcoming.

[4] See "*ger*," *HALOT* 1:201.

[5] See, e.g., Lev 16:29; 17:8–13; 18:26; 24:22; Num 9:14; 15:14, 26, 29; 19:10–11; Deut 14:29; 26:13.

[6] See "*nekhar*," *HALOT* 1:700.

Exodus, Leviticus, Numbers, and Deuteronomy), and **torah** with a lowercase *t* will be used to refer to teaching or instruction. Torah is an unfinished story that culminates in the teaching, death, and resurrection of the Messiah. The narratives of Israel's Scriptures unfold in the shadow of Torah and move the Israel story toward the gospel.

Modern conventions refer to the dating of Old Testament events as **BCE,** meaning Before the Common Era. These dates count down to the time of the Messiah. Thus, the northern kingdom of Israel fell in 722 BCE, more than a century earlier than the fall of Jerusalem in 586 BCE. Just as modern dates beginning with 20 (e.g., 2001) are part of the twenty-first century CE, so too the fall of Jerusalem in 586 occurred in the early sixth century BCE.

The **Old Testament** refers to the first section of the Christian Bible. In the days of Messiah and the earliest Christians before the New Testament was written, what we call the Old Testament was simply thought of as Israel's Scriptures. The New Testament refers to them as the Torah and Prophets or Torah, Prophets, and Psalms.[7]

Israel's Scriptures were originally written in Hebrew, with a few later parts in Aramaic. The rise of the Mesopotamian empires, which changed hands many times, in the ancient Near East altered many things for the people of God. When the Greeks took over the region in 333 BCE, they imposed their culture on their subjects. This is called Hellenization. Many Jews of the **Diaspora** (those exiled from their homeland and forcibly relocated) needed to have Israel's Scriptures translated into Greek so they could understand them. The Greek translation of Israel's Scriptures is called the **Septuagint** or **LXX** (see Ancient Connections I.1).

ANCIENT CONNECTIONS I.1: SEPTUAGINT

The Letter of Aristeas, written between 250 and 100 BCE, presents an account of the translation of Israel's Scriptures into Greek in the mid-third century BCE. It says that seventy-two translators, six from each of the twelve tribes of Israel, independently translated the Torah in seventy-two days.

> You will therefore act well . . . by selecting elders of exemplary lives, with experience of the Law and ability to translate it, six from each tribe. . . . The result was such that in seventy-two days the business of translation was completed, just as if such a result was achieved by some deliberate design. (Letter of Aristeas, 39, 307, in *OTP*)

---

[7] Cf., e.g., Matt 5:17; Luke 24:44.

The letter's account was so famous in antiquity that the Greek version of Israel's Scriptures became known simply as the Septuagint, meaning "seventy," or by the Roman numeral LXX, also meaning "seventy." Though most today view this origin story as an exaggeration, the name stuck.

The origin story of the Septuagint in the letter was enhanced with imaginative details in ancient times. The Jewish scholar Philo (c. 20 BCE–50 CE) claimed the translators of the Septuagint independently made identical translations.

> Sitting . . . in seclusion with none present save the elements of nature . . . they [the translators] became as it were possessed, and, under inspiration, wrote, not each several scribe something different, but the same word for word, as though dictated to each by an invisible prompter.[a]

[a] Philo, *Moses II*, §37, in *Philo*, trans. F. H. Colson, LCL (Cambridge, MA: Harvard University Press, 1984), 6:467.

The date of authorship of biblical narratives is often a long time after the events in the narratives. Biblical authors frequently referred to historical sources as they compiled and composed the narratives (e.g., Josh 10:13; 2 Sam 1:18; 1 Kgs 11:41; 2 Kgs 23:28; 1 Chr 29:29–30; 2 Chr 33:18–19; Ezra 7:11; Neh 7:5). Evaluation of the reliability of biblical narratives must be based on evidence. As the following chapters will show, the evidence provides a strong basis for readers to have confidence in the historical narratives of Israel's Scriptures.

The Judaic and Christian traditions that lay claim to Israel's Scriptures arranged them in different sequences, including the narratives (see table I.1).

Table I.1: Two Traditional Arrangements of Israel's Scriptures

Judaic Scrolls in the Synagogue

Torah	Prophets	Writings
Genesis	*Former Prophets*	Psalms
Exodus	Joshua	Job
Leviticus	Judges	Proverbs
Numbers	Samuel	
Deuteronomy	Kings	*Megillot*
		Ruth
	Latter Prophets	Song of Songs
	Isaiah	Ecclesiastes
	Jeremiah	Lamentations
	Ezekiel	Esther
	The Twelve	
	Prophets	Daniel
		Ezra-Nehemiah
		Chronicles

Christian Old Testament according to the LXX

Torah	Narratives	Poetry	Prophets
Genesis	Joshua	Job	Isaiah
Exodus	Judges	Psalms	Jeremiah
Leviticus	Ruth	Proverbs	Lamentations
Numbers	Samuel	Ecclesiastes	Ezekiel
Deuteronomy	Kings	Song of Songs	Daniel
	Chronicles		Minor Prophets
	Ezra-Nehemiah		
	Esther		

The stories of Joshua, Judges, Samuel, and Kings were included in the Former Prophets because they were narrated from a prophetic point of view. In that sense these four narratives complemented the Latter Prophets, which critically evaluated the Hebrew kingdoms by the Torah's standards.

The Writings of the synagogue arrangement house several exile and restoration narratives. The short stories of Ruth and Esther were included with the other short scrolls (*Megillot*) that are read during the festivals—Ruth at Pentecost and Esther at Purim.[8] Daniel, Ezra-Nehemiah, and Chronicles tell stories of exile, restoration, and the temple for postexilic readers.

The Christian Old Testament arrangement apparently follows the Septuagint. Most of the narratives were collected after the Torah in more or less chronological order.

The oddities of the Christian sequence include collecting Lamentations and Daniel among the prophetic writings. Ancients noticed that Jeremiah sometimes used the rhetoric of weeping, that the male figure of Lamentations weeps, and other similar imagery.[9] They surmised Jeremiah must have written Lamentations, so they placed the two books side by side. Daniel was a bureaucratic administrator, not a prophet, and he did not produce prophetic oracles like Isaiah, Amos, and others. It seems the narrative was collected with the Prophets because Daniel interpreted visions and had his own visions that offered prophetic views of things to come. Even Jesus referred to Daniel as a prophetic writing in the broad sense of the term (Matt 24:15). The present textbook series includes chapters on Daniel in both the volumes on narratives and prophetic writings since some study it with the narratives while others study it with the Prophets.

Long ancient scrolls were difficult to use. So, the long narratives of Samuel, Kings, Ezra-Nehemiah, and Chronicles were broken into two parts each (e.g., 1 Samuel and 2 Samuel). In this textbook these will all be treated in their original form as four single stories.

The narratives of Israel's Scriptures can be thought of in two groups. The books of Joshua, Judges, Samuel, and Kings make up a four-part serial known as the **Deuteronomistic narrative**.[10] The serial narrates the rise and fall of the Hebrew

---

[8] Ecclesiastes is read during Tabernacles, Song of Songs at Passover, and Lamentations on the Ninth of Av, which memorializes the destructions of Solomon's temple in 586 BCE and the Second Temple on the same day in 70 CE.

[9] Cf., e.g., Jer 13:17; 14:17; Lam 3:48–49.

[10] Deuteronomy dates from the time of Moses and is not part of the Deuteronomistic narrative, which depends on it. On the complications of dating Deuteronomy, see Gary Edward Schnittjer, *Torah Story: An Apprenticeship on the Pentateuch,* 2nd ed. (Grand Rapids: Zondervan Academic, 2023), 389–91.

kingdoms through the covenantal lens of Deuteronomy. The story moves forward toward the fall of Jerusalem.

The people taken into exile were shell-shocked, wondering, *How could this happen?* Up to that point they thought the kingdom could not fall because of God's forever promises to Abraham and David. The destruction of the temple and Jerusalem and the exile of the people contradicted everything they once believed. The prophets had long told them to turn back to Yahweh or face his wrath.[11] No one listened.

The Deuteronomistic narrative responds to this crisis of faith and demonstrates why the exile had to happen. The exile did not show God as unfaithful. Yahweh's faithfulness to the covenant with his people made exile necessary. The people badly needed this serial narrative to adjust their history, their identity, and their hope for the future.

The serial begins with the conquest of the land in **Joshua**. The **Judges** story grew out of the gap between Yahweh's fidelity to give the land and Israel's failure to obey. Again and again Israel was bullied by regional predators until they called out to Yahweh, who sent deliverers. The downward slide of Israel landed them in a moral cesspool wherein everyone did what is right in their own eyes.

The **Samuel** narrative presents the rise of King David. Yahweh made a promise to David that turned out to be the centerpiece of his redemptive plan within the entirety of Israel's Scriptures. Yahweh promised that David's offspring would be the son of God ruling over his kingdom forever. **Kings** narrates the inevitable fall of Jerusalem from Solomon through the two competing Hebrew kingdoms to the last Davidic rulers of the city of God.

The other Old Testament narrative books are mostly one-off **stories of exile and restoration**. In this study they will be approached chronologically, with Chronicles representing the entire story line. The **Ruth** narrative features an ancient matriarch of King David to show the challenges of how Israel should respond to the outsider. **Daniel** as dream-interpreter as well as having his own visions reveals that Israel's God is the Most High sovereign over all of history. Because it left out all elements of covenant, **Esther** forces its readership into a do-it-yourself situation. God is never mentioned, requiring readers to supply the story's theology from elsewhere in the Bible.

Ezra-Nehemiah starts on a high note. It begins with the edict of the Persian ruler Cyrus, inviting God's people to return to their homeland and rebuild the temple as an effect of Yahweh's word through his prophet Jeremiah. The story ends badly, with

---

[11] See, e.g., Jer 25:3–7; Zech 1:4.

rebellion running rampant in Jerusalem. By the end of the book it seems as if the exile never happened. **Chronicles** sets the story of the Davidic kingdom and its support for the temple within the entire Old Testament story line. The very first word is *Adam*. The story ends with the edict of Cyrus calling the people of Yahweh to rebuild his temple in Jerusalem. Together these narrative books tell the Israel story.

Connections

This section explains the connections that help make sense of the biblical narratives. Every main chapter except this introductory chapter provides a dedicated focus on ancient, biblical, gospel, and life connections.

The **Ancient Connections** sidebars feature excerpts from ancient Near Eastern writings. They relate to historical, cultural, and social realities of the story's setting.

The sections on **Biblical Connections** highlight cases where the narrative alludes to earlier Scriptures or where later Scriptures allude to the narrative. Focusing on biblical connections offers a concrete way to think with the biblical authors as well the people in their stories.

The **Gospel Connections** sections present selected examples of how the narrative points toward the gospel of the Messiah. Though discussions of gospel connections within this book typically are short, they are critical. There is no need for clever attempts to find Jesus in every verse. Instead of trivializing gospel connections, they must unfold from the redemptive structure of the narrative. The big story is redemptive because it moves toward God's own remedy for human rebellion.

Jesus of Nazareth never read the New Testament. Not one verse. He lived before it was written. But this did not cause him any trouble. The Son of God knew better than anyone that the Torah and Prophets bear witness to the gospel. The study of the great narratives of Israel's Scriptures offers a ripe opportunity to make the kind of gospel connections that are badly needed today.

The sections on **Life Connections** draw attention to key implications that call for response. Many important life connections begin within the framework of the narratives of Israel's Scriptures. The New Testament calls believers to regard the persons of the scriptural narratives as a great cloud of witnesses that surround Christians (Heb 12:1). Paul and Sosthenes told their Gentile listeners that the stories of Israel's temptation "were written for our instruction" (1 Cor 10:11).

These kinds of connections help, but they all require careful study of biblical narratives. The painting called *Dickens' Dream* made shortly after the death of the famous English writer in 1870 illustrates immersion in narrative. Charles Dickens sits in his study chair dozing off amid ethereal imagined scenes from many of his beloved novels. Faithful Christians would do well to surround themselves with scenes from the narratives of Israel's Scriptures.

How Biblical Narratives Work

Biblical narratives differ from one to the next. This reality calls for careful study of each one on its own terms. The main chapters of this book take up the distinctives of each narrative of Israel's Scriptures.

The present section explains key elements of how biblical narratives work in general, including the beginning, the ending, narrative sequence and dischronological narrative, literary structure, and narrative shaping. These elements need to be kept in mind all the time when interpreting narrative.

Narratives begin. **The beginning** of every biblical narrative provides the framework to make sense of the story. As readers work through the story, every new element needs to be apprehended within the context of the beginning and the story line up to that point. It matters that Judges begins with Yahweh declaring that Judah shall go up first against the peoples of Canaan. Everything in Ezra-Nehemiah was measured against the edict of the Persian king Cyrus, which sprang from Yahweh stirring his heart to fulfill the word of the prophet Jeremiah.

Other historical events occur before the beginning of a narrative. Though these realities are of great importance historically, the beginning provided by the storyteller provides the determinative context to interpret the events within the narrative.

Narratives end. **The ending** can be thought of as the goal or destiny of the narrative. From the very beginning everything within a narrative moves toward its ending. The ending places everything within the narrative in a new light.

The ending of the movie *Munich* (2005), directed by Steven Spielberg, sets its entire story in a new perspective. The movie was released four years after the destruction of the Twin Towers in New York City, better known as 9/11. The story of *Munich* is set in the early 1970s. The story line pivots on the idea of "an eye for an eye" payback as the lead characters strike down terrorists who are replaced by others who strike again.

The last scene is set at the edge of Queens with the Manhattan skyline across the East River in the background. As the lead character exits stage left, a caption is superimposed over the scene. Notice the way the term "Ultimately" ends on the Twin Towers. The next part of the phrase says "Nine of the Eleven" (figure I.1).

Figure I.1: Final scene of *Munich*

Sketch by Gary Edward Schnittjer

This message could be framed in dozens of ways. But the story needed to end with the phrase "Ultimately, Nine of the Eleven . . ." on the Twin Towers. Viewers get the message. Back-and-forth eye-for-an-eye unsanctioned attacks on terrorists escalate to bigger attacks. The assassination of the Munich terrorists had nothing to do with the Twin Towers. But the movie ends this way to make a point about where back-and-forth nationalistic attacks may lead. In this case the characters in the story could not be aware of what would happen to the Twin Towers in the future. The message is for viewers who know exactly what happened. The filmmakers used this ending to invite viewers to reevaluate the entire story line.

Likewise, biblical narratives are never *about* who they are *for*. The last scenes of Judges hold a big surprise for readers because they are flashbacks. Only after readers puzzle over how bad things have gotten does the narrator reveal that these events happened at the beginning of the days of the judges. This changes how to understand the entire Judges narrative. The ending of Ezra-Nehemiah shows what the restoration assembly did with the mighty work of God for his people. They turned the restoration into a failure. This forces readers to go back through the story to figure out what went wrong. Chronicles ends with the edict of Cyrus in midsentence: "Yahweh . . . has appointed me to build a house for him at Jerusalem in Judah. Whoever among all his people, may Yahweh their God be with them and *let them go up*" (2 Chr 36:23 AT, emphasis added). By ending in the middle of the sentence readers feel the weight of Cyrus's invitation to go up to worship in Jerusalem. In this way, the ancient worship in Jerusalem narrated in Chronicles challenges readers to renew their own worship of Yahweh.

Narratives begin, and narratives end. The beginning provides the framework to interpret the characters, events, and everything else within the story. The ending of a narrative is critical to the meaning of the entire story. Once readers arrive at the ending—its destiny—they have a new perspective by which to reevaluate every part of the narrative.

When **narrative sequence** differs from chronological sequence it is called **dischronological narrative**.[12] This is different from the normal conventions of modern historiography and requires close attention. The first thing that happened when David was anointed king of all Israel was a battle with the Philistines (2 Sam 5:17). But that is not what the Deuteronomist puts first. He fronts David taking Jerusalem (vv. 6–7). The Chronicler rearranges several parts of the David story that he took from Samuel to center everything on worship. For example, the Chronicler retains the fronting of the capture of Jerusalem but then places David getting the ark of the covenant as his next action (1 Chr 13:1–14).

The point is not to rearrange things into their proper chronological sequence. Ancient storymakers would have found it ridiculous to follow the chronological sequence of events if it did not frame the story's theology to its best advantage. Readers need to identify the importance of the narrative's sequence.

Dischronological narrative is very common in the Bible. Moses goes to the tabernacle in Exod 33:7–11, but the tabernacle is not built until Exodus 40. John the baptizer gets locked up in Luke 3:20 before he baptizes the Messiah in v. 21.

Dischronological narration serves several purposes. Sometimes thematically similar episodes are collected together, like many of David's battles in 2 Samuel 8 or many of Messiah's miracles in Matthew 8–9. In other cases, rearrangement placed causes and effects side by side. For example, placing Hezekiah's illness and his showing off to the Babylonians (2 Kings 20) after the defeat of Sennacherib of Assyria (18–19) allowed it to occur immediately before his wicked son Manasseh ruined everything (21). But the episode of Hezekiah's illness is a flashback because God promised he would deliver Jerusalem from the king of Assyria (20:6). Other examples will be discussed in later chapters.

Narrative sequence requires close consideration in every case, not just when it is dischronological. If biblical narrators arranged stories to their best theological advantage, then sequence always matters. Readers need to think with narrators.

---

[12] See Schnittjer, *Torah Story*, 10; *OTUOT*, 708–10, 893; David A. Glatt-Gilad, *Chronological Displacement in Biblical and Related Literatures* (Atlanta: Scholars Press, 1993).

For the present purposes, leading examples of **literary structure** used widely in biblical narratives can be summarized as a list.[13]

Characterization refers to the tendencies and qualities of persons. More developed biblical characters exhibit realistic conflicted and complex tendencies.

Comparison/contrast refers to the effects of placing or juxtaposing (dis)similar elements together.

Denotation refers to that which is signified by a word or phrase, and *connotation* refers to the inferences and qualities of that which is signified (see "setting" later in this list).

Extended echo effect refers to building a later episode so it sounds like an earlier episode, such as a-b-c, a-b-c. For example, the story of the Levite's concubine in Judges 19 closely follows the pattern of the two strangers who visit Lot in Sodom in Genesis 19.

Formula refers to repeated organizing phrases. Examples include "in those days there was no king in Israel" (Judg 17:6; 18:1; 19:1; 21:25) and the royal formula used to organize the presentation of the kings in Kings and Chronicles (see chapter 4).

Framing or *inclusio* refers to using the same or a similar element to bracket a unit, such as: a*b*xyz*b*cd. For example, Yahweh promises to be with Joshua before and after encouraging him (Josh 1:5, 9). Framing is used to enclose and make connections. See "resumptive repetition" later in this list.

Irony refers to saying one thing but meaning another, with readers in the know.

Juxtaposition is often closely related to comparison/contrast and refers to the placement of narrative elements next to one another.

Leading word refers to the abundant use of a term or set of terms for emphasis.

Mirror imaging refers to the second half of a narrative that repeats elements from the first half in reverse order such as a-b-c, c-b-a, or with a pivot such as a-b-c-d-c-b-a. Many interpreters have distorted mirror imaging

---

[13] See Schnittjer, *Torah Story*, 12–15, 18–19; *OTUOT*, 889–903.

by overemphasizing the central element as the pivot and focus. This rarely occurs and even then should not eclipse the design of stories that always move toward their ends or destinies. Many have failed to see how mirror imaging emphasizes elements through repetition. This commonplace structuring device is often called *inverted parallelism*, or a *chiasm*, so named for connecting the reversed elements in the second line of poetry forming the Greek letter *chai* (χ).

A-line: a $\diagdown$ b
B-line: b $\diagup$ a

Repetition refers to repeating words, expressions, phrases, or the like for emphasis and overlaps with comparison/contrast and leading word.

Resumptive repetition (also called *repetitive resumption*) refers to an ancient scribal technique of repeating a narrative element before and after an insertion of a new element, such as a*b*xyz*b*cd. For example, the mention of the building of the temple coming to a stop in Ezra (4:4, 24) brackets a series of previews of kindred trouble from later days. Many resumptive repetitions also serve literary ends and function as framing, or *inclusio* (see earlier in this list).

Setting refers to the narrative time and narrative space in which the story plays out. For example, referring to Bethlehem in the days of the judges in Ruth 1:1 does more than denote physical time and place. It also connotes a time when everyone did what was right in their own eyes (Judges 17–21) in David's own hometown (1 Sam 16:1). See "denotation/connotation."

Turning point (or pivot) refers to an element that causes the story to move in a new direction.

Typological patterns refers to intentional shaping of the text by biblical authors to draw analogies between persons, events, institutions, or teachings by which an earlier text prophetically expects a fulfillment in a later biblical text. For example, Isa 11:16 expects a return from Mesopotamian exile like the exodus from Egypt, which was fulfilled in an initial way in the return from exile in Ezra 1.

Wordplay refers to a variety of elements—puns, sound-alike words, alliteration, and so on—that shape the text, create irony, link its contents, and perform many other functions. For example, extensive use of humor in Judges creates a pervasive irony.

Narrative shaping refers to the activities of storymakers to present historical narrative to convey a theological message. Historical narratives are not just recitals of facts. They are shaped. No case of narrative shaping is more important than the gospel story.

That Jesus died is a fact. The gospel conveys more than this since any eyewitness enemy of Jesus could proclaim it while rejecting the gospel. To say, "Messiah died for sin according to the Scriptures" represents narrative shaping of the gospel message.

While narrative shaping is present everywhere in biblical stories, it can be seen most clearly in **synoptic narratives** (two versions of the same story). Consider the different ways to handle what David's soldiers did with the Philistine plunder.

> The Philistines abandoned their idols there, and David and *his men carried them off.* (2 Sam 5:21, emphasis added)

> The Philistines abandoned their idols there, and David *ordered that they be burned in the fire.* (1 Chr 14:12, emphasis added)

The Deuteronomistic narrative seeks to explain the inevitability of exile and makes readers worry about what David's troops were doing with the false gods. The Chronicler wants to underline the path to worship Yahweh and shows them getting rid of the idols.

Some modern interpreters wrongly assert that historical and ideological accounts are incompatible. This not only tries to superimpose a modern view on ancient narratives, but it is badly mistaken. All narratives are ideological. An ancient scholar of narratives observed that even poetic dramas could be historical: "[T]he poet should be more a maker of plots than of verses . . . even should his poetry concern actual events, he is no less a poet for that."[14]

Biblical narratives exemplify sophisticated literary artistry in presenting historical events. Modern readers can benefit both by studying the art of biblical narration and by attending to its ancient context.

---

[14] Aristotle, *Poetics*, ed. and trans. Stephen Halliwell, LCL 199 (Cambridge, MA: Harvard University Press, 1995), 1451b, 27–30.

Ancient Context of Old Testament Narratives

Some sense of the ancient context is essential to make the most of the main chapters in this book focused on the narratives of Israel's Scriptures. Everything that follows in this chapter is critical even while it is stated concisely. Readers may want to return to this discussion when working through the main chapters and the respective biblical narratives.

The ancient context of the narratives of Israel's Scriptures includes the lands and social realities in which they were set. Social realities like economic, political, military, and religious forces not only intertwined but greatly changed across the ten centuries treated by the narratives.

Modern Bible readers need to keep in mind that 100 years in antiquity was just as long and just as complicated as 100 years today, even though the kinds of complications may differ. Pause and think about the changes over the last century. Consider all that has happened that relates to your homeland over the last ten centuries. If an ancient person lumped together the last ten centuries as "modern," we might want to explain the difference between medieval versus colonial dominion as well as between industrial versus informational forces. The last millennium can hardly be lumped together in any meaningful way. Likewise, modern readers need to recognize the basic complications of the ancient world and not simply group it all together.

As noted above, narratives are never *for* who they are *about*. The accounts about ancient Israel first entering the land are part of a serial narrative for the exiles of Judah many centuries later. Even stories of very early days such as in the generation of Moses's grandson come to us from an exilic perspective, whether of Israel or Judah (Judg 18:30).

The present purpose is to provide a broad framework. The ancient historical context of Israel's narratives can be evaluated according to several periods of transformation: the regional situation of early Israel, the rise of the empires, and exile and return to provincial life.

The Regional Situation of Early Israel

Israel faced many challenges in the land of promise, from the conquest of the land to the early period of the Hebrew kingdoms.

Details of the debate regarding the so-called early and late dates of the exodus cannot be taken up here.[15] Proponents of the early date identify Israel's invasion of

---

[15] See Schnittjer, *Torah Story*, 188–90; *The Exodus: Historicity, Chronology, and Theological Implications*, ed. Mark D. Janzen (Grand Rapids: Zondervan Academic, 2021).

the land in 1406 BCE while the proponents of the late date put it in the late 1200s BCE. Both views accept the historical testimony of pharaoh Merneptah's monument as the earliest mention outside the Bible of Israel as a people, not a land (see Ancient Connections I.2). Referring to Israel as a people rather than a land fits with the days of the conquest and the judges.

ANCIENT CONNECTIONS I.2: THE STELE OF MERNEPTAH

The following figure is the ancient Egyptian hieroglyphic expression for "Israel" that appears on the Merneptah stele (c. 1208 BCE). The bent throw stick in front of the male figure signifies Israel as foreigners (non-Egyptian). The three vertical marks under the two persons signify that Israel is a people, not a geographic region (James K. Hoffmeier, "Stela of Merneptah," *COS* 2.6:41).

Sketch by Gary Edward Schnittjer

Here is a translation of the context in which the term *Israel* is mentioned.

> The (foreign) chieftains lie prostrate, saying "Peace." Not one lifts his head among the Nine Bows [expression for enemies]. . . . Canaan is plundered, Ashkelon is carried off, and Gezer is captured. Yenoam [south of Sea of Galilee] is made into non-existence; *Israel* is wasted, its seed is not; and Hurru [Syria] is become a widow because of Egypt. All lands united themselves in peace. Those who went about are subdued by the king of Upper and Lower Egypt . . . Merneptah ("Stela of Merneptah," *COS* 2.6:41, emphasis added).

The Levant refers to the region running down the eastern side of the Mediterranean Sea. Many different peoples lived in this area, including the coastal peoples of Ugarit, Phoenicia (Sidon and Tyre), and Philistia. Further inland the Scriptures refer to seven peoples: Hethites, Girgashites, Amorites, Canaanites, Perizzites, Hivites, and Jebusites (Deut 7:1). Since many of the seven peoples descended from Canaan according to Genesis 10, they have traditionally all been called Canaanites (Gen 10:15–19). The present study will likewise use the umbrella term *Canaanites* for the various peoples who lived in the land of promise before Israel. The Scriptures sometimes also use the term *Amorites* as a general term for the diverse peoples of this region (15:16, 19–21).

Besides the Canaanites the region was home to distant relatives of Israel. The people's namesake, Israel (Jacob), had a brother, Esau. While Jacob was honored by being renamed Israel, Esau was renamed Edom to shame him and his people for trading his birthright for red soup (25:30; 32:28; 35:10). The ancient name forever reminded Israel that the Edomites were the red-soup people. The troubles of Abraham's nephew Lot did not end when he escaped the doomed cities of the plain without his wife. His daughters, who remembered their father offering to let the men of the city gang-rape them, repaid him by getting him drunk and raping him. These incestuous relations gave birth to the namesake ancestors of Ammon and Moab (19:36–38).

When Israel invaded the land of promise in the lower part of the Levant, they entered a region of diverse peoples (figure I.2). The social diversity included many challenges, from military predators to local economic rivalries. Frequent aggression from rival peoples plagued Israel throughout the period of the judges who were divinely raised up to deliver the people. But external troubles did not cause Israel's downfall. Military and economic oppression tended to turn Israel back to their God. The root of Israel's troubles stemmed from their attraction to the advantages of the nations of Canaan and to their gods.

One constant attraction was the desire of Israelite parents to secure marriage matches with established families of the land to give social and economic advantages to their children. Ancient Israelite parents wanted to help their children, and this included the right marriage covenants. Yahweh repeatedly prohibited marriage matches with those who refused to come into the covenant.

> Do not make a treaty with the inhabitants of the land. . . . Then you will take some of their daughters as brides for your sons. Their daughters will prostitute themselves with their gods and *cause your sons to prostitute themselves with their gods.* (Exod 34:15–16, emphasis added)

> You shall not intermarry with them, and you shall not give your daughters to their sons or take their daughters for your sons, because *they will turn your children away from me to serve other gods.* Then Yahweh's anger will burn against you, and he will swiftly destroy you. (Deut 7:3–4 AT, emphasis added)

Figure I.2: Levant, Including Several Regional Rivals

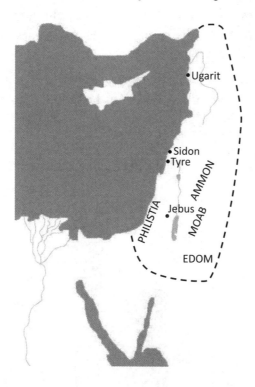

Despite the repeated strong warnings, intermarriage with those who worshiped other gods remained a constant attraction throughout Israel's history. The long-running problem of apostasy marriages seems highest during times of economic hardship, like during the original invasion and during the return and restoration after the exile.

For all of the diversity of the Canaanites, the evidence suggests a broadly accepted set of religious traditions. The creator and chief god of the Canaanite pantheon was named El—his name is the word for God. Their hero god is one of his sons, the storm god, Hadad, known by his title Baal (figure I.3). The Hebrew term *baal* means "owner," "master," or "husband," depending on the context. Referring to this god by his title was somewhat like the practice of referring to Yahweh by one of his titles— the Hebrew word for "lord" (*adonai*).

The consort (sexual partner) of El is the goddess Asherah, while the consort of Baal is the goddess Astarte. Asherah is a matron figure who gave birth to the other gods. She is associated with fertility worship that frequently included relations with local shrine prostitutes. Meanwhile Astarte is a youthful goddess of love and war. Sometimes people wonder how love and war can be themes of the same goddess (also Ishtar of Mesopotamia). In the Baal myths Astarte has frequent relations with Baal as well as throwing a tantrum while wading through the blood of the warriors she slaughtered. Astarte even threatened El as he sat upon his throne (see Ancient Connections I.3).

Figure I.3: Sculptural Relief of the Canaanite Storm God Baal[‡]

Sketch by Gary Edward Schnittjer

[‡] Sculptural reliefs present figures that project out from the background or wall, like shallow sculptures, but that belong to the background or wall. The fifteenth-century BCE relief of Baal from Ugarit (see figure I.2) is housed in the Louvre. Baal's upper lip is shaved, yet he has a long beard and long hair that ends in coils. In his left hand is lightning in the form of a stylized cedar and spear. The figure hanging from the sword may be the king of Ugarit. The waters below Baal's feet are likely the sea and river that he defeated in one of the surviving myths.

ANCIENT CONNECTIONS I.3: ASTARTE/ANAT THREATENS EL

The roles of the gods within ancient polytheistic cultures may surprise modern readers accustomed to the supreme deity of a monotheistic religion. Notice how the young female goddess of the Canaanites warns the high god not to be prideful:

> Maiden Anat spoke: "Don't rejoice in your well-built house, in your well-built house, El, don't rejoice in the height of your palace. Or else I will seize it . . . with my mighty arm. I'll smash your head, I'll make your gray hair run with blood, your gray beard with gore." ("The Palace of Baal," 3 v 19–26, in *SFAC*, 123–24)[a]

[a] Though some regard Anat and Astarte as two separate goddesses, the approach here accepts these as alternate names of the same goddess since these names sometimes appear in parallel lines (e.g., 2 i 40–41, in *SFAC*, 113).

Israel was highly attracted to the gods of Canaan. And why not? Canaanite worship of Baal and Asherah, for example, focused on fertility and prosperity. Israelite families depended on the rains and desired safety from outlaw and military predators. The majority of ancient Israelites worshiped the God of their ancestors as well as the regional gods in the hope of safety and prosperity. Many modern Christians shake their heads at ancient Israel's folly, even while seeking God on Sunday and pursuing prosperity and entertainment the rest of the week.

Mixing true and false religious devotion was the norm. Biblical narrators even used the title Baal and the name Astarte or Asherah in the plural to refer to false worship in general in the same way a modern person might use the brand name of tissues or the brand name of bandage strips to refer generally to all tissues and bandages: "Again the Israelites did evil in the eyes of Yahweh. They served *the Baals and the Ashtoreths*, the gods of Aram, the gods of Sidon, the gods of Moab, the gods of Ammon, and the gods of the Philistines. They abandoned Yahweh and they did not serve him" (Judg 10:6 AT, emphasis added).

Besides the pantheon of the prevailing Canaanite culture, the patron deities of other regional rivals also attracted a worship base in Israel. These other gods included Milcom, the god of Ammon, and Chemosh, the god of Moab (cf. 10:6; 1 Kgs 11:5, 7, 33).

The situation of ancient Israel transitioned from decentralized local tribal culture to a central civil kingdom. Individual struggles with regional peoples continued even when Israel achieved a collective military power.

A high point of Israel's early regional situation came in the days of David and Solomon. David the warrior-king subdued or made peace treaties with nearly all local rivals to establish a modest regional empire (table I.2).

Table I.2: Davidic Kingdom Subjection of and Alliances with Regional Rivals[‡]

Rival	Reference	Relationship
Tyre	2 Sam 5:11 (cf. Solomon, 1 Kgs 5:1, 12)	Alliance
Philistines	2 Sam 8:1 (cf. 5:17–25)	Subjection
Moab	2 Sam 8:2	Subjection
Zobah	2 Sam 8:3–4	Subjection
Damascus/Aram	2 Sam 8:5–8 (cf. revolt in 1 Kgs 11:23–25)	Subjection
Hamath	2 Sam 8:9–11	Tribute
Edom	2 Sam 8:14	Subjection
Ammon	2 Sam 12:26–30 (cf. 2 Kgs 14:25)	Subjection
(Egypt)	(cf. Solomon, 1 Kgs 3:1; 9:16, 24)	Alliance
Canaanite nations	1 Chr 22:2, 15–16 (cf. Solomon, 1 Kgs 9:20–21)	Enslavement

[‡] Table adapted from *OTUOT*, 389.

Based on David's dominion on the battlefield, Yahweh took away from him the honor of building a temple. The normal arc of ancient Near Eastern kings was to secure victory on the battlefield and then build palaces or temples to signal the favor of the gods on the king.[16] David complained, "God said to me, 'You are not to build a house for my name because you are a man of war and have shed blood'" (1 Chr 28:3).

Solomon would be a king of peace and would build the temple David had been denied. David amassed materials and wealth by plundering the regional rivals for Solomon's building projects (22:3–4, 14; 29:2–5). Many of Solomon's political alliances and strategies may have been planned and initiated under David's rule, like Solomon's marriage to Naamah the Ammonitess during David's tenure

---

[16] See Douglas J. Green, *"I Undertook Great Works": The Ideology of Domestic Achievements in West Semitic Royal Inscriptions* (Tübingen: Mohr Siebeck, 2010), 302–4.

(1 Kgs 14:21, 31). The rule that David established on the battlefield Solomon retained by a large number of treaty marriages to royal wives, who continued to serve the gods of their homelands. The worship of other gods by treaty wives signified peace between Solomon and the nations.

Even while Solomon was building a temple for the name of Yahweh in Jerusalem, he made high places of worship for his many treaty wives on the hills around Jerusalem. When people came to worship at the temple, they came into a region with places of worship for every god of Solomon's hundreds of treaty wives.

> Solomon followed Ashtoreth, the goddess of the Sidonians, and Milcom, the abhorrent idol of the Ammonites. . . . At that time, Solomon built a high place for Chemosh, the abhorrent idol of Moab, and for Milcom, the abhorrent idol of the Ammonites, on the hill across from Jerusalem. *He did the same for all his foreign wives,* who were burning incense and offering sacrifices to their gods. (1 Kgs 11:5, 7–8, emphasis added)

In the next generation the kingdom that David and Solomon had established broke into two kingdoms, with Israel in the north and Judah in the south. The first king of Israel, Jeroboam, defied the prohibition against images by setting up golden calves to the God of Israel in Dan and Bethel at the far north and south of his domain (see figure I.4).

Figure I.4: Worship Centers in the Hebrew Kingdoms to Israel's God and Other Gods

The northern kingdom of Israel provided royal support for the two golden calves in Dan and Bethel. In addition, King Ahab of the northern kingdom married a Phoenician queen, Jezebel, and built a shrine to worship the Canaanite deities in the capital city.

Then, as if following *the sin of Jeroboam* son of Nebat were not enough, he married Jezebel, the daughter of Ethbaal king of the Sidonians, and then proceeded to serve Baal and bow in worship to him. *He set up an altar for Baal in the temple of Baal that he had built in Samaria.* Ahab made an Asherah and did more to arouse the anger of Yahweh, the God of Israel, than all the kings of Israel who were before him. (16:31–33, emphasis added; v. 33 AT)

In sum of the regional situation of early Israel, though Yahweh honored his word of giving the people the land of promise, the rich religious heritage of diverse rival nations allured Israel. The people worshiped God but also served the gods of their rivals. The divided commitments of Israel ran directly against the very first of the Ten Commandments: "Do not have other gods besides me" (Exod 20:3//Deut 5:7). And in the northern kingdom of Israel the golden calves in Bethel and Dan broke the second commandment: "Do not make an idol for yourself, whether in the shape of anything in the heavens above or on the earth below or in the waters under the earth" (Exod 20:4//Deut 5:8).

The Rise of the Empires

The empires of Assyria and Babylon, the predecessors of the Persian Empire, effected many changes in the ancient Near East that dramatically affected Israel and Judah (figure I.5). Whereas the previous section considered the Levant, this section turns toward Mesopotamia, the land between the Euphrates and Tigris Rivers. The purpose is not to provide a historical survey of rulers and military-political control. Rather, this section explains the prophetic view of the rise of the Neo-Assyrian Empire, as well as the Chaldeans, as these relate to understanding the biblical narratives. An overview of the dates of the major rulers, including Persian rulers associated with the next subsection, provides a resource for this discussion as well as for later chapters (table I.3).

Figure I.5: Overview of Ancient Near Eastern Empires‡

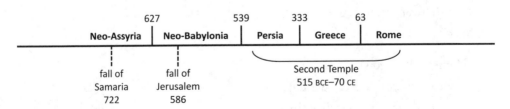

‡All dates BCE unless stated otherwise.

Table I.3: Rulers of the Empires of Mesopotamia and Persia with Selected Biblical References‡

Rulers of Neo-Assyrian Period

Ashurnasirpal II (883–859 BCE)

Shalmaneser III (858–824)

> humiliation of Jehu depicted on the Black Obelisk
> (period of weakness 823–745)

Tiglath-pileser III (744–727)

> c. 740, Menahem commits tribute to Tiglath-pileser III (2 Kgs 15:19–20)
> 734–732, Syria-Ephraim debacle (Isa 7:1)
> 733, Ahaz asks Tiglath-pileser for help (2 Kgs 16:5–9)

Shalmaneser V (726–722)

Sargon II (721–705)

> 721, the fall of Samaria (2 Kgs 17)
> 711, Jerusalem is preserved apparently in relation to the sign-act of Isaiah's nakedness (Isa 20:1–5), though the sign was against Egypt and Cush (Ethiopia)

Sennacherib (704–681)

> 701, Assyrian conquest of Judah and siege of Jerusalem (2 Kings 18–19; Isaiah 36–37)

Esarhaddon (680–669)

Ashurbanipal (669–626?)

Chaldean Rulers of Neo-Babylonian Period

Nabopolassar (627–605)

Nebuchadnezzar II (son of Nabopolassar) (605–562)

> 605, forced migration of aristocratic youth of Jerusalem (Dan 1:1)
> 597, forced migration of prominent citizens of Jerusalem (2 Kgs 24:8–12; Ezek 1:2)
> 586, Jerusalem and temple destroyed and forced migration of new prominent citizens (2 Kings 25; Jeremiah 52)

Amel-marduk (Evil-merodach) (son of Nebuchadnezzar) (562–560) (2 Kgs 25:27–30)

Neriglissar (conspirator and brother-in-law of Amel-marduk) (560–556) (Jer 39:3, 13)

Labashi-marduk (son of Neriglissar) (briefly in 556)

Nabonidus (conspirator) (555–539)

Belshazzar (co-regent and son of Nabonidus) (549–539)

Achaemenid Rulers of the Persian Period

Cyrus (559–530; ruler of Babylon, 539–530)

> 538, Sheshbazzar returns to Jerusalem with temple vessels (Ezra 1:8)

Cambyses (530–522)
Darius I (522–486)
> 520, Haggai and Zechariah prophesy to encourage rebuilding the temple (Hag 1:1; Zech 1:1; cf. Ezra 5:1)
> 515, completion of the rebuilt temple (Ezra 6:14–15)

Ahasuerus (Xerxes) (486–465)
> sometime after 479, salvation of the Jews at Purim (Esth 2:16; 9:21–22)

Artaxerxes (464–424/423)
> 458, Ezra returns to Jerusalem (Ezra 8:31–32)
> 445, Nehemiah returns to rebuild the walls of Jerusalem (Neh 6:15)

‡ Dates based on A. Kirk Grayson, "Mesopotamia, History of," *ABD*, 4:741–46; *ANE*, 2:592, 597; *PE*, 879.

The Hebrew prophets explained the significance of the rise of the Neo-Assyrian Empire in relation to the Hebrew kingdoms. The Assyrian crisis gave rise to a new form of revelation. The prophets Amos and Hosea preached against the northern kingdom of Israel, Isaiah preached against the southern kingdom of Judah, and Micah preached against both kingdoms. All four prophets left behind written collections of their prophetic ministries that offer enduring testimony to Yahweh's use of the Assyrians (and Babylonians) to bring his wrath on his people.

The people rebelled against the covenant. The prophets interpreted the economic sanctions and military aggression of the Assyrians as God's own judgment against his people. Notice the irony in Yahweh's using Assyria to punish his people, which then incited his wrath against Assyria.

> Woe to *Assyria, the rod of my anger*—the staff in their hands is *my wrath. I will send him* against a godless nation; *I will command him* to go against a people destined *for my rage,* to take spoils, to plunder, and to trample them down like clay in the streets.". . . But when the Lord finishes all his work against Mount Zion and Jerusalem, he will say, "I will punish the king of Assyria *for his arrogant acts* and the proud look in his eyes." (Isa 10:5–6, 12 emphasis added)

Meanwhile, the Assyrians interpreted their acts of aggression as justified force to subjugate peoples from the Mediterranean Sea to the Persian Gulf. While their control fluctuated, at its high points the empire ruled over most of Mesopotamia and the Levant (figure I.6).

Figure I.6: Assyrian Empire in the Late Eighth Century BCE

Assyrian rulers reveled in self-aggrandizement. A comparison between the royal Assyrian inscriptions and the scriptural narratives of the Hebrew kingdoms shows sharp contrasts between these bodies of literature (table I.4).

Table I.4: Comparing Royal Assyrian Inscriptions and the Book of Kings

Royal Assyrian Inscriptions	Book of Kings
• King as central figure	• God as central figure
• First-person account of the king	• Third-person account about kings
• Self-aggrandizing	• Prophetic critical

The scriptural narratives measure rulers by their commitment to God's Torah. The book of Kings indicts most kings with a common summary evaluation: "He did what was evil in the eyes of Yahweh" (e.g., 2 Kgs 21:2a AT). The contrast with the royal inscriptions of contemporary Assyrian rulers could not be more dramatic. Compare the statements regarding two contemporary kings: Esarhaddon of Assyria (680–669 BCE) and Manasseh of Jerusalem (698–642 BCE).

Esarhaddon, the great king, the mighty king, king of the universe, king of Assyria, viceroy of Babylon, king of Sumer and Akkad, king of Karduniash (Babylonia), all of it. . . . I am powerful, I am all powerful, I am a hero, I am gigantic, I am colossal, I am honored, I am magnified, I am without an equal among all kings, the chosen one of Assur, Nabû and Marduk, called of Sin, favorite of Anu, beloved of the queen, Ishtar, goddess of all (the world); the unsparing weapon, which utterly destroys the enemy's land, am I. (*ARAB* 2:224, 226).

Yahweh spoke by his servant the prophets, "Since King Manasseh of Judah has committed all these detestable acts—worse evil than the Amorites who preceded him had done—and by means of his idols has also caused Judah to sin. Therefore, thus says Yahweh, the God of Israel, 'See, I am bringing such disaster upon Jerusalem and Judah that the ears of all who hear about it will tingle. I will stretch over Jerusalem the measuring line used on Samaria and the mason's level used on the house of Ahab, and I will wipe Jerusalem clean as one wipes a bowl—wiping it and turning it upside down.'" (2 Kgs 21:10–13; vv. 10, 12 AT)

The self-glorification of Assyrian rulers was stunning by ancient standards. For many centuries the stamp used for royal tribute—discovered even in Samaria—featured an Assyrian king stabbing an attacking lion that the king holds in his bare hand.[17] In one version of the palace reliefs of his traditional royal lion hunt, Ashurbanipal had the artisans remove his armor and revive the nearly dead lion with arrows protruding from his back in the previous panel.[18] This way the relief of Ashurbanipal could stab the attacking lion that he holds in his bare hand just like the tribute seal (left panel of figure I.7). Many centuries later Darius the Great, king of Persia, had his artisans mimic the famed Assyrian royal art with images of himself killing a mythologized, attacking, horned, and winged lion in several doorways of his palace in Persepolis (right panel of figure I.7).[19]

---

[17] See A. R. Millard, "The Assyrian Royal Seal Type Again," *Iraq* 27, no. 1 (1965): 15 [12–16].

[18] See Julian E. Reade, *Assyrian Sculpture*, 2nd ed. (London: British Museum Press, 1998), 79; Julian E. Reade in *Art and Empire: Treasures from Assyria in the British Museum*, ed. J. E. Curtis and J. E. Reade (London: British Museum Press, 1995), 87.

[19] For pictures of reliefs in the figure, see Reade, *Assyrian Sculpture*, 79; *PE*, 546.

Figure I.7: Royal Lion-Kill Scenes‡

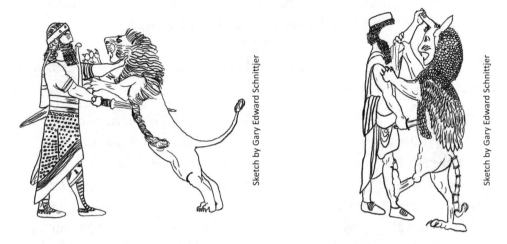

‡ *Left:* Ashurbanipal's (669–626? BCE) lion hunt sculptural relief in the British Museum. *Right:* sulptural relief of Darius (522–486 BCE) in doorways of Persepolis.

A major innovation of Neo-Assyrian warfare was its extreme cruelty, depicted both in graphic palace reliefs and narrated in many inscriptions. The literary and visual propaganda repeatedly glorified Assyrian power to torture, maim, and display corpse trophies of any who refused to pay crushing tribute. Defeated dignitaries allowed to live often had their noses, ears, or hands cut off. Many defiant leaders were skinned alive so their skin could be put on display to encourage abject submission (figure I.8).

Figure I.8: Sculptural Relief of Skinning Alive an Elamite from the Palace of Sennacherib

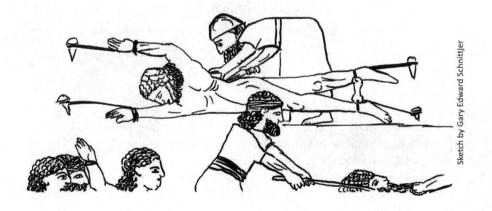

In one version of the eighth military campaign of Sennacherib (late 690s), the scribes enhanced the battle against the Elamites with imagery from their myths. The literary embellishments included several allusions to the creation myth known by its first words *Enuma Elish* ("When on high") signified by underlining, one allusion to Erra and Ishum signified by italics, and one allusion to the Law Collection of Hammurabi signified by bold.[20]

> Like a lion I raged. I put on (my) coat of mail. (My) helmet, emblem of victory (battle), I placed <u>on my head</u>. My great battle chariot, which brings low the foe, I hurriedly mounted in the anger of my heart. The mighty bow which Assur had given me, I seized in my hands; the javelin, <u>piercing to the life</u>, I grasped. Against all of the hosts of wicked enemies, I raised my voice (*lit.*, cried out), rumbling like a storm. Like Adad I roared. . . . [S]peedily I cut them down and established their defeat. I cut their throats like lambs. I cut off their precious lives (as one cuts) a string. Like the many waters of a storm, *I made (the contents of) their gullets and entrails run down* upon the wide earth. My prancing steeds harnessed for my riding, plunged into the streams of their blood as (into) a river. The wheels of my war chariot, **which brings low the wicked and the evil**, were bespattered with blood and filth. With the bodies of their warriors I filled the plain, like grass. (Their) testicles I cut off, and tore out their privates like the seeds of cucumbers of Simânu (June). Their hands I cut off. (*ARAB* 2:126–27, emphasis added)

Later versions of the eighth military campaign were revised to exclude the mythic elements.[21] While Sennacherib's boasting of horrific violence is commonplace, the Assyrian scribes may have been embarrassed by the mythical descriptions of a battle Sennacherib lost. The same battle recounted in the quotation above is presented very differently in the standard Babylonian chronicles: "Mushezib-Marduk . . . effected an Assyrian retreat."[22]

---

[20] For these and other parallels, see Elnathan Weissert, "Creating a Political Climate: Literary Allusions to *Enūma Eliš* in Sennacherib's Account of the Battle of Halule," in Hartmut Waetzoldt and Harald Hauptmann, eds., *Assyrien im Wandel der Zeiten,* Rencontre Assyriologique International 39 (Heidelberg: Heidelberger Orientverlag, 1997), 191–202. For the parallels to Enuma Elish, see *COS* 1.111:397 (4.58; 4.30–31); Erra and Ishum, see *COS* 1.113:412 (4.35); Law Collection of Hammurabi, see Roth, 76 (i.35–36).

[21] See Weissert, "Creating," 199–202; cf., e.g., *ARAB* 2:158.

[22] See *ABC* 1 iii 13, 18 (p. 80).

Knowing the Assyrian reputation for excessive cruelty helps explain the willingness of both Menahem of the northern kingdom of Israel and Ahaz of the southern kingdom of Judah to submit to vassalage under Tiglath-pileser (2 Kgs 15:19–20; 16:7–8). A suzerain-vassal treaty guaranteed safety to vassals who paid extremely high tribute (taxes) to the suzerain. Menahem of Israel and Ahaz of Judah each bartered away sovereign independence to retain their personal positions of power. And in both cases vassalage to Assyria marked a first step on the pathway to exile.

The rise of the Chaldeans in the late seventh century BCE instigated major shifts in power across the ancient Near East (see table I.3). They took over Babylon and defeated the Assyrians. The son of King Nebopolassar was the ruthless general named Nebuchadnezzar II. Shortly after becoming king, he defeated the Egyptians decisively at the battle of Carchemish, effectively ending their dominance for good. The rebellions of Jerusalem against Nebuchadnezzar led to prolonged sieges and forced migrations of prominent citizens. The last few decades of Jerusalem's rule played out amid momentous political and military events across the ancient Near East (see figure I.9).

Figure I.9: The Final Years of the Rule of Davidic Kings in Jerusalem

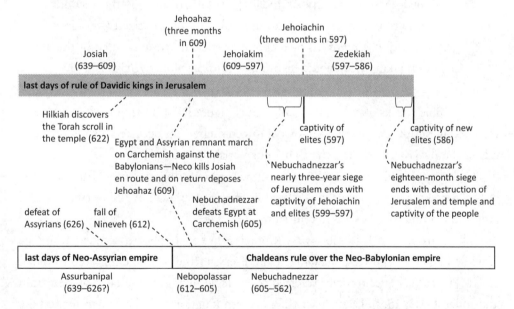

Exile and Return to Provincial Life

Nothing changed Israel and Judah more than the forced migrations of their people from their homelands. Attention needs to be given to the exiles of the northern kingdom of Israel, the exile of the southern kingdom of Judah, and the return of Yahwistic Judeans to their homeland as a minor sub-province of the Persian Empire.

Biblical scholarship often refers to two exiles: the forced migration of many citizens of the northern kingdom of Israel in 722 BCE and the forced migration of the upper class of Jerusalem in 586 BCE (see Ancient Connections I.4). But these were only the two most important forced migrations when the capitals of Samaria and Jerusalem were sacked and their rules ended.

ANCIENT CONNECTIONS I.4: NEO-BABYLONIAN CHRONICLE OF NEBUCHADNEZZAR

The Neo-Babylonian Chronicles tell of Nebuchadnezzar's siege of Jerusalem that resulted in its surrender in 597 BCE. At that time Nebuchadnezzar took king Jehoiachin and the royal family as well as the upper-class citizens into captivity. Nebuchadnezzar set up Zedekiah as king in place of Jehoiachin.

> The seventh year: In the month of Kislev the king of Akkad [Nebuchadnezzar] mustered his army and marched against Hattu. He encamped against the city of Judah [Jerusalem] and on the second day of the month of Adar he captured the city (and) seized (its) king [Jehoiachin]. A king of his own choice [Zedekiah] he appointed in the city (and) taking vast tribute he brought it to Babylon. (*ABC* 5 ii 11–13)

The Bible speaks of ten exiles (table I.5; cf. figure I.10). There may be others not recorded in Scripture. The two seasons of forced migrations occurred during the periods of the Assyrian crisis and the Babylonian crisis.

Older scholarship mistakenly spoke of the "lost ten tribes of Israel." But Sargon II only claimed to take into exile 27,290 people after Samaria fell in 722 (see table I.5).[23] And the Chronicler takes a different view.

There are no ten lost tribes in Chronicles. When Jeroboam seceded from the Davidic kingdom, Yahwistic Israelites from every northern tribe emigrated to Judah (2 Chr 11:16). The Chronicler referred to all Israel living in the land of Benjamin and Judah (11:3; 15:9). Later, after the northern kingdom fell, Hezekiah invited the faithful among its remnant to rejoin the Davidic kingdom for worship in Jerusalem (30:11, 18).[24]

---

[23] See *ARAB* 2:26. For evidence of the Israelites in Assyrian exile, see *BFE*, 35–53.

[24] See *OTUOT*, 776–77, 813.

Table I.5: Ten Recorded Exiles

Date	Reference	Forced Migrations
c. 734 BCE	2 Chr 28:5, 8	Judeans to Damascus by Remaliah of Syria, and other Judean captives to Samaria by Pekah of Israel[a]
c. 733	2 Chr 28:17; 2 Kgs 16:6	Judean villages by the Edomites to Elath
c. 733	1 Chr 5:26	Transjordan tribes of Reuben, Gad, and half tribe of Manasseh by Tiglath-pileser III of Assyria[b]
c. 733	2 Kgs 15:29	Several northern cities in the lands of Naphtali and Galilee by Tiglath-pileser III
c. 722	2 Kgs 17:3–6	Samaria besieged by Shalmaneser V and people taken by Sargon II (27,290)[c]
701	2 Kgs 18:13; Isa 36:1; 2 Chr 32:1	Many Judean cities sacked and people taken by Sennacherib of Assyria[d]
605	Dan 1:1–3	Several aristocratic Judean youths[e] forced into governmental service in Babylon and some temple vessels taken
597	2 Kgs 24:10–13; Jer 24:1; 27:21–22; 52:28	Jehoiachin and the prominent citizens of Jerusalem (3,023) and many temple vessels taken by Nebuchadnezzar
586	2 Kgs 25; Jer 27:21–22; 39:1–2; 52:29; 2 Chr 36:17–20	Temple destroyed and Zedekiah and the new prominent citizens of Jerusalem (832) and remaining temple vessels taken by Nebuchadnezzar
582	Jer 52:30	Remnant of Judeans (745) taken by Nebuchadnezzar

[a] Second Chronicles 28:8 says 200,000 Judean exiles to Samaria. Raymond Dillard says this is hyperbole to emphasize the defeat of Ahaz (2 Chronicles, WBC [Grand Rapids: Zondervan, 1987], 222).

[b] See RINAP 1:105 (42.6), 131 (49.rev.3–4), 134 (50.3–4).

[c] See ANET 284–86.

[d] Sennacherib claims he took 201,105 Judeans into exile (ANET 287–88). Others suggest this is an exaggeration and estimate c. 120,000 exiles (RT, 120).

[e] The youths included Daniel (Belteshazzar), Hananiah (Shadrach), Mishael (Meshach), and Azariah (Abednego) (Dan 1:7).

Figure I.10: Judeans of Lachish Forcibly Migrated
to Assyrian Captivity in 701 BCE‡

Sketch by Gary Edward Schnittjer

‡ This sculptural relief once adorned the palace of Sennacherib to celebrate the defeat of the
Judean town Lachish and is now housed in the British Museum. The ancient artisans' detail of the
ribs showing on the youth and cattle may signify hunger brought on by the siege.

Virtually all of the regional people groups around the Hebrew kingdoms lost
their national identity and assimilated when the empires forcibly migrated them from
their homelands and sometimes forcibly migrated other peoples into their homelands.
The exception is Judah.[25]

What was different about Judah? The most important elements in Judah retaining its covenantal identity pivot on what may be called *canonical consciousness*. The
exiles took with them scrolls that they regarded as the word of God. The exiles studied the Torah and Prophets to understand how the exile could have happened when
Yahweh had made enduring promises to Abraham and David. As much as anything
else the scriptural witness to Yahweh's fidelity sealed the identity of the Yahwistic
Judeans as his people.

Recent archaeological finds have begun to provide a view of Judah in exile. Some of the
people were placed into villages in the lower Mesopotamian region such as Sha-Nashar
and āl Yahudu ("City of Judah"). Others were moved into neighborhoods in established
cities like Sippar and Nippur (figure I.11). The Scriptures mention several other exilic
villages whose locations remain unknown: Tel-abib along the Chebar Canal (Ezek 3:15);
Tel-melah, Tel-harsha, Cherub, Addan, and Immer (Ezra 2:59); and Casiphia (8:17).

---

[25] Observed as early as Haman (Esth 3:8).

Figure I.11: Villages of Judah in Babylonian Exile‡

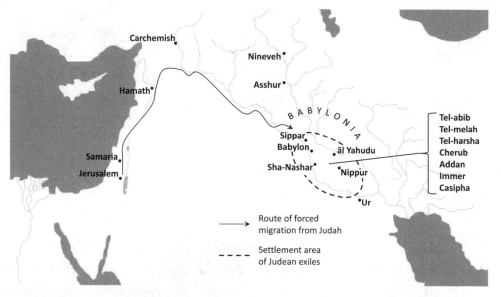

‡ Details on map indebted to *BFE*, 139.

The evidence shows that the Judean captives owned property, paid taxes, and participated in the economics of society.[26] They were also put into forced labor for Nebuchadnezzar's building projects like any other group of exiles (Ancient Connections I.5).

ANCIENT CONNECTIONS I.5: FORCED LABOR OF NEBUCHADNEZZAR

In a monument related to building two ziggurats (Mesopotamian-style pyramids) Nebuchadnezzar mentioned the labor he forced on his captives. This would include the people of Judah.

I mobilized [all] countries everywhere, [each and] every ruler [who] had been raised to prominence over all the people of the world [as one] loved by Marduk, from the upper sea [to the] lower [sea,] the [distant nations, the teeming people of] the [world, kings of remote mountains

---

[26] See *BFE*, 145–55; David S. Vanderhooft, "Babylonia and Babylonians," in *The World Around the Old Testament: The People and Places of the Ancient Near East*, ed. Bill T. Arnold and Brent A. Strawn (Grand Rapids: Baker Academic, 2016), 133–34 [107–37].

and far-flung islands in the midst of the] upper and lower [seas,] whose lead-ropes [my] lord Marduk placed in [my] hand so [that they should] draw [his] chariot (*lit.*, pull his chariot-pole), and I imposed corvée-duty on the workforces of the gods Šamaš and [Marduk] in order to build E-temen-[anki][a] and E-ur-meimin-anki.[a] (Andrew R. George, "A Stele of Nebuchadnezzar II," in *Cuneiform Royal Inscriptions and Related Texts in the Schøyen Collection*, ed. Andrew R. George [Bethesda, MD: CDL, 2011], 160)

[a] E-temen-anki "House, Foundation Platform of Heaven and Underworld" and E-ur-meimin-anki "House that Controls the Seven Divine Decrees of Heaven and Underworld" (George, "Stele," 159).

The dynamics of the relationships between one wave of exiles and the next shows signs of strain and disharmony among the Judeans. One set of problems would naturally stem from the nonelites who moved into the vacated homes, jobs, and positions of social standing when the rulers and prominent citizens were exiled in 597 BCE. That is, the officials and upper-class citizens of Jehoiachin's pre-597 BCE Jerusalem and the new replacement officials and upper-class citizens of Zedekiah's 597–586 BCE Jerusalem could not both enjoy the same privileged lives, if the 597 exiles had been returned home as the false prophets had promised (Jer 29:8–9). The divide between these Judeans was underlined by Jeremiah, who called the 597 exiles "good figs" and the 586 exiles "bad figs" (24:4–10). This may be one of the underlying fractures that helps explain some of the troubles the exiles faced when they returned to the Judean homeland.

One of the first things Cyrus did when Persia defeated and took over the empire formerly in the hands of the Chaldeans was to grant limited privileges to many captives. He allowed people to return to their ancestors' homelands and rebuild temples. The importance of the edict of Cyrus as testimony to Yahweh's faithfulness to his promises can be seen in the inclusion of four versions of it in the Bible (2 Chr 36:23; Ezra 1:2–4; 5:13–15; 6:3–5).

A significant innovation in the Achaemenid Empire of the Persians was to move the royal court routinely between four important capital cities: Babylon, Susa, Persepolis, and Parsagarda (figure I.12). Moving the royal court among the powerful peoples of Mesopotamia, Elam, and Persia gave the Achaemenid Empire enduring stability in comparison to previous Near Eastern empires. The administrative city of Ecbatana in the region of Media further stabilized the empire.[27]

---

[27] Cf. Herodotus I, 98; Polybius, X, 27.5–6, in *PE*, 35, 501.

Figure I.12: Four Capital Cities of the Persian Empire

God was faithful to bring back many Yahwistic Judeans to rebuild the temple and the walls of Jerusalem. Most Jews never returned to their homeland but permanently remained in the Diaspora. Centuries later, at the time of the Messiah after the empire had changed hands a few more times, 80 percent of Jews continued to live in the Diaspora.

The rebuilt house of God in Jerusalem is known as the Second Temple in relation to Solomon's temple that was destroyed by the Babylonians. The Second Temple stood from 515 BCE until 70 CE, when the Romans looted and destroyed it (see figure I.5). It is where the Messiah worshiped and faced off against his rivals.

The returned exiles in the days of the Persian Empire in many ways represent groups of faithful people who desired to reestablish a covenantal community in Judah. They faced significant challenges in the severely economically depressed region of Judah. It took centuries to recover from the decimation of the entire social and economic infrastructure by Nebuchadnezzar.

The restoration failed. The people fell into the same sins that got their ancestors exiled. It was as though they had never left. The addiction to covenant breaking by the restoration assembly demonstrated that the exile did not work in terms of reforming God's people.[28] If Yahweh was going to fulfill his covenantal promises, he would need to do it in some other way.

---

[28] See Gary Edward Schnittjer, "The Bad Ending of Ezra-Nehemiah," *BSac* 173 (2016): 46–49 [32–56].

Fulfillment awaits the arrival of a teacher from Nazareth.

In sum, under the Assyrians Judah maintained limited, relative autonomy though suffering from Assyrian pressures. Under the Neo-Babylonians Judah lost independence, statehood, their place of worship, and life in the land. And under the Persians Judah regained life in their ancestors' homeland and freedom to worship their God as long as they remained submissive to Persian taxation and rule.

Interactive Questions

How do Old Testament narratives provide a framework for the gospel?

How do narrative beginnings and endings work?

Why is it important to take note of dischronological narration?

What is an example of a literary pattern used by a biblical author to shape a narrative?

How can biblical narratives promote an agenda and ideology, use artistic literary forms, and at the same time be considered historical and reliable?

What factors in the regional situation of early Israel help make sense of the narratives set in that period?

Why was Israel attracted to the gods of Canaan?

How does the rise of the empires provide a context for explaining the purpose of biblical narratives set within that period?

What was the situation of Judah during the Neo-Assyrian Empire?

What was the situation of Judah during the Neo-Babylonian Empire?

In what sense is exile the major turning point of the Old Testament narratives?

Why did Judah retain its identity in exile when virtually all other displaced peoples lost their identities and assimilated?

What made return to Judah difficult for the Judean captives? Why did the restoration fail?

Study Resources

Biblical Narratives

Berlin, Adele. *Poetics and Interpretation of Biblical Narrative*. Winona Lake, IN: Eisenbrauns, 1994.

Chisholm, Robert B., Jr. "History or Story?: The Literary Dimension in Narrative Texts." In *Giving the Sense: Understanding and Using the Old Testament Historical Texts*. Edited by David M. Howard Jr. and Michael A. Grisanti, 54–73. Grand Rapids: Kregel, 2003.

———. *Interpreting the Historical Books: An Exegetical Handbook*. Grand Rapids: Kregel Academic & Professional, 2006.

Dutcher-Walls, Patricia. *Reading the Historical Books: A Student's Guide to Engaging the Biblical Text*. Grand Rapids: Baker Academic, 2014.

Hays, J. Daniel. "An Evangelical Approach to Old Testament Narrative Criticism." *BSac* 166 (2009): 3–18.

Long, V. Philips. *The Art of Biblical History*. Grand Rapids: Zondervan Academic, 1994.

Schnittjer, Gary Edward. "An Apprenticeship on the Torah." In *Torah Story: An Apprenticeship on the Pentateuch*, 4–19. 2nd ed. Grand Rapids: Zondervan Academic, 2023.

Ancient Near Eastern Context

The Ancient Near East in Pictures Relating to the Old Testament. Edited by James B. Pritchard. 2nd ed. Princeton: Princeton University Press, 1969.

Cogan, Mordechai. *Bound for Exile: Israelites and Judeans Under Imperial Yoke*. Jerusalem: Carta, 2013.

———. *The Raging Torrent: Historical Inscriptions from Assyria and Babylonia Relating to Ancient Israel*. Jerusalem: Carta, 2008.

Coogan, Michael D., and Mark S. Smith, eds. and trans. *Stories from Ancient Canaan*. Louisville, WJK, 2012.

Kuhrt, Amélie. *The Persian Empire: A Corpus of Sources from the Achaemenid Period*. New York: Routledge, 2007.

PART 1

Narratives of the Rise and Fall of the Hebrew Kingdoms

1

Joshua

Outline

Rehearsing commitment to invade the land of promise (1)

    Joshua selected to lead (1:1–11)

    Commitment of Transjordan tribes (1:12–18)

Military invasion of Canaan (2–12)

    Preparations for warfare (2–5)

    Jericho (6)

    Ai (7:1–8:29)

    Ceremony at Mount Ebal and Mount Gerizim (8:30–35)

    Gibeon's deception (9)

    Campaign against southern alliance (10)

    Campaign against northern alliance (11)

    Summary of military invasion (12)

Tribal distribution of the land (13–21)[1]

Transition to settlement (22–24)

    Trouble in the Transjordan (22)

    Final speeches of Joshua (23–24)

---

[1] See figure 1.4 for a detailed outline of Joshua 13–21.

Author, Date, and Message

The author of the book of Joshua is unknown. In composing the narrative, the author used many old sources such as the records of the tribal distribution of the land and a poem from the scroll of Jashar/the upright one (cf. Josh 10:13 CSB text note).

The book of Joshua was assembled long after the events therein as can be inferred by the series of updates that say "to this day."[2] It could not come into its present form until after Jerusalem was conquered by David (c. 1010–970 BCE), since the city was still called Jebus in the days of Joshua but is referred to as Jerusalem in the book (18:28). Joshua is not unusual on this account. Genesis includes a note that looks back at the establishment of Israel's kingship at some distance in the past, Deuteronomy looks back to the long-gone days of the conquest of the land, and Judges refers to the exile of Israel or Judah as a past event (Gen 36:31; Deut 2:12; Judg 18:30). Though scholars are divided, the reference to Beth-aven (a name meaning "House of Iniquity") next to Bethel (a name meaning "House of God") in Josh 7:2 may reflect Hosea mocking Bethel by calling it Beth-aven because of its shrine with a golden calf (c. 750–720 BCE).[3] In any case, Joshua was written sometime after the rise of the Davidic kingdom and before the compilation of the Deuteronomistic narrative perhaps in c. 561–560 BCE (see chapter 4).

Joshua stands as the first in a four-part serial narrative—Joshua, Judges, Samuel, and Kings—known as the Deuteronomistic narrative. These books narrate the rise and fall of the Hebrew kingdoms with special attention to breaking the covenant as expressed in Deuteronomy. The central theme of this collection hinges on explaining the inevitability of the exile (see introduction).

Joshua opens the Deuteronomistic narrative with Yahweh's faithfulness to his promises. Yahweh told Abraham that his descendants would inherit the land, and he assured Joshua that he would be with him in the military invasion of the land (Gen 15:16, 18–21; Deut 3:21–22, 28–29; 31:7–8, 23; Josh 1:2–9).

---

[2] See Josh 4:9; 5:9; 7:26; 8:28, 29; 9:27; 10:27; 13:13; 15:63; 16:10. A couple of the updates could refer to a time not long after the days of Joshua (6:25; 14:14) and a few others to the latter days of Joshua (22:3, 17; 23:8, 9).

[3] See Hos 4:15; 5:8; 10:5; and NET note on 4:15. Also see Thomas B. Dozeman, "Bethel in the Wars of Ambush in Joshua 7–8 and Judges 19–21," in *Writing, Rewriting, and Overwriting in the Books of Deuteronomy and the Former Prophets: Essays in Honour of Cynthia Edenburg*, ed. Ido Koch, Thomas Römer, and Omer Sergi (Leuven: Peeters, 2019), 112 [105–19].

Four themes run through Joshua: covenant, land, devoting the nations (*herem*, see later discussion), and fear. These themes interrelate with each other as well as with the message of the narrative. Yahweh provided proximate initial fulfillment of granting the land promised in the Abrahamic covenant. Israel's partial obedience to the law of devoting the nations was the vehicle for Yahweh's giving the land. Israel's fear of failure, their fear of the nations of Canaan, and the Canaanites' fear of Israel drive much of the story line.[4]

No one has captured the message of the book better than Joshua himself in his final speeches. Just as the Torah ends with Moses explaining Torah in Deuteronomy (cf. Deut 1:5), Joshua wraps up by interpreting the conquest (Joshua 23) and setting the conquest within a larger narrative framework (chap. 24). But notice both sides of Joshua's interpretation.

On one side the book emphasizes empirical evidence of Yahweh's faithfulness by repeating that it is still like this "to this day" as well as emphasizes eight piles of stones that bear witness to what they mark (see table 1.2). So, too, Joshua said, "*You yourselves have seen all that Yahweh your God has done* to all of these nations for your sake, for it is Yahweh your God who was fighting for you." (23:3 AT, emphasis added).

But on the other side, Joshua worried that Yahweh's faithfulness still left room for Israel's failure in the land they did not completely conquer. He warned Israel and encouraged them using the very words Moses and Yahweh had once used to encourage him (italics signify shared language and bold signifies the danger).

> [Yahweh:] Above all, *be strong* and *very* courageous *to observe carefully the whole instruction* my servant *Moses* commanded you. *Do not turn from it to the right or the left,* so that you will have success wherever you go. (1:7)

> [Joshua:] *Be very strong to observe carefully all* that is written in the book of *instruction of Moses, not turning from it to the right or the left,* so that you do not associate with **these nations remaining among you**. (23:6–7a AT)

Joshua had it right. Yahweh is faithful. And Israel almost obeyed. They obeyed during Joshua's lifetime. But his intuitive anxieties saw the underlying problem. Israel did not want to get rid of the remaining nations of Canaan. Israel longed to serve the Canaanite gods. But that is another story for the days of the judges.

---

[4] For fear themes, see Josh 2:9–11, 24; 5:1; 10:1–2; cf. 6:1; 9:3–4; 11:1.

Interpretive Overview

The narrative begins with Yahweh revealing to Joshua what he had previously mediated to him through Moses. He said three times, "Be strong and courageous" (Josh 1:6, 7, 9). That is exactly what he had told Moses to say to Joshua (Deut 31:7, 23) and what Yahweh had said to Israel using plural imperatives (31:6). This repeated call to strength and courage came with help of two kinds: Yahweh's presence and Torah.

If the covenant is embodied by Yahweh's proclamation that he is Israel's God and they are his own people (see introduction), then assurance formulas of his presence are closely associated. Yahweh brackets his revelation to Joshua with "*I will be with you,* just as I was with Moses. I will not leave you or abandon you" (Josh 1:5, emphasis added); and "*Yahweh your God is with you* wherever you go" (v. 9 AT, emphasis added). This is why Joshua and the people did not need to be in fear (cf. Deut 31:6).

The other basis for courage comes from the Torah. Those who obey Torah and talk of it all the time do exactly what those who love God with all their hearts do (Josh 1:7–8; Deut 6:4–9). At this point many readers trip.

Many think the passage says biblical study and obedience always lead to success: "so that you will have success wherever you go," and "for then you will prosper and succeed in whatever you do" (Josh 1:7–8). But this gets things turned around. A good analogy is misunderstanding when the psalmist said, "Delight yourself in Yahweh, and *he will give to you the desires of your heart*" (Ps 37:4 AT, emphasis added). Many readers wonder, *If I do what the verse says, will God give me whatever I want?* Sort of. But listen to the psalmist again: "*Delight yourself in Yahweh,* and he will give to you the desires of your heart" (AT, emphasis added). Those who delight in Yahweh have him as their heart's desire. It only seems like a trick from a self-serving perspective. In a similar manner the successful life of Joshua 1 does not mean getting whatever a person wants. It defines Torah obedience and biblical study as characteristics of success and prosperity.

All of this relates to securing the land Yahweh had promised to the Hebrew ancestors. Consider how the land stood as one of the major elements of God's promise to Abraham that unfolded in a series of revelations (table 1.1).[5]

The land connects Joshua with the Abrahamic and Mosaic covenants. Both covenants points toward the land (emphases added).[6]

---

[5] Table adapted from *OTUOT*, 12.

[6] See Daniel I. Block, *Covenant: The Framework of God's Grand Plan of Redemption* (Grand Rapids: Baker Academic, 2021), 86.

Table 1.1: Expansions of the Abrahamic Covenant

Genesis	Land	Descendants	Relationship
12:1–3	Land that the deity will show	Great nation	Families of the earth will be blessed
13:14–18	All the land Abraham can see, forever	Like dust of the earth	—
15:16–21	Return when Amorite iniquity complete; from Brook of Egypt to Euphrates	—	—
17:1–16	Land of Canaan	Renamed Abraham; sign of circumcision; forever	Multitudes of nations; kings
22:16–18	—	Like the sand	All nations of the earth will be blessed

<u>I am Yahweh who has brought you out from</u> Ur of the Chaldeans **to give to you this land** to possess. (Gen 15:7 AT)

<u>I am Yahweh</u> your God <u>who brought you out from</u> the land of Egypt **to give to you the land** of Canaan, to be your God. (Lev 25:38 AT)

This shows why commitment to the Torah of Moses was critical for Joshua.

Fronting the story of the Canaanite prostitute points toward the urgency of interpreting the law of devoting the nations of Canaan.[7] Modern readers are not the first ones to be troubled by the law that commands getting rid of the Canaanites. It starts in the Bible.

Joshua only sent two scouts, secretly. Readers may smile when they remember that Joshua himself was once one of the two scouts who gave a minority report against the other ten (Num 14:38). Readers may smile again when the two scouts went immediately to the house of a prostitute. But the dischronological narration creates drama to put aside the smiles. Readers are informed that the scouts were being hunted before a flashback of the prostitute hiding them (Josh 2:4).[8]

---

[7] See David G. Firth, *Including the Stranger: Foreigners in the Former Prophets* (Downers Grove, IL: IVP Academic, 2019), 22.

[8] See David G. Firth, *The Message of Joshua* (Downers Grove, IL: IVP Academic, 2015), 47.

Rahab the prostitute's act of delivering the scouts was backed up by her words. She recounted Yahweh's mercies and expressed her faith more directly than anyone in Israel. Rahab used the very words of the Torah (emphases signify parallels).

> Then the chiefs of Edom will be terrified; trembling will seize the leaders of Moab; **all the inhabitants of** Canaan **will panic [fear]**; **terror** and dread **will fall on** them. (Exod 15:15–16)

> Know this day and take to heart that <u>Yahweh is God in heaven above and on earth below</u>. There is no other. (Deut 4:39 AT)

> I know that Yahweh has given you the land because **terror has fallen upon us**, and **all the inhabitants of** the land **are fearful** before you . . . for <u>Yahweh</u> your God, he is <u>God in heaven above and on earth below</u>. (Josh 2:9, 11b AT)

Rahab's faithful actions secured a commitment from the scouts to spare her and her family. This was an exception in how Joshua applied the law of devoting (6:17). The law of devoting the nations of Canaan used the loaded Hebrew term *herem* (Deut 7:1–2; see Ancient Connections 1.1). Devoting everything that breathed to destruction would have included Rahab and her family (20:16–17; cf. Josh 10:40; also vv. 28, 35, 37, 39).

The rationale for the law of devoting the nations in Torah includes several issues. Devoting the nations of Canaan was Israel's idea, not Yahweh's (Num 21:1–3), though he held Israel to their vow and added it into the law (Deut 7:1–2). The law of devoting the Canaanites was a temporary law for the initial invasion of the land (v. 1a; 12:29a). The reason for the law was to protect Israel from sin and Yahweh's wrath (7:3–4). The judgment against the nations of Canaan was not racial but because they deserved it (9:4–6; cf. Gen 15:16). Yahweh treated rebellious Israel exactly the way he treated the nations of Canaan (Lev 18:24–30; 20:22–23; Deut 29:22–25). All of these issues have been explained in detail elsewhere.[9]

The basis of the Rahab exception stemmed from the rationale of the law of devoting. Devote them to destruction and do not intermarry with them "because they will turn your sons away from me to worship other gods" (Deut 7:4a; cf. 20:18). This did not apply to Rahab. Just as Paul stated in Rom 9:6 that not all Israel is Israel, so too Joshua realized that not all Canaanites were Canaanites.[10]

---

[9] See Schnittjer, *Torah Story*, 2nd ed., 428–32 (see intro., n. 10).

[10] See Schnittjer, 442.

ANCIENT CONNECTIONS 1.1: DEVOTING TO DESTRUCTION

An important parallel to the Hebrew term for "devote" (*ḥrm*) is the Moabite term *devote* (*ḥrm*) that appears in the Mesha inscription (830 BCE). Just as devoting the nations of Canaan to destruction was initiated by a vow of Israel in a time of crisis and later integrated into law because of what Israel vowed (Num 21:1–3; Deut 7:1–2), so, too, notice the parallel usage by King Mesha of Moab.

> Then Chemosh said to me [King Mesha], "Go, seize Nebo from Israel." So I went by night and I waged war against it from the break of dawn until midday. I seized it and **I killed everyone**—seven thousand m[e]n and boys and g[ir]ls and young women of marriageable age—**because I had devoted it** (*hḥrmth*) to Ashtar-Chemosh. Then I took from there th[e ves]sels of Yahweh and I dragged them before Chemosh (14b–18a, emphasis added).[a]

[a] Green, *"I Undertook Great Works,"* 104–5 (see intro., n. 16).

Yahweh did not part the waters of the Jordan River so that Israel could escape—as he did at the sea crossing forty years earlier—but to initiate an attack. The remarkable invisible damming up of the water is bracketed by the feet of the worship personnel first touching the water until they stepped out on the other side (Josh 3:15; 4:18).

The amount of detail is one of the signals of the importance of the event. Other indicators of its importance include dating the event only forty days after Moses's death to the tenth day of the first month (Deut 1:3; 34:8; Josh 4:19); connecting the sea and river crossings in a way that effectively brackets the entire wilderness experience (Josh 4:23; cf. Ps 114:3); and twice anticipating children asking about the stone monument (Josh 4:6, 21).

The stone monument that children would ask about in years to come referred to twelve stones taken from the empty riverbed, one by a representative of each tribe. But there was a second stone monument in the riverbed proximate to where the worship personnel stood with the ark while the waters stopped and the people passed through (v. 9). These were the first two of eight memorials of stone that bore witness to events in Joshua (see table 1.2). Many of these stone memorials include the notation that they remain "to this day." The twice-repeated youthful question, "What is the meaning of these stones?" invites the same question for all of the piles of stones (v. 21; cf. v. 6).

Table 1.2: Eight Stone Memorials in Joshua

	Witnesses to Yahweh's Fidelity	Witnesses to Rebellion
4:8, 20–24	Twelve stones in Gilgal	
4:9	Twelve stones in riverbed of Jordan where worship personnel stood with ark	
7:25–26		Heap of stones over Achan
8:29		Heap of stones over king of Ai
8:32	Blessings and curses of torah of Moses	
10:27		Large stones entombed the kings of Jerusalem, Hebron, Jarmuth, Lachish, and Eglon in a cave
22:26–28	Transjordan nonfunctional altar since they worship at the tabernacle	
24:25–27	Large stone under the oak at Shechem covered a Torah scroll of the people's commitment to obedience	

Crossing the Jordan River sent fear into the rulers of the nations of Canaan (5:1). Before attacking Jericho the narrator included three vignettes that connected with the days of redemption from Egypt in sobering ways.

First, the entire generation of Israel born and raised in the wilderness was uncircumcised and needed to take the sign of the covenant (vv. 2–7). This reminds readers in the know of Yahweh meeting up with Moses to kill him on his way to Egypt. His wife, Zipporah, delivered Moses from Yahweh by performing an emergency circumcision on their son (Exod 4:24–26). Instead of learning anything from his near-death experience, Moses led Israel for forty years without making any of them commit to the covenant by its entry sign. Circumcision served as a physical sign of Israelite faith and commitment to the covenant and its obligations. Yahweh framed the covenantal obligations in broad terms to Abraham: "Walk before me and be blameless" (Gen 17:1 NET). In Yahweh's mercy he gave the gift of the Mosaic covenant, beginning with the Ten Commandments, to Israel to flesh out his covenantal standards.

Second, when Israel celebrated their first Passover in the land the manna ceased (Josh 5:10–12).

Third, Joshua saw the commander of Yahweh's army with his sword drawn. The commander told Joshua to remove his sandals because he stood on holy ground (v. 15). This obscure event connected with Moses removing his sandals before the burning bush (Exod 3:5).

Just as the narrative explicitly connected crossing the river with crossing the sea, the three vignettes of Joshua 5 established continuities with the generation of the redemption from Egypt. Yet, these connections come with theological baggage. Unlike crossing the sea when Yahweh killed the Egyptian army himself, the river crossing led Israel into warfare, requiring them to get their own hands dirty. The shocking reality that an entire generation spurned the sign of the covenant leaves a bitter aftertaste when reminded of Moses's failure to circumcise his son until his own life hung in the balance. The manna ended because the people now had the land. But the land was not automatic like manna. It required cultivation, adequate rain, and safety from predatorial enemies. These were all things for which the gods of Canaan were known (see introduction). The statement of the commander of Yahweh's army that he was not for Israel nor for the enemy also gives pause (v. 14). Entering into Yahweh's covenant did not somehow obligate him to Israel's will. That is not what kind of covenant it is. Yahweh is the suzerain, and the people are his subjects (see introduction). In sum, the three vignettes offer positive ways forward, but trouble lingered nearby each continuity.

The narrative presents only four conquest episodes—or five if Gibeon's non-conquest is counted—to represent a much larger, extended military campaign implied from the evidence of the list of defeated rulers in Joshua 12. These four conquest episodes plus one nonconquest episode foreground the theological implications that Joshua himself draws out in one of his last speeches in chapter 23. The present purpose includes considering how the narrator develops the theological implications of the conquest in relation to Joshua's speech (table 1.3).

The attack on Jericho included an elaborate seven-day procession featuring the ark, worship personnel, and seven trumpets. The fortified city known for its great walls was defeated when Israel shouted and Jericho's walls simply collapsed. As promised, the prostitute who delivered the scouts and her whole family was spared. While Rahab's family initially lived outside the camp (6:23), they later assimilated into Israel (v. 25). The battle ended with Joshua pronouncing a curse on anyone who would rebuild the city (v. 26; see Ancient Connections 1.2).

Table 1.3: Military Episodes of the Conquest Aligned with Joshua 23

Chapter	Locale	Military Episodes	Joshua 23
6	Jericho	"Look, **I have handed Jericho ... to you** ... Then the city wall will collapse (6:2a, 5b).	"Yahweh your God ... **was fighting for you**" (23:3b AT).
(7)	(Achan)	"Achan ... took the devoted things and **the anger of Yahweh was kindled against Israel**" (7:1b AT).	"If you violate the covenant of Yahweh your God ... **then Yahweh's anger will be kindled against you, and you will quickly perish from this good land that he has given you**" (23:16 AT).
8	Ai	"Yahweh said to Joshua, 'Stretch out the javelin that is in your hand over the city, **for I will give it into your hand**'" (8:18a AT; cf. v. 1).	"Yahweh has driven out before you great and powerful nations, and **no one has been able to stand before you**" (23:9 AT).
(9)	(Gibeon)	"The Israelites took some of their provisions, **but they did not ask for Yahweh's direction**" (9:14 AT).	"**Watch yourselves carefully to love Yahweh your God.** For if you turn away and seek the remnant of these nations that remain with you ..." (23:11–12 AT).
10	Northern campaign	"**Yahweh threw them into confusion** before Israel, and he soundly defeated them ... **Yahweh threw large stones** upon them from heaven ... because **Yahweh, the God of Israel, fought for Israel**" (10:10a, 11a, 42b AT; cf. vv. 13–14).	"Yahweh your God ... **was fighting for you**" (23:3b AT).

Chapter	Locale	Military Episodes	Joshua 23
11	Southern campaign	"All the military went out with them—**many people, like the sand upon the seashore** . . . Yahweh gave them into the hand of Israel, and **they defeated them and they pursued them . . .**" (11:4a, 8a AT; cf. v. 6).	"Yahweh has driven out before you great and powerful nations, and no one has been able to stand before you to this day. **One of you causes a thousand to run away**" (23:9–10a AT).

ANCIENT CONNECTIONS 1.2: UTTERLY DESTROYING CITIES

Modern people tend to recoil at the biblical accounts of killing all the people of a defeated city. Modern warfare only rarely includes killing entire cities inclusive of civilians and children, like when the United States dropped atomic bombs on two Japanese cities in 1945. Even though those who served in the Pacific theater of World War II could explain the importance of these two events, that fact does not remove the gravity of civilian deaths.

Ancient warfare sometimes included killing everyone in defeated cities. An example of this is seen in the royal inscriptions of the Assyrian king Tiglath-pileser I (1114–1076 BCE). Similar to Joshua's destruction of Jericho (Josh 6:26), Tiglath-pileser knocked down the walls and warned against rebuilding the city (emphasis added):

> I overwhelmed the city of Hunusu, their fortified city, (so that it looked) like a ruin hill (created by) the deluge. Violently I fought with their mighty army in city and mountain (and) brought about their defeat. I laid low their men-at-arms in the mountains like sheep. Like lambs I cut off their heads (and) made their blood flow into the hollows and plains of the mountains. (Thus) I conquered that city. I took their gods (and) brought out their possessions (and) property. I burnt the city. *The three great walls* which were constructed with baked brick and the entire city I razed, destroyed, turned into a ruin hill and strewed *şipu*-stones over it. I made bronze lightning bolts (and) inscribed on them (a description of) the conquest of the lands which with my god, my lord, I conquered *(and a warning) not to occupy that city and not to rebuild its wall.* (*ARI* 2:15)

To prepare for an attack against Ai, for the last time Joshua sent ahead scouts, who assured him that a mere 3,000 troops could defeat the insignificant town in the hill country. When Ai soundly defeated them, Joshua and Israel lost courage (Josh 7:5–9). Yahweh assured Joshua that they were defeated because someone in Israel had taken devoted things (v. 11). Though generally plunder was not devoted to Yahweh, Jericho was a special case (6:18–19). What was devoted to Yahweh became extremely holy and could not be redeemed (Lev 27:28–29). Though the cause of devoting an entire town to destruction differed, the expression for taking devoted things applies to Achan: "Let nothing that has been doomed *stick to your hand* (Deut 13:17 NJPS, emphasis added; cf. Josh 7:21).

At the moment of judgment Joshua made a wordplay on Achan's name. He said, "Why have you troubled (*achar*) us? Yahweh shall trouble (*achor*) you this day!" (Josh 7:25a AT). The stones used to kill Achan and his family stood as the third heap of stones in the Valley of Trouble/*Achor* (see table 1.2). Since Achan's individual crime brought collective judgment on Israel—the Israelites broke faith (v. 1)—the punishment fell collectively on Achan's family. Interpreters struggle with this and wonder if Achan's family is to blame along with him. The collective judgment on Achan and his family for taking devoted plunder stands in stark contrast to the collective deliverance of Rahab and her family from the destruction of Jericho.

Israel's second attack on Ai involved ten times as many troops (7:3; 8:3) as well as an elaborate scheme to draw out Ai's military from the city. Joshua stood with an outstretched javelin until Ai had been utterly devoted (8:18, 26). Joshua's outstretched javelin connects with the drawn sword of the commander of Yahweh's army, even while the different weapons make them distinct (5:13). This time the plunder belonged to Israel (8:2, 27).

The last section of Joshua 8 features a significant intermission halfway through the four battle episodes. Israel held a prescribed formal covenant ceremony making an altar of unfinished stones according to the altar law (Exod 20:25) and writing torah on stone monuments on Mount Ebal (Josh 8:30–32). Then Israel stood before Mount Gerizim and Mount Ebal, half and half, for the pronouncement of blessing and curses according to the twice-repeated expectation for this ceremony in Deuteronomy (vv. 33–35; Deut 11:29; 27:2–8, 11–14). This ceremony demonstrates that the conquest was covenantal, and it draws attention to Yahweh's faithfulness to fulfill his word as well as Israel's obligations to the covenant under the threat of curse and the hope of blessing.

The deception of Gibeon relates to the version of the law of devoting in Deuteronomy 20 as well as the warning against collective treaties with the people of the land in Exod 23:32. As opposed to the land of promise, Israel could make peace and put under subjection peoples who lived "far away" (Deut 20:15; cf. vv. 16–18). The narrative of Israel's debacle with Gibeon uses "far away" three times to show Israel's failure in making a treaty with a quartet of towns in their midst (Josh 9:6, 9, 22).[11] The people of Gibeon dressed up in old clothes and took old food to secure a treaty by deception—pretending they were all new and fresh when they left their supposedly distant home. Israel tried to honor the law by actually eating the bad food. Heavy voiceover narration tells readers what is missing: "They did not ask for Yahweh's direction" (v. 14 AT). Readers discover that obedience is more than mere compliance to the letter of the law. True obedience can only happen within a relationship to Yahweh.

The outcome of Gibeon's deception is Joshua accepting a quartet of towns in the heart of Israel inhabited by Hivites (figure 1.1). Tragically, in days to come the ark would remain at one of the sister-towns, Kiriath-jearim, and the tabernacle would remain at Gibeon, forgotten by Israel (cf. 1 Sam 7:1; 1 Chr 13:3, 5; 16:39). This arrangement makes sense practically because the people of Gibeon were permanently tasked with tending to the sanctuary (Josh 9:23, 27). Even more tragically, Joshua is immediately called on to honor his treaty and defend Gibeon (10:6).

Figure 1.1: Joshua's Early Victories and Failures (Joshua 6, 7, 8, 9)

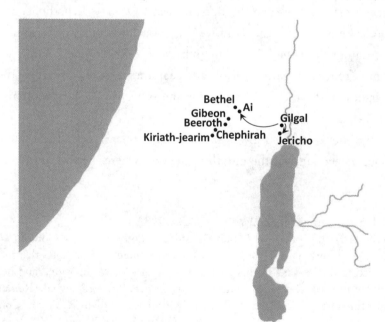

---

[11] See "*rahoq*," Even-Shoshan, 1071 (nos. 59, 60, 69).

The southern campaign includes several sensational cosmic acts of Yahweh against the coalition of five southern kings who banded together against Gibeon (figure 1.2). Yahweh directly fights for Israel. The narrator uses "Yahweh" as the subject of a series of active verbs describing his fight for Israel (bold signifies third-person singular finite verbs with "Yahweh" as the subject, and italics signify a nonfinite verb).

> **Yahweh put them into a turmoil** before Israel. **He struck them down** in a great rout at Gibeon and **pursued them** on the road to the Bet-horon ascent, and **struck them down** as far as Azekah and as far as Makkedah. While they were fleeing from before Israel (they were on the Bet-horon descent), **Yahweh threw** big stones at them from the heavens, as far as Azekah. . . . The sun stood still, the moon halted, until a nation took redress from its foes. (It's written on the Document of the Upright One [Jashar], isn't it.) The sun stood in the middle of the heavens and didn't hasten to set, the like of a whole day. There hasn't been anything like that day before it or after it *for Yahweh's listening* to someone's voice, because **Yahweh was battling** for Israel. (10:10–11a, 13–14 FT)

Since the days of Galileo, many interpreters have balked at the sun standing still because of the grave implications of stopping the earth's rotation. They often suggest the language from the poetry in the Book of Jashar (v. 13) is hyperbolic, or exaggerated for literary emphasis, in the narrative.[12] The Baal myth may use a similar expression: "The Luminary of the Gods, Sun, [burn]s. *The heavens stop.*"[13] In any case, the victory comes from God. Notice the difference in the nonfinite verb form of verse 14 above in italics versus the finite verbs for the other divine interventions in bold (vv. 10, 11, 14).[14]

The "large stones" (AT) Yahweh threw from the heavens (v. 11) anticipated the "large stones" Israel put over the mouth of the cave where the five dead kings of the

---

[12] See discussion in Firth, *The Message of Joshua*, 123.

[13] "Palace of Baal," 3 v 25–26 (emphasis added), quoted in Cyrus Gordon, *Ugarit and Minoan Crete* (New York: W. W. Norton, 1966), 56. Elsewhere Gordon notes that the Ugaritic term *la* applied to the heavens in this context may signify "weak" or "stop," and he observes the similarity to Josh 10:12–13. See Cyrus Gordon, *Ugaritic Textbook*, rev. ed. (Rome: Editrice Pontificio Istituto Biblico, 1998), 426a (no. 1341). And see William A. Ward, "Comparative Studies in Egyptian and Ugaritic," *Journal of Near Eastern Studies* 20, no. 1 (1961): 35 [31–40].

[14] For other examples of the infinitive of purpose getting at circumstances akin to "Yahweh's *listening to*" (Josh 10:14 FT, emphasis added), see GKC §114i.

Figure 1.2: Joshua's Southern Campaign to Defend Gibeon (Joshua 10)

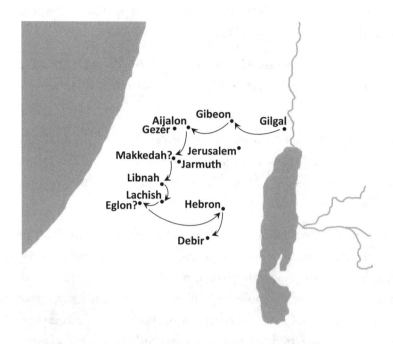

coalition were buried (v. 27). These large stones made up the sixth such testimony in Joshua (see table 1.2). The account concludes by backtracking and repetitively telling of Joshua's devoting to destruction a series of cities that had banded with the five southern kings against Gibeon.[15]

Upon hearing of Joshua's victories in the southern campaign, a large coalition of northern peoples of Canaan come together to battle against Israel. The coalition's army had horses, chariots, and large numbers—"a multitude as numerous as the sand on the seashore" (11:4). Yahweh directly reveals victory to Joshua as he had in the past battles, except for the first aborted attack on Ai and the treaty with Gibeon's quartet of towns (v. 6). The narrative jumps to Joshua's sudden attack on the northern Canaanite coalition at the waters north of Merom (v. 7; figure 1.3). The decisive victory is followed by dedicating Hazor to destruction and by the complete defeat of the enemy troops who had gathered against Israel. The narrator includes a final note to explain the entire era of Israel's conquest of the land of promise: Yahweh hardened the heart of the Canaanites (see Biblical Connections, page 60).

---

[15] See Lissa M. Wray Beal, *Joshua*, SGBC (Grand Rapids: Zondervan Academic, 2019), 235–36.

After the battle story comes the distribution of the land of promise. Joshua 13–21 has been carefully arranged. Note the resumptive repetition or *inclusio* around it (emphasis added).

> **Joshua was old and advanced in years,** and Yahweh said to him, "*You are old and advanced in years* but much of the land remains to be conquered. (13:1 AT)

> A long time later after Yahweh had given rest to Israel from all their surrounding enemies, **Joshua was old and advanced in years.** So Joshua summoned all Israel, including its elders, leaders, judges, and officers, and said to them, "*I am old, advanced in age.*" (23:1–2, v. 1 AT)

This *inclusio* sets the distribution of the land as background to the story proper.

Within the outer frame of Joshua's old age is another contrastive outer frame that begins with much of the land still needing to be taken (13:2–6; cf. Exod 23:29–30) and concludes with Yahweh completely fulfilling his word and giving Israel rest from all her enemies (Josh 21:43–45). The tension between Israel's incomplete obedience and Yahweh's complete faithfulness ripples across the days of the judges.

Figure 1.3: Joshua's Northern Campaign (Joshua 11)

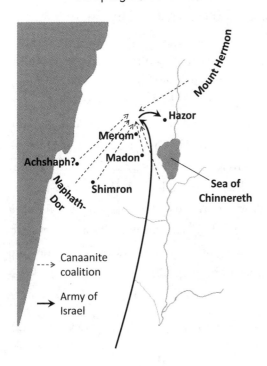

Next, within the outer contrastive frame of Israel's almost obedience and Yahweh's complete faithfulness stands the distribution of the land. The account of distribution first rehearses the inheritance under Moses of the Transjordan tribes—the land on the east side of the Jordan River—and then explains the inheritance under Joshua of Judah, Joseph (Ephraim and Manasseh), and the other seven tribes (figure 1.4). The placement of the Transjordan tribes near the catastrophic building of a giant altar beside the Jordan River in Joshua 22 plays a part in framing the entire book (1:12–18; 22:1–34).

Figure 1.4 provides a reading guide for Joshua 13–21. It identifies some surprises, such as tribes named after Joseph's two sons Ephraim and Manasseh treated as "Joseph"; the remaining unsettled land among Judah, Ephraim, and Manasseh that would be taken up in Judges; and special notice of land granted to Caleb and Joshua. Other surprises await a close reading. For example, consider how the narrator highlights women who demanded and got allotments—Achsah (15:16–19; cf. Judg 1:12–15) and Zelophehad's daughters (Josh 17:3–4; cf. Num 27:1–11; 36:1–12). It may also help to consider a general geographical orientation of the tribal allotments (figure 1.5).

The tribes of the Transjordan—Reuben, Gad, and the half-tribe of Manasseh—had a habit of taking actions that brought all of Israel to the brink of disaster. The opening of the book of Joshua pauses to let the Transjordan tribes reiterate their commitment to the conquest of the land of promise on the west side of the Jordan River (Josh 1:12–18). This reminds readers of the time the tribes told Moses that since he had defeated the enemies of the Transjordan, they would stay back and settle their towns there. When Moses confronted them as traitors, they assured him of their full intention of going with Israel to take the lands west of the Jordan River and then settle

Figure 1.4: Literary Framework of Tribal Inheritance

Joshua's old age (13:1a)
Israel's incomplete conquest of the land (13:1b–6)
    Transjordan tribal inheritance by Moses (13:8–33)
    Land allotment by Eleazar and Joshua by casting lots (14:1–5)
        Caleb inherits Hebron (14:13–15)
    Judah's inheritance (15:1–62), except settling Jebus/Jerusalem (15:63)
        Caleb inherits Hebron (15:13–15)
        Joseph's inheritance (16:1–4)
    Ephraim's inheritance (16:5–10), except settling Gezer (16:10)
    Manasseh's inheritance (17:1–11), except settling Canaanite towns (17:12–13)
        Joseph needs more land (17:14–18)
        Casting lots for the other seven tribes (18:1–10)
    Benjamin's inheritance (18:11–28)
    Simeon's inheritance within Judah (19:1–9)
    Zebulun's inheritance (19:10–16)
    Issachar's inheritance (19:17–23)
    Asher's inheritance (19:24–31)
    Naphtali's inheritance (19:32–39)
    Dan's inheritance (19:40–48)
        Joshua's inheritance in Ephraim (19:49–50)
        Conclusion of inheritance by casting lots (19:51)
    Towns of refuge (20:1–9)
    Towns for Levites including cities of refuge (21:1–42)
Yahweh's complete fulfillment to give rest from Israel's enemies (21:43–45)
Transjordan tribes' nearly catastrophic giant altar of witness (22:1–34)
Joshua's old age (23:1–2)

Figure 1.5: General Geographical Orientation of the Tribal Allotments

their own towns (see Numbers 32). After the tribal distribution of the land, the Transjordan tribes made another seemingly traitorous move. They constructed a giant altar by the Jordan River (Josh 22:10).

The narrator of Joshua builds the account of the seemingly traitorous giant altar of the Transjordan tribes according to the template of their rebellion-like actions in Numbers 32 (table 1.4).

Both Moses and Phinehas worried that the Transjordan tribes were "turning from Yahweh" (Num 32:15 AT; Josh 22:16, 18 AT).[16] Though civil war had been averted, readers need to remember the Transjordan tribes' habit of bringing Israel to the edge of disaster. This is a clue for what lies ahead. In the days of the judges, any time the scene shifts to the Transjordan, watch out. It is wild on that side of the Jordan River.[17]

The setting of Joshua's final speech exudes the covenant. After the battle of Ai the people had performed a covenant ceremony proclaiming the blessings from Mount Gerizim and the curses from Mount Ebal, as called for by Moses (Josh 8:30–35; cf. Deut 11:29). Joshua gives his final speech at Shechem nestled as it is between these two mountains (Josh 24:1; figure 1.6).[18]

Joshua tells the story of Yahweh's covenantal faithfulness. He goes from the election of Abraham, through the redemption from Egyptian slavery, through the wilderness trials, and up to the conquest of the land of promise. While nearly all of the panoramic retrospective comes from the Torah, Joshua adds two elements not in the Torah.

---

[16] See Lissa Wray Beal, "The Past as Threat and Hope: Reading Joshua with Numbers," *BBR* 27, no. 4 (2017): 467–71 [461–83].

[17] Thank you to Michael Carasik for this observation.

[18] For a similar observation, see Block, *Covenant*, 257.

Table 1.4: Similarities between Numbers 32 and Joshua 22

Numbers 32	Joshua 22
Transjordan tribes requested staying put rather than going to war alongside Israel (vv. 1–5).	Transjordan tribes made a giant altar near the Jordan River (vv. 10–12).
Moses accused Transjordan tribes of revolution (vv. 6–15).	Phinehas and tribal representatives accused Transjordan tribes of revolution (vv. 13–20).
Transjordan tribes claimed Moses misunderstood because they were going to war alongside Israel (vv. 16–19, 25–27).	Transjordan tribes claimed Phinehas misunderstood because the altar bore witness to their support of only worshiping at the altar of the tabernacle (vv. 21–29, 34).
Moses accepted the commitment of the Transjordan tribes to military service alongside Israel (vv. 20–24).	Phinehas and tribal representatives accepted that the Transjordan tribes had not revolted (vv. 30–31).
Transjordan inheritance (vv. 33–42).	Transjordan inheritance (vv. 1–9).

Figure 1.6: Shechem between Mount Gerizim and Mount Ebal

Mount Gerizim

Mount Ebal

Shechem

Sketch by Gary Edward Schnittjer

Joshua said that the family of Terah, father of Abraham, served other gods when they lived in Mesopotamia (24:2). He also said that the exodus generation worshiped the gods of Egypt (v. 14). Torah says nothing about either of these.[19] Joshua filled in this essential backstory to get to the point of his covenantal retrospective. His angst pivoted on his belief that when he died Israel would turn away from Yahweh to other gods. At the high point Joshua asked a damning question:

---

[19] Elsewhere Ezekiel recounts the exodus generation worshiping the gods of Egypt (Ezek 20:8).

If it is evil in your eyes to serve Yahweh, then choose this day *who you will serve, whether the gods your ancestors served beyond the Euphrates River or the gods of the Amorites, in whose land you are living*. But I and my household, we will serve Yahweh. (v. 15 AT, emphasis added)

Caleb and Joshua alone trusted Yahweh and made it out of the wilderness alive. Joshua concludes his last speech with the same minority view. Even if all of Israel served other gods, he and his household would follow Yahweh.

Joshua's bold faith moved the people to say they would follow Yahweh also. This started a back-and-forth because Joshua did not believe the people.

"We will too," they said.

"No you won't," he said.

"Yes we will."

Joshua finally accepted the congregation's claims and said, "You are witnesses against yourselves," to which they replied, "We are witnesses!" (v. 22). This leads to the eighth of eight stone memorials in the narrative (see table 1.2). Joshua put the covenant oath of the people in writing on a stone and set it up under the oak at Shechem.

Unfortunately, Joshua's anxieties were well founded. The days of the judges found Israel repeatedly breaking the covenant renewed at Shechem.

Biblical Connections

The biblical connections that can be taken up here involve the nations of Canaan: large-size Canaanites, law of devoting, and avoiding covenants. Many modern readers do not realize that interpreting the laws about Canaanites is a leading concern of the authors of the Torah and the Deuteronomistic narrative.

When the twelve scouts gave their report to Israel at Kadesh only Caleb and Joshua dissented. The other scouts mythologized the Anakites, saying they were from the preflood Nephilim.[20] They were so large it made Israel seem like locusts—the smallest animal allowed in the dietary regulations (Num 13:33; cf. Lev 11:22). The singular faith of Caleb and Joshua in Yahweh explains why they alone cross the Jordan River and enter the land of promise forty years later. They are given an opportunity to live up to their bold report as scouts. The narrator credits Joshua and Caleb with defeating the large-sized Anakites (Josh 11:21; 15:13–14; cf. 14:14–15). The only

---

[20] See Schnittjer, *Torah Story*, 346–48.

Anakites remaining were in three cities, including Gath, where a large champion would later emerge to taunt Israel in the days of Saul (11:22; cf. 1 Sam 17:4).

The Joshua narrative is dominated by allusions to the law of devoting the nations of Canaan in Deut 7:1–5 and 20:16–18. The story of Rahab the prostitute shows that the issue is not racial or ethnic. The four battle accounts of Joshua plus the deception of Gibeon all allude to the law of devoting.

The final allusion to the law of devoting the nations in the military invasion section of Joshua provides decisive insight. At the close of the fourth of four narrated battle episodes the narrator pauses to provide a backstage theological rationale. The narrative connects the military victories of Joshua with Yahweh's redemptive terrors against Egypt. Before, after, and between every one of the ten cosmic terrors inflicted on Egypt in Exodus the narrative offers readers an ultrasound of Pharaoh's heart. Pharaoh often hardened his own heart. But when he did not, God hardened it for him.[21] Notice how the narrator of Joshua connects the law of devoting and the hardening of the hearts of the nations of Canaan (emphases added).[22]

> Yahweh said to Moses, "When you go back to Egypt, see that you do before pharaoh all the wonders that I have put in your hand. But I **will harden** his **heart** so that he will not let the people go." (Exod 4:21 AT)[23]

> When Yahweh your God gives them over to you and you defeat them, you must completely destroy them. Do not make a covenant with them and show them no mercy. (Deut 7:2 AT)

> For it was Yahweh who **hardened their hearts** to do battle against Israel so that they might destroy them and not give them mercy, as Yahweh had commanded Moses. (Josh 11:20 AT)

Devoting the nations of Canaan did not stem from cultural hatred or ethnicity. Their hardness of heart stemmed from divine judgment for wickedness (Gen 15:16; Deut 9:4–5). When Israel rebelled, Yahweh treated them in precisely the same manner (Lev 18:28; Deut 29:23).[24] Wickedness had serious consequences for the nations of Canaan and for Israel.

---

[21] See Schnittjer, *Torah Story*, 193–94 (letter "d" 11x in table 13-E).

[22] See *OTUOT*, 159–60.

[23] Most cases of the hardening of Pharaoh's heart use the same term (*ḥzq*) appearing in Josh 11:20 (see Exod 4:21; 7:13, 22; 8:19; 9:12, 35; 10:20, 27; 11:10; 14:4, 8, 17). A few other cases use synonyms with an identical sense in context (*qshh*, 7:3; *khvd*, 8:15; 10:1).

[24] See Schnittjer, *Torah Story*, 431.

When the Gibeonites deceived Israel, the people made a collective treaty with them. In the first of Joshua's two final speeches, he warns the congregation against making personal treaties with the nations of Canaan by intermarriage. Torah speaks against both collective (Exod 23:32; Deut 7:1–2) and personal treaties with the nations of Canaan (Exod 34:15–16; Deut 7:3–4). Joshua's warning builds off the law against personal treaties through apostasy marriages (thematic parallels emphasized).

> Be careful not to make a treaty with the inhabitants of the land that you are going to enter; otherwise, they will **become a snare** among you. . . . <u>Then you will take some of their daughters as brides for your sons</u>. Their daughters will prostitute themselves with their gods and cause your sons to prostitute themselves with their gods. (Exod 34:12, 16)

> For if you turn away and seek the remnant of these nations that remain with you, and <u>if you intermarry with them and establish relations with them</u>, then know for certain that Yahweh your God will no longer drive out these nations before you. They will **become** a trap and **a snare** to you, to be a whip on your back and thorns in your eyes until you perish from this good land that Yahweh your God has given to you. (Josh 23:12–13 AT)

In the context of arranged marriages in the ancient world it is natural that parents want to help their children with beneficial marriage matches. Israelite parents as wandering newcomers could see how marriage matches to the established peoples of the land would offer financial and social stability to their children. This grave temptation persists from the conquest until the restoration after the exile.

Moses put in vivid terms the tragic outcome of trying to help one's children in this way: your children will "go a whoring after" false gods (Exod 34:16 KJV). Joshua speaks of gouging the flesh and the eyes (Josh 23:13). As attractive as apostasy marriages always seem to be, they ruin people.

Gospel Connections

Before narrating the conquest, the author tells of Rahab the prostitute. This is the right place to start because not all Canaanites were Canaanites. By faith Rahab and her family fully assimilate into Israel (Josh 6:25). Her faith places her side by side with Abraham and the near sacrifice of his son in the New Testament (James 2:25). Rahab even marries into the tribe of Judah and has a son named Boaz, the great-grandfather of King David.

Rahab is a matriarch of the Messiah (Matt 1:5). Messiah came to save people like those in his own family line.

Life Connections

Joshua begins with a written Torah scroll in the story (Josh 1:8). The book ends by placing the people within the Torah's story. There is no gap, bump, or seam between Joshua 24 verses 10 and 11. After "you" were delivered from Balaam's damning curse (v. 10), "you" were delivered from the nations of Canaan (vv. 11–12). The Torah's story of Israel in the wilderness flows directly into the Joshua story in the land because they are part of the larger redemptive narrative that culminates in the teaching, death, and resurrection of the Messiah.

The place of the Torah within Joshua and the place of the people of Joshua's day within the Torah narrative models the Christian situation. Those who think of the Bible merely as an app on a device or a book on a shelf only get it half right. Treating the Bible only as a book about them and not as telling our story is a breeding ground for the pandemic of deformed Christian views stretching across many lands. It is crucial to read Scripture into our lives as well as define our identity and destiny within scriptural narrative. The Bible is an app. But it also needs to be our own story.

Interactive Questions

How does the book of Joshua function within the Deuteronomistic narrative?

How does the Joshua narrative relate to the Abrahamic and Mosaic covenants?

What role do fear and courage play in Joshua?

What is the meaning of devoting (*herem*) the nations of Canaan?

How do stone memorials play a role in Joshua?

How should collective versus individual responsibility be interpreted in the accounts of Rahab and Achan?

What does the Gibeonite deception teach about obedience to God's commands?

How does the first of Joshua's final speeches (Joshua 23) offer an interpretation of the military campaigns in the days of Joshua?

How can the statements of securing rest from all Israel's enemies (Josh 21:43–45) be understood in light of the fact that many areas of the land remain not conquered (13:2–6, 13; 15:63; 16:10; 17:12)?

What are the implications of the Torah as a book in Joshua and Joshua as a continuation of the Torah's story?

Study Resources

Butler, Trent C. *Joshua 1–12* and *Joshua 13–24*. 2nd ed. WBC. Grand Rapids: Zondervan, 2014.

Firth, David G. *Including the Stranger: Foreigners in the Former Prophets.* Downers Grove, IL: IVP Academic, 2019.

Wray Beal, Lissa M. *Joshua.* SGBC. Grand Rapids: Zondervan Academic, 2019.

———. "The Past as Threat and Hope: Reading Joshua with Numbers." *BBR* 27, no. 4 (2017): 461–83.

2

Judges

Outline

First introduction: Tribal failures (1:1–2:5)
Second introduction: Moral decline generation by generation (2:6–3:6)
Delivering judges (3–16)

[Judges with full cycle]	**[Minor judges]**
Othniel of Judah against assault of Aram-naharaim (3:7–11)	
Ehud of Benjamin against assault of Moab (3:12–30)	
	Shamgar son of Anath (3:31)
Deborah of Ephraim against assault of Canaan (4–5)	
Gideon of Manasseh against assault of Midian and his concubine's son Abimelech (6–9)	
	Tola of Issachar (10:1–2)
	Jair of Gilead (10:3–5)

Jephthah of Gilead against assault of Ammon
(10:6–12:7)

Ibzan of Bethlehem (12:8–10)
Elon of Zebulun (12:11–12)
Abdon of Pirathon (12:13–15)

Samson of Dan against assault of Philistia
(13–16)
First epilogue: Levitical and Danite distortions (17–18)
Second epilogue: Benjamite distortions spread to all Israel (19–21)

Author, Date, and Message

The author of Judges is unknown. It could not have come into its present form until at least 722 BCE after the northern kingdom was taken into exile (18:30). It stands within the Deuteronomistic serial narrative—Joshua, Judges, Samuel, Kings—that goes from Israel's entry into the land until its exile. Judges goes a long way toward the purpose of showing readers of the Deuteronomistic narrative why the exile was inevitable. It tells of Israel's profound and fully developed rebellion from the beginning.

The main characters of the book are known as judges. They should not be confused with modern judges with gavels and robes. The roots for "deliver" (*ysh'*) and "judge" (*shpht*) are used interchangeably: "Yahweh raised up *judges* [*shpht*], and they *delivered* [*ysh'*] them out of the hand of the predators" (2:16 AT, emphasis added). Ideally, the judges should have delivered Israel to justice. This ideal strengthens the irony of the days of the judges.

To get at the message of Judges requires consideration of the ending and the book's satirical humor. The author moves the story along episode by episode, building toward a surprise ending. No biblical author uses more irony or humor than the author of Judges.

At first, readers are unsure if they should laugh at the ancient polemical humor. It is easier for modern readers to smile when the same kind of biting ridicule turns on the hapless judges and people of Israel. Yet somewhere it stops seeming funny as the increasingly dark humor builds to the perverse ending.

The use of dark humor as a tool of covenantal narrative points toward a prophetic author. The profile of the prophetic storymakers of Judges aligns with prophets like Amos who weaponized the Torah to taunt the moral failure of religious elites. Amos mocked the hypocritical, affluent worshipers who did not help those in need by exaggerating both their religious devotion and their shameful treatment of the disadvantaged.[1] The ironic, satirical stories of the prophets of the northern kingdom of Israel scattered across Kings and appearing in Jonah stand in the same general orbit. The use of scornful humor in Judges does not demand but suggests prophetic authorship. The tone of prophetic scorn is so important in Judges that its pervasiveness needs to be observed.

To say humor is "omnipresent" in Judges may be an overstatement but points in the right direction.[2] Consider a partial list of humorous elements to look for: maiming of Adoni-bezek the mutilator (1:6–7); Achsah's bold demands of the mighty warriors Othniel and Caleb (1:14–15); the left-handed savior from the tribe of Benjamin ("Son-of-the-right-hand"; 3:21); Eglon ("Little-calf") the fat king of Moab (3:22); the toilet joke (3:24); the "fat" (*shamen*) Moabite army (3:29); the defeat of the Canaanites, who worshiped the storm god Baal by timid Barak ("Lightning"), apparently by means of a storm from Yahweh (4:8; 5:20–21); Jael giving milk and covering to Sisera before driving a peg through his skull (5:24–26); Deborah imagining Sisera's women imagining two wombs (girls) for every guy (5:30); Gideon refusing kingship, then naming his son Abimelech ("My-father-is-king"; 8:23, 31); Abimelech worrying about being remembered as being killed by a woman (9:54, which is how Joab and maybe David remembers it; see 2 Sam 11:21); the illegitimate son and outlaw Jephthah ruling over the upstanding citizens who cast him out (11:1, 11); Jephthah's errant "diplomacy" naming the wrong god in a message to the king of Ammon (11:24); the Ephraimites' "speech impediment" (12:6); the powerful savior against the Philistines, Samson, repeatedly succumbing to Philistine females, especially the sequence of entrapments by Delilah (14:1, 17; 16:1, 4–20); the once mighty Samson doing a lowly female job at the grinding mill (16:21); Micah's mother dedicating silver to Yahweh for her son to disobey Yahweh and make an idol with the silver (17:3); the Levite refusing to stay with foreigners at Jebus but going on to stay with Sodom-like Israelites at Gibeah (19:12); expert left-handed slingers of the tribe of Benjamin ("Son-of-the-right-hand"; 20:16); and the formerly morally outraged opponents of the men of Gibeah for their treatment of a woman now advising them to take by force females from Shiloh (21:21). The careful reader will find many more cases of satire and scornful humor in Judges, though most of it is dark humor. Again, this heavy-handed mocking of Israel and its leaders in the days of the judges suggests prophetic authorship.

---

[1] See *OTUOT*, 386.

[2] See A. Graeme Auld, *Joshua Retold: Synoptic Perspectives* (Edinburgh: T&T Clark, 1998), 103.

Spoiler Alert: If you want to see the surprise ending for yourself, please read Judges before proceeding.

The prophetic storymakers of Judges pull off a shocker. The main story trick is dischronological narration. The narrative opens by suggesting things get worse from one generation to the next—"But when the judge died, the people returned to ways *even more corrupt than those of their ancestors*" (2:19 NIV, emphasis added). And so it seems. Each judge was worse than the one before.[3] The last judge, Samson, confirms the downward spiral since Israel no longer cried out to Yahweh, and the deliverer did no delivering except as it related to his addiction to Philistine ladies.

The closing set of refrains—"In those days there was no king in Israel" (17:6; 18:1; 19:1; 21:25) and "all the people did what was right in their own eyes" (17:6//21:25 NRSVue)—condemns the moral failure of the people in the days of the judges as well as invites comparison to the days of the kings.

The closing epilogues of Judges are set in a backward world. The standard of measurement ceased to be "in the eyes of Yahweh" (3:7, 12; 4:1; 6:1; 10:6; 13:1 AT). The two epilogues had nothing to do with Yahweh's covenant, for "all the people did what was right in their own eyes" (17:6//21:25 NRSVue). Everything about the epilogues is backward, even timing. The end is the beginning.

The first closing episode of the Levitical and Danite distortions (what is right in their own eyes) in chapters 17–18 is set in the youthful days of Jonathan, the grandson of Moses (17:7; 18:30).[4] The second closing episode of the Benjaminite distortion that spread to all Israel is set in the days of Phinehas, the grandson of Aaron (20:28). Jonathan's father, Gershom, was born before Moses went to Egypt to deliver Israel (Exod 2:22). And Jonathan was still young in Judges 17 (see later discussion). Phinehas was a grown man already when Israel was in the wilderness (Num 25:7–13). The two episodes that close Judges are flashbacks to the days immediately following the conquest of Joshua.

In Judges things get worse and worse (Judg 2:19). It gets so bad with Gideon, Jephthah, and Samson that it seems as if it cannot not be worse, but then it indeed gets much worse.[5] However, that is the dischronological trick of these two flashbacks

---

[3] See examples in Klaas Spronk, "Parallel Structures in Judges and the Formation of the Book," *JSOT* 46, no. 3 (2022): 310, 313 [306–18].

[4] The textual issue of Judg 18:30 will be taken up later in this chapter.

[5] On the problems with Gideon, Jephthah, and Samson, see later discussion. Abimelek is not listed here since he is not a judge but a political usurper who, as Gideon's son, puts an additional negative layer on the judgeship of Gideon.

in Judges 17–18 and 19–21. They do not tell of eventual moral disintegration. The times when things were so bad that they could only be described as when everyone did what was right in their own eyes was how bad it was immediately—in the days of the grandchildren of Moses and Aaron and the exodus generation.

Anyone who reads Judges may empathize with Israel longing for the good old days when Israel first entered the land. But the concluding episodes make it clear: there is no such thing as the good old days, at least not in Dan or in the hill country of Benjamin and Ephraim. However bad things could get is the way things were from the first.

Judges helps seal the certainty of exile. Israel had been in full rebellion from the beginning. That is the message of Judges.

Interpretive Overview

Two of the most prominent aspects of the Judges story have been mentioned already: satirical and dischronological narration. Paying attention to a few other challenging elements will make it easier to focus briefly on the major episodes of Judges: tribal culture, regional focus, narrative sequence, timing, geography, and minor judges.

Readers will do well to attend to the tribal and other affiliations made explicit throughout Judges. The tribal relations in Judges can be compared to earlier biblical books. The namesakes of the tribes and most of Israel's enemies appear in Genesis. The intratribal relations in Numbers are Genesis-shaped in many ways including Judah first, the deadly zeal of Levi, and a double portion for Joseph (Ephraim and Manasseh).[6] Judges is Genesis-shaped and Joshua-shaped as can be seen most clearly in the tribal fault lines.

Readers need to remember that narratives are never written *about* who they are written *for*. As noted above, the final form of Judges dates from the time of the fall of the northern kingdom of Israel at its earliest. The later realities of the tribal fractures in the days of Israel's first king, Saul of Gibeah (Benjamin), versus the second king, David of Bethlehem (Judah), shape the Judges narrative. This goes beyond the first two judges that came from Judah (Othniel) and Benjamin (Ehud). Notice the role of Gibeah in Judges 19. The smearing of Saul's hometown is no accident, nor is it a coincidence that Judah was called by Yahweh as first to battle the Canaanites and as first to battle the rebellious Benjamites (Judg 1:1–2; 20:18). Also, notice the centers of worship located in Dan and Bethel from the early days of the judges (18:30; 20:26). This foreshadows

---

[6] See Schnittjer, *Torah Story*, 2nd ed., 327–28 (see intro., n. 10).

Jeroboam setting up shrines to two golden calves in Bethel and Dan when the northern kingdom broke away from the Davidic kingdom of Judah (1 Kgs 12:28–30).

The issues of regional focus, narrative sequence, geography, and timing overlap. Brief consideration of each can help show the importance of the narrative sequence of Judges. If everything in Judges was stacked end to end, it would not fit between the exodus and the building of Solomon's temple in 966 BCE (figure 2.1).[7] Many scholars have made charts that list all the chronological data between the exodus and the building of Solomon's temple, including the wilderness wandering; Joshua's conquest; 410 years of Judges; Eli, Samuel, Saul, David, and the first four years of Solomon before he began to build the temple. Adding these together comes to 593 years.[8] This is too much time for the late date or the early date of the exodus. The goal here is not to solve the issue.[9] It is enough to note that if read sequentially with no overlap, there is not enough time for everything that happens in Judges in any of the views.

Figure 2.1: Not Enough Time for All Episodes of Judges without Overlap[‡]

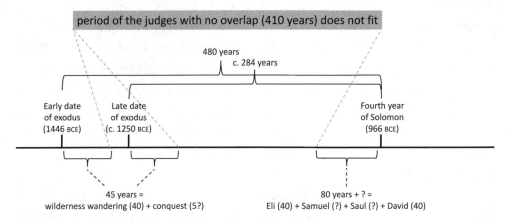

[‡] (1) The possibility of five years of conquest is based on Caleb's retrospective (Josh 14:7, 10). (2) Among other issues not depicted in the figure: ending of forty years of Philistine rule (Judg 13:1)—by Samuel (1 Sam 7:13) (?), Saul (14:46) (?), or David (2 Sam 5:25; 8:1) (?); from the time of Eli the ark is in Philistia seven months and then at Kiriath-jearim for twenty years, the last seven and a half of which David ruled Judah in Hebron (1 Sam 6:1; 2 Sam 2:11; 5:4–5).

---

    [7] On the early and late dates of the exodus, see Schnittjer, 188–90.

    [8] See, e.g., Daniel I. Block, *Judges, Ruth*, NAC (Nashville: B&H, 1999), 59–61. For another approach with 554 years plus Joshua's conquest (unknown years) plus Saul's rule (unknown years), see S. J. De Vries, "Chronology of the OT," *IDB* 1:583.

    [9] For an overview of several "solutions," none of which add up without additional tweaks, see Mordecai Cogan, "Chronology [Hebrew Bible]," *ABD* 1:1005. For a thoroughgoing review of failed chronological approaches along with a literary and chronological solution,

Most scholars agree that the episodes in Judges maintain a regional focus—the exception being the last episode that included all twelve tribes (19:29–20:1). Many of the periods of local oppression and deliverance could have overlapped chronologically since they took place in regions remote from one another (figure 2.2).

Figure 2.2: Chronologically Overlapping Episodes in the Sequence of Judges 3–16

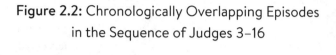

Figure 2.2 raises another question: Why favor the sequence of major judges in Judges 3–16 versus the other two sequences in Scripture? Samuel presented the judges as Jerubbaal (Gideon), Barak, Jephthah, and Samuel (1 Sam 12:11, cf. CSB text note). The author of Hebrews lists the judges as Gideon, Barak, Samson, and Jephthah (11:32). Before drawing a provisional conclusion, geography needs to be considered.

If the major judges are arranged by the geography of their tribal locations, a south-to-north pattern emerges, except for the last one.[10] Othniel is considered here relative to Judah's tribal allotment in the south, wherever he faced off against the oppressors of Aram-naharaim. Though Dan never took their tribal land but settled in the north, Samson lived on the fringes of Dan's assigned territory, where he fell for Philistine women (Josh 19:41–47). The minor judges—"minor" because the accounts are short—provide a similar pattern moving northward, except for Abdon.[11] Figure 2.3 shows a nearly consistent south-to-north sequential arrangement of judges except for the sixth major and sixth minor judges.

---

see Robert B. Chisholm Jr., *A Commentary on Judges and Ruth*, KEL (Grand Rapids: Kregel Academic, 2013), 34–53.

[10] The Assyrian royal inscriptions, written in roughly the same period as Judges, were frequently arranged geographically (e.g., *RT*, 82, 89) or topically (e.g., 112), rather than chronologically. Also see the discussion of dischronological narrative in the introduction and its footnotes for other biblical examples.

[11] On Bethlehem of Zebulun in the north, see Henri Cazelles, "Bethlehem," *ABD* 1:714. On Pirathon in the hill country of Ephraim, see Robert W. Smith, "Pirathon," *ABD* 5:373.

Figure 2.3: General Geographical Sequence of the Major and Minor Judges

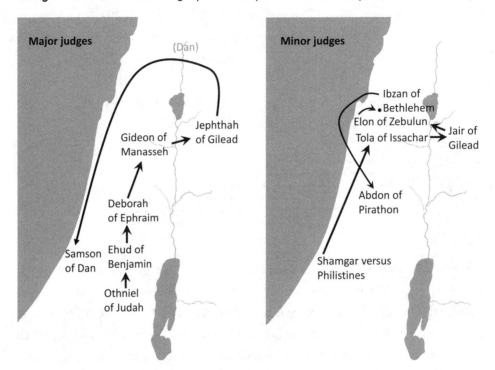

In sum, the evidence of regional focus, narrative sequence, geography, and timing elements can be put together. The Bible presents the sequence of the major judges in three different ways. The major and minor judgeships relate to regional oppressions and tribal situations that could overlap chronologically with one or more of the others. The geographical sequence of the judges moves from south to north except the last judge. All of these lines of evidence eliminate the "problem" of too much time. The expectation for a nonoverlapping chronological sequence of judges is a modern imposition.[12]

For these reasons the present approach interprets Judges by its narrative sequence (see outline at the beginning of the chapter and table 2.1). The narrative sequence moves progressively toward greater rebellion (Judg 2:19) even while the last two episodes are flashbacks to a time immediately after the conquest (18:30; 20:28).

The minor judges serve to reinforce the larger narrative in several ways. Most important, the regular appearance of other judges suggests the six major judges were merely representative of a larger set of rebellions and judgments. This is much like the four narrated battle episodes in Joshua that represent the entire era of conquest. Also,

---

[12] On the nonchronological arrangement of Judges, see Block, *Judges*, 145.

just as the lists of Ishmael and Edom serve as dividers between stories of Abraham, Jacob, and the sons of Jacob in Genesis (cf. Gen 25:12–18; 36:1–43), so too the three sets of minor judges serve to segment the major judges into ever-increasing moral disintegration among the judges themselves (see outline at the beginning of the chapter). In sum, the minor judges in many ways reinforce the major themes and flow of Judges as a whole.[13]

All of the special issues of Judges explained so far need to be kept in mind as we turn our attention briefly to the story line of Judges based on the outline at the beginning of this chapter.

The first introduction presents tribal failures mostly drawn from Joshua. The exception is Judah, who appears first and gets the most attention by a wide margin. The first verses help to frame the entire book (emphases added).

> After the death of Joshua, the Israelites asked of Yahweh, "<u>Who among us is to go up first to fight</u> against **the Canaanites**?" <u>Yahweh said, "Judah</u> will go up. See, I have given the land into their hands." (Judg 1:1–2 AT)

> The Israelites went up to Bethel and asked of God, "<u>Who among us is to go up first to fight</u> with **the Benjamites**?" <u>Yahweh said, "Judah</u> will go first." (20:18 AT)

Though it seems the Canaanites are the problem at the beginning of Judges, the increasing troubles of Israel in the days of the judges reveal that Israel themselves were the real problem.

One of the new elements not carried over from Joshua shows a rare example of Israel torturing a captive of war—something commonplace in some ancient Mesopotamian empires (see Ancient Connections 2.1). But Adoni-bezek himself admitted that he deserved to have his thumbs and big toes amputated because he had done the same to seventy other rulers (1:7).

Another surprise is that Judah burned Jerusalem (1:8). This must refer to an incomplete attack since elsewhere Scripture says that this city that sat between Judah and Benjamin was not taken until the time of David (cf. 1:21; Josh 15:63; 2 Sam 5:6–9). Telling of Judah burning Jerusalem at the beginning stages of securing their tribal allotment seems to already anticipate the Babylonians burning Jerusalem when they forced Judah into exile (2 Kgs 25:9).

---

[13] See Kenneth Way, "The Meaning of the Minor Judges: Understanding the Bible's Shortest Stories," *JETS* 61, no. 2 (2018): 275–85.

ANCIENT CONNECTIONS 2.1: MAIMING CAPTIVES

Ashurnasirpal II (883–859 BCE) frequently recounted horrific atrocities he meted out on cities who revolted against his onerous rule. Here is what he said of defeating the city of Tela:

> I burnt many captives from them. I captured many troops alive: I cut off some of their arms (and) hands; I cut off of others their noses, ears, (and) extremities. I gouged out the eyes of many troops. I made one pile of the living (and) one of heads. I hung their heads on trees around the city. I burnt the adolescent boys (and) girls. I razed, destroyed, burnt, (and) consumed the city. (*ARI* 2:126)

The narrator of Judges recycled the account of Caleb taking Hebron but replaced his name with his tribe and referred to the Anakites as Canaanites. This illustrates how individual acts can be reframed within the tribal focus of Judges.

> **Caleb** drove out from there [Hebron] **the three sons of Anak**: *Sheshai, Ahiman, and Talmai*, descendants of Anak. (Josh 15:14, emphasis added)

> **Judah** also marched against **the Canaanites** who were living in Hebron (Hebron was formerly named Kiriath-arba). They struck down *Sheshai, Ahiman, and Talmai*. (Judg 1:10, emphasis added)

The author of Judges recycled from Joshua the story of Achsah—the daughter Caleb gifted to Othniel for attacking Kiriath-sepher (Debir)—to introduce a major theme: women in the days of the judges (1:11–15; Joshua 15–19; cf. 10:38–39). Achsah represents an ideal covenantal attitude by her proactive seeking of springs in Judah's land allotment. The text quietly implies that she needed to make this request from her father, Caleb, since Othniel did not after she had urged him. Achsah's boldness stands out within a decidedly patriarchal culture that gave daughters as gifts to battle heroes—especially since she was compared to Othniel, the first and model judge. Careful readers will notice many ways that the author used female characters to satirize and shame the patriarchal establishment of Israel's tribal days.

The majority of the rest of Judges 1 highlights the tribe-by-tribe failure to drive out the Canaanites. The reasons offered are telling. Some tribes could not drive out the Canaanites because of their military strength (vv. 19, 21, 29, 31–32, 34). Other tribes decided to enjoy the economic advantages of enslaving Canaanites (vv. 28, 30,

33, 34). The weakness and greed of the tribes provided two reasons for the persistent troubles of the tribes.

The second introduction of Judg 2:6–3:6 lays out the expected moral and social decline that played out in the six episodes of the major judges and the two epilogues. As noted earlier the sense of increasing decline spelled out in Judg 2:19 establishes the downward arc of the story line.

The second introduction also provides the literary formulas that trigger the cycles of the major judges' episodes. Several formulaic phrases shape the repetitious story line: rebellion → Yahweh gave over Israel to a military predator → Israel cried out (without repentance) → Yahweh raised a deliverer or judge → the land rested or the judge led (table 2.1).

Table 2.1: Formulaic Structure of the Major Judges

	Second Introduction	Othniel	Ehud	Deborah	Gideon	Jephthah	Samson
Israel did evil in the eyes of Yahweh	2:11	3:7	3:12	4:1	6:1	10:6	13:1
Yahweh gave them over/sold them, etc.	2:14	3:8	3:12	4:2	6:1	10:7	13:1
Israel cried out/groaned	2:18	3:9	3:15	4:3	6:7	10:10	--
Yahweh raised up a judge/deliverer; spirit came upon the deliverer	2:16	3:9	3:15	4:6–7	6:34	11:29	13:25; 14:4, 6, 19; 15:14

land rested X years (3:11, 30; 5:31; 8:28) ⏐ judge led X years (12:7; 15:20; 16:31)

The only fully consistent formula is "Israel did evil in the eyes of Yahweh" to open each narrative cycle. Two indications of the downward spiral are (1) the shift from the land resting for X years to a judge merely ruling for X years and (2) the lack of Israel's crying out in the Samson narrative. The reason Israel did not cry out was that the Danite tribe affected by the local oppression had already left their allotment to live in unsanctioned territory (see flashback in Judges 18). It must be noted that crying out for relief from oppression is not equivalent to repentance from sin.

The formula "Israel did evil in the eyes of Yahweh" is more or less parallel to disobeying Torah. The second introduction spells out the leading infraction as devotion to false gods: "The Israelites did evil in the eyes of Yahweh and they served the Baals" (2:11 AT; cf. v 13). The hero god of the Canaanite pantheon is Baal, the storm god (see introduction). The gods and goddesses of Canaan primarily represented fertility and prosperity. An agrarian culture depends on the rains. This made Baal worship highly attractive (see Ancient Connections 2.2).

ANCIENT CONNECTIONS 2.2: PROSPERITY ACCORDING TO THE BAAL MYTH

The effects of the absence and presence of the storm god Baal directly relates to the ancient Canaanites' view of times of famine and times of plenty. The goddess Anat explains to the sun god the effects of Baal's absence:

> Sun, *the furrows in the fields have dried*, the furrows in El's fields have dried; Baal has neglected the furrows of his plowland. Where is Baal the Conqueror? Where is the Prince, the Lord of the Earth? ("Baal and Death," 6 iv 12–16, in *SFAC*, 149, emphasis added)

El speaks in his dream of the effects of Baal's return and then it is fulfilled:

> "But if Baal the Conqueror lives, if the Prince, the Lord of the Earth, has revived . . . the heavens rain down oil, the wadis run with honey." . . . *[T]he heavens rained down oil, the wadis ran with honey*. El the Kind, the Compassionate, was glad: he put his feet on a stool, his brow relaxed and he laughed. He raised his voice and declared: "Now I can sit back and relax; my heart inside me can relax; for Baal the Conqueror lives, the Prince, the Lord of the Earth, is alive." ("Baal and Death," 6 iii 3–7, 12–21, in *SFAC*, 148–49, emphasis added)

The most important outcome of the formula-driven major judges' cycles is placing Yahweh in the foreground and the human enemies in the background. The reasons for oppression of the tribes are not explained by the greed or military ambition of Israel's rivals. The Judges story pivots on the covenantal relationship between Yahweh and the tribes of Israel.

The people of Israel did not stop believing in Yahweh, who had brought up their ancestors from Egypt and had given the land of promise to a previous generation. They simply ceased to worship him exclusively. The past acts of Yahweh seemed irrelevant to the daily challenges of tribal living. Israel needed to work to grow crops and raise cattle. The desires of the people to assure fertility that lead to prosperity begin to explain why most Israelites worshiped the gods of Canaan.

The Othniel cycle provides the ideal narrative prototype (3:7–11). Narrative formulas naturally invite variation, which explains why no two sets of formulas are exactly the same in Judges (see table 2.1). Othniel is from Judah, which fulfills Yahweh's call for Judah to go up first (1:1–2). The Othniel cycle includes both formulas, "Yahweh raised up a deliverer" and "the spirit of Yahweh came upon him," setting up some of the variations in future judge narrative cycles.

Othniel defeats King Cushan-rishathaim of Aram-naharaim. Naharaim means "of the two rivers," referring to Aram in the area of modern Syria north of Israel. This is a significant victory if such a distant enemy is aligned with other local enemies in southern Canaan. The king's name means "Doubly-Evil" (3:8 CSB text note), which suggests a later intentional scribal distortion.[14] The lean narrative provides no extra details, which goes a long way toward making Othniel the ideal judge.

Ehud comes from Benjamin. It is a little surprising that a seemingly good judge comes from Benjamin since the final epilogue of Judges goes to the nth degree to smear the character of the Benjamites and King Saul's hometown of Gibeah. Yet, the first three more "positive" judges fit with the expected pattern spelled out in the second introduction—namely, an encouraging start before decline (2:19). The narrator's silence on God's role in Ehud's deliverance asks unanswered questions about this clever and brutal judge.[15]

The Ehud story overflows with wordplays, mostly at the expense of the hapless Moabite oppressors (see the beginning of this chapter).[16] The clever left-handed judge of Benjamin (which means "Son-of-the-right-hand") anticipated the expert left-handed slingers of Benjamin that made an appearance in the civil war in the second epilogue (20:16). The Benjamite judge easily musters the troops of Ephraim to help him finish off the Moabite forces. This sets up the increasingly bad relations between the tribes and Ephraim in later episodes, further strengthening the theme of decline (3:27–28; cf. 8:1–3; 12:1–6).

The Deborah story begins when the Israelites again does evil in the eyes of their God. Yahweh sold them into the hand of the Canaanite king Jabin of Hazor and his military general Sisera with his 900 chariots of iron.[17] Joshua had defeated Hazor, burned their chariots, and hamstrung their horses in a previous generation

---

[14] See "*kushan rish'atayim*," *HALOT* 1:467.

[15] See Block, *Judges*, 171.

[16] Also see Ryan D. Schroeder, "Eglon's Fat and Ehud's Oracle: A Reconsideration of Humour in Judges 3.12–30," *JSOT* 46, no. 4 (2022): 460–79.

[17] The reference to "iron" seems to refer to a small piece of iron that improved the chariot's function. See Mary Aiken Littauer and J. H. Crouwel, "Chariots," *ABD* 1:890. And for

(Josh 11:9). But since they did not finish off the Canaanites of this region, they were back with better chariots.

Deborah is a prophetess matron of Ephraim. Her judgeship represents the last relatively good narrative cycle. The narrative treatment of Barak already anticipates increasing trouble from the deliverers themselves.

Barak showed a reluctance to attack Sisera unless Deborah goes with him. She agrees but assures him that "you will not be honored on the way that you are going, for Yahweh will deliver Sisera into the hand of a woman" (Judg 4:9b AT). Deborah makes explicit the loss of glory for the patriarchal establishment.

To make sense of the battle requires reading the narrative in chapter 4 with the song of Deborah in chapter 5—much like the story and song of the sea crossing in Exodus 14–15. Deborah, Barak, and their forces assemble at Mount Tabor on the eastern side of the Valley of Jezreel. The plan is to meet Sisera in battle on the western side of the valley near the Kishon River. Compare the narrative and poetic explanation of the battle (emphases added).

> *Yahweh threw* Sisera and all his chariots and his militia *into a panic* before the sword of Barak. Then Sisera got down from his chariot and fled on foot. (4:15 AT)

> The stars fought from the heavens; the stars fought with Sisera from their paths. *The river Kishon swept them away,* the ancient river, the river Kishon. March on, my soul, in strength! (5:20–21; cf. v. 4)

Reading the narrative and poetic accounts of the battle together suggests Yahweh unleashed a storm that flooded the Kishon and rendered the chariots useless. This put the charioteers at a sharp disadvantage against Barak's ground troops. The irony cuts both ways here. Barak, whose name means "lightning," gets assistance from a storm and flash flood. The Canaanites who serve Baal the storm god lost the battle because of a sudden storm (see Ancient Connections 2.3).

In Sisera's lone flight he happens upon the tent dwelling of Heber and Jael. They are not of the tribes of Israel. They are foreigners. The narrator fills in the backstory of the peaceful relations between King Jabin and the clan of Heber. This explains why Sisera trusts Jael, who is home alone. Though he asks for water she gives him milk and puts him to bed like a child. Then Jael takes a hammer and drives a spike through

---

iron-rimmed wheels, see Robert Drews, "The 'Chariots of Iron' of Joshua and Judges," *JSOT* 45 (1989): 15–23.

Sisera's head, reported in detail in narrative and poem (4:21; 5:26–7). In the narrative, after Jael drives the spike through Sisera's head, the narrator adds "and he died" with an undercurrent of dark humor. The poetic version slows down, offering two long verses detailing the kill.

ANCIENT CONNECTIONS 2.3: BAAL THE STORM GOD

The use of a storm by Israel's God to help his people defeat the peoples of Canaan is highly ironic. Ancient Canaanites looked to the storm god Baal for rains that brought prosperity. Yet, storms also testified to the god's power.

> Asherah says: "Now Baal will provide his enriching rain, provide a rich watering downpour; and he will sound his voice in the clouds, flash his lightning to the earth.". . . Then Baal opened a break in the clouds, Baal sounded his holy voice, Baal thundered from his lips. ("The Palace of Baal," 4 v 6–9; 4 vii 27–30, in *SFAC,* 132, 137)

Yahweh's use of a storm to defeat the Canaanites in Judges 4–5 demonstrated his sovereignty over the gods of the nations.

Reading narrative and poem together ridicules the male characters with sexual expressions used in nonsexual ways. In the narrative Jael shows Barak the corpse. Of the nine biblical uses of the exact phrase "he went into her" (AT), only Judg 4:22 does not refer to sexual relations. This verse uses a figure of speech in an unconventional way to emasculate the man who gives his honor to a woman.[18] The expression "between her legs" appears three times in Scripture, including twice in 5:27 with the verbs *knelt, fell,* and *lay*—"knelt" is rarely used sexually (Job 31:10), but "lay" is used of relations frequently.[19] Sisera was between Jael's legs because she just drove a spike through his skull. These cases of sexually suggestive phrases used in nonsexual ways ironically underscore the impotence of the male establishment.

Deborah immediately shifts her song to the women of Sisera's hometown and employs vulgar sexual lyrics. Deborah imagines how Sisera's mother and her ladies

---

[18] See Chisholm, *Judges,* 233; cf. Gen 29:23; 30:4; 38:2, 18; Judg 16:1; Ruth 4:13; 2 Sam 12:24; Ezek 23:44. The phrase "into her" (*'eleyha*) cannot be translated "into it," meaning the tent (against ESV), because the term for "tent" is grammatically masculine (BDB, 13).

[19] The phrase "between her feet" (AT) is a euphemistic expression for "between her legs," as Deut 28:57 makes clear (see *"regel,"* Even-Shoshan, 1061, nos. 201–3).

would interpret his delay. Deborah gives voice to the musing of Sisera's mother: "Are they not finding and dividing the spoil—a womb or two wombs for each man?" (Judg 5:30 AT). Though the context allows for the interpretive translation "a girl or two for each man to rape!" (NET), elsewhere in Judges the Benjaminite survivors "pick up" (AT) and steal virgin girls of Shiloh to marry (21:23). In that case they merely abduct one each. However severely Deborah means to insult Sisera's mother is less important than glorifying Yahweh for the victory over the Canaanite bullies.

The Gideon narrative has been widely misunderstood. Many interpret Gideon as an ideal judge. So he seems—that is, until he crosses the Jordan River. Once he gets to the Transjordan, the shy, upright facade gives way to a ruthless, greedy man set on personal vengeance.

The first half of the Gideon story seems to continue the mighty deliverances of Yahweh, much akin to Othniel, Ehud, and Deborah. And so it is. Yahweh is faithful and merciful to his people oppressed by the locust-like Midianites. This half of the story includes an elaborate calling. Gideon thinks of himself humbly, from a weak clan of Manasseh and least in his own family (6:15). Yet Gideon distinguishes himself by tearing down his father's altar to Baal and its Asherah pole. His own father defends him against the altar's angry constituents, and Gideon gets the taunting nickname Jerubbaal, "let Baal contend" (vv. 31–32). Gideon remains unsure, needing two signs of a fleece as well as hearing visions of doom given to the Midianites. Does Gideon's need for assurance already signal his wavering faith? In any case, Yahweh goes to great lengths to have Gideon and his 300 men scare the Midianite soldiers in the middle of the night so they begin killing each other.

The second half of the Gideon story begins in the Transjordan, where things get wild. Gideon threatens to torture the people of Succoth and Penuel, who refuse hospitality to his 300 men. After he captures the two Midianite kings, Gideon makes good on his word, torturing and killing the people of both towns (8:15–17).

The major surprise comes not from the narrator but from the embedded speeches of Zebah and Zalmunna, captured kings of Midian. They taunt Gideon, saying they killed men just like Gideon because they resembled a king. Gideon replied, "They were my brothers, my mother's sons. As Yahweh lives, if you had let them live, I would not have killed you" (8:19 FT). Readers are stunned. After all of Gideon's reluctance and posturing as a humble servant of Yahweh, he exceeds his role as deliverer to exact personal vengeance for the loss of his loved ones. It does not end there.

In addition to his torture and personal vengeance in the Transjordan, Gideon also makes a golden ephod for false worship (v. 27). He then lives like a king, taking many wives and concubines and siring seventy sons. Though he refuses to be made a king, he names the son of one of his concubines Abimelech, which means "My father is king" (v. 31).

After Gideon dies, Abimelech's ambition and treachery as a leader incites extended civil warfare between several cities in the heart of the hill country of middle Israel. Finally, a woman of Thebez drops an upper millstone on his head, reminding readers of how Jael killed Sisera (9:53). As he is dying, he begs his armor bearer to finish him off to avoid the shame of being killed by a woman (but cf. 2 Sam 11:21).

What should be made of the debacle of Gideon and his son Abimelech? Positively, Yahweh displays his mercy by delivering Manasseh from the vast forces of Midian using Gideon and a mere 300 men. But this deliverance comes with Gideon's baggage, which turns out to be the negative turning point of Judges. Gideon leverages his judgeship for his personal agenda of vengeance and his lust for gold and women. Not only does Israel prostitute itself before Gideon's golden ephod, but many Israelites die fighting over nothing with Abimelech. Though it would seem that things could only get better, that is not how Judges works. Nothing gets better in Judges.

The illegitimacy of Jephthah as the son of a prostitute drives much of the drama in his rule. Trouble from Ammon forces the elders of Gilead to seek deliverance from the outcast Jephthah and his band of outlaws. Jephthah agrees but only if he is made ruler of Gilead (11:10).

As ruler, Jephthah sends a long letter to the king of Ammon, apparently to get the Ammonites to release their hold on the Transjordan lands belonging to Manasseh. The letter requires readers to compare the details of Israel's conquest of the Transjordan region recorded in Numbers and Deuteronomy.[20] The most significant problems arise from Jephthah's bad theology. Like the ancient foreign poets, Jephthah gives credit to other gods, but he needs to contradict Deuteronomy to do so. And, significantly, Jephthah "accidentally" mixes up Milcom the god of Ammon with Chemosh the god of Moab. Notice the bold and underlined contradictions:[21]

> Therefore the poets say: . . . Woe to you, **Moab**! You have been destroyed, people of **Chemosh! He gave up** his sons as refugees, and his daughters into captivity to Sihon the Amorite king. (Num 21:27a, 29)

> Yahweh said to me [Moses], "Do not harass <u>Moab</u> and do not provoke them to war, because I have not given <u>their land</u> to you as a possession. <u>I have given</u>

---

[20] See table in *OTUOT*, 169.

[21] See *OTUOT*, 169–71, 294; Jillian L. Ross, *A People Heeds Not Scripture: Allusions in Judges* (Eugene, OR: Pickwick, forthcoming), chap 7.

Ar to the descendants of Lot as a possession. . . . When you get close to the Ammonites, don't show any hostility to them or provoke them, for I will not give you any of the Ammonites' land as a possession; I have given it as a possession to the descendants of Lot." (Deut 2:9, 19; v. 9 AT)

[Jephthah, to Ammon:] "Will you not possess that which **Chemosh your god** has given you? And all that Yahweh our God has conquered for us we will possess." (Judg 11:24 AT)

Maybe Jephthah accidentally makes these blunders. Or maybe he misspeaks intentionally to pick a fight with Ammon. It is not clear if he is ignorant, a bully, or an ignorant bully. In any case, the God-given defeat of Ammon stands in the background, taking up a mere two verses in the midst of Jephthah's most (in)famous blunder (11:32–33).

Jephthah vows to make a burnt offering of whatever first came out of his house even while the Spirit of God had come upon him (vv. 29–30). The folly of Jephthah while the Spirit of God is upon him cautions against any kind of simplistic theology of the Spirit. Jephthah's only child comes out of his household to greet him upon his return. Chisholm offers an interpretation of where the text seems to point—Jephthah's daughter as a burnt offering:

> The scene is Jephthah's altar, covered with the charred remains of his daughter. Just weeks before, this vibrant young woman, gyrating to the beat of her tambourine, was the first to greet her victorious father as he returned home from battle. But now she is reduced to a pile of ashes and bones.[22]

The horrific vow of Jephthah has led many interpreters to read this passage against the sense of the text and claim he did not sacrifice her. Instead, clever interpreters say that Jephthah's daughter was assigned to be a perpetual virgin as a replacement for the burnt offering (cf. v. 38).[23] However, a natural reading of the syntax of verses 31 and 39 suggests that Jephthah indeed offers his daughter as a burnt offering.[24]

Readers who know the Scriptures may be aware of two silences that raise unanswerable questions. First, why do local leaders fail to stop Jephthah from acting on his rash vow like they did for Saul, who was prevented from acting on his rash

---

[22] Robert B. Chisholm Jr., "The Ethical Challenge of Jephthah's Fulfilled Vow," *BSac* 167 (2010): 404.

[23] See Chisholm, 406–7, n. 8.

[24] See Chisholm, 405–9; Chisholm, *Judges*, 355–58.

oath and killing his son (1 Sam 14:24, 45)?[25] The moral outrage to make a collective counteroath was predictably absent in the days of the judges. Second, where is the delegate of Yahweh who stopped Abraham before he sacrificed his son? Abraham, of course, was being tested, but Jephthah makes the vow for himself.

Samson's humorous and disappointing story works between two points of reference. First, as a lifelong Nazirite, Samson needs to abstain from wine, dead bodies, and haircuts (Judg 13:4–5; Num 6:1–21). Samson has no scruples about handling dead animals. His feast of honey from a lion's carcass provides an on-ramp that leads to killing many Philistine men and ruining their crops (Judg 14:8). The narrator uses the rare term *fresh* to describe the fresh jawbone in order to indicate that Samson touches a dead donkey to get a weapon to slaughter 1,000 Philistines at Lehi (15:15–17).

Second, as a deliverer from the Philistines, Samson should have avoided intermarriage and fornication with Philistine women. On this second issue, heavy voiceover narration signified by italics explains why Samson needed to get into a series of failed relationships with Philistine women: "His father and mother did not know that *this was from Yahweh, for he was seeking an opportunity to make trouble with the Philistines*" (14:4a AT, emphasis added). The story of Samson shows that he killed exactly zero Philistines except as it relates to his love of or lust after Philistine women.

Samson's relationship with Delilah exhibits a delightful three-plus-one storytelling structure. After two failed attempts to bind his strength, Samson gets closer by telling Delilah that his seven locks of hair needed to be woven together and tightened with a pin to take away his strength. When Samson awakes with his hair woven together young readers want to scream that he needs to get away. Not Samson. He spends day after day with Delilah until he finally tells her the truth and wakes up bald and weak.

The Philistines blind Samson, which may have helped with his lust for Philistine women.[26] The Philistine captors humiliate the weakened hero by forcing him to grind at the mill. This may have been a way of making Samson do work fit for female slaves (16:21; cf. Exod 11:5; Lam 5:13). Samson spends his last hours being mocked by a crowd at a Philistine temple until he prays and pushes over its supporting pillars. The narrator reports the tragic reality that Samson killed more Philistines by his death than he ever did in his life (Judg 16:30).

---

[25] Oaths are unconditional assertions or promises, while vows are conditional promises. See Jacob Milgrom, *Numbers*, JPS Torah Commentary (Philadelphia: Jewish Publication Society, 1990), 488–90.

[26] See Chisholm, *Judges*, 428.

After the spectacular failure of Samson readers may think that things could only get better. Wrong. These are the days of the judges.

Variations on the phrase "There was a man/young Levite/Levite" (17:1, 7; 19:1) open units in the closing episodes and continue into Samuel (1 Sam 1:1; 9:1). This connects the two books. The use of the expression "and there was" or "and it came to pass" typically marks new narrative units.[27] The author of Judges uses this construction to open new episodes chronologically detached from the preceding major judges' cycles. As noted in the opening of this chapter, the two epilogues are both flashbacks dating to the earliest days of the tribes in the land—the generation of the grandchildren of Moses and of Aaron (Judg 18:30; 20:28). Yet the narrator withholds revealing the timing of these apostasies until the end of the first and middle of the second epilogues to let readers continue to think things are getting worse generation by generation (2:19).

Two refrains or formulas frame and punctuate the two closing epilogues of Judges. Four times readers hear, "In those days there was no king" (17:6; 18:1; 19:1; 21:25)—the first and last of which are combined with "all the people did what was right in their own eyes" (17:6//21:25 NRSVue). The Biblical Connections section at the end of this chapter explains how a biblical allusion strengthens the negative connotation of the latter phrase.

The two epilogues present everything upside down and distorted. The replacement of the disapproving evaluation, "Israel did what is evil in the eyes of the Yahweh," in Judges 3–16 (see table 2.1) with "everyone did what was right in their own eyes" in 17–18, 19–21 signals that these final episodes are untethered from the covenant. The surreal moral disfigurement of Israel becomes most evident whenever Yahweh is mentioned.

Upon recovering her stolen silver, Micah's mother declares, "*I solemnly consecrate the silver to Yahweh for my son to make an idol of sculpted metal*" (17:3b AT, emphasis added). Readers might blink and say, "What?" No one can consecrate silver to Yahweh in order to break the prohibition against making images in the Ten Commandments. This forces a second look. Yes, she cursed the silver. Yes, she said, "May my son be blessed by Yahweh" because he returned it (v. 2 AT). And, yes, she consecrated the silver to Yahweh for her son to make an idol and put the curse back on him and on the silver used to make objects of false worship.[28]

---

[27] See GKC §111f; *IBHS* §33.2.4a, b.

[28] On the curse on one who makes a carved image and a silver idol in Judg 17:3–4 as an allusion to the curse in Deut 27:15, see Ross, *A People Heeds Not Scripture*, chap. 9.

Micah recruits a young Levite—Moses's own grandson (18:30)—to preside over his personal shrine of false worship. Like his mother, he invokes the covenantal name of Yahweh in a bizarre way. "Micah said, 'Now I know *that Yahweh will cause me to prosper because the Levite has become my priest*'" (17:13 AT, emphasis added). Again, readers might blink and say "What?" No one but Yahweh could appoint priests, as Korah and the other rebels found out when the ground swallowed them into Sheol (Num 16:32–33). And worship anywhere except the tabernacle is expressly prohibited, as the Transjordan tribes learned in Joshua 22 (cf. Deut 12:5–14).

When leaders of the tribe of Dan reject Yahweh's land allotment to confiscate northern land belonging to a peaceful people, the young Levite makes an absurd pronouncement: "Go in peace. *Yahweh grants favor* to your mission" (Judg 18:6 AT, emphasis added). The Danites take the renegade young Levite with them. Their five scouts echo and distort the report of the scouts who returned to Moses at Kadesh in Numbers 13. The scouts of Dan falsely declare it is God's will to take land other than what God gave them (Judg 18:10; cf. Deut 1:25).

The narrator waits until the Danites take land that was not theirs and set up their traitorous shrine with their young Levite to reveal his name: Jonathan son of Gershom, son of Moses (Judg 18:30). This revelation masterfully stuns readers. It is so upsetting that a well-meaning scribe in the days before Jesus tried to "fix" it and save Moses's good name by adding a single letter.[29] At that time Hebrew was written with only consonants. Without vowels Moses is spelled MSH, but adding one letter could make it MNSH, "Manasseh." Yet the scribe must have had misgivings because he did not put the letter on the same line but left it elevated (figure 2.4). Hebrew scribes were so meticulous that over the centuries they continued to copy the scroll of Judges with the single letter raised. Nearly 100 percent of biblical scholars agree that the original text said Moses.

Figure 2.4: Intentional Scribal Change to Judges 18:30‡

M^NSH   מנֿשה

‡ Read the English letters left to right and the Hebrew letters right to left.

---

[29] See Natalio Fernández Marcos, *Judges: Biblia Hebraica Quinta* (Stuttgart: Deutsche Bibelgellschaft, 2011), 104*–5*.

Who gave support to the deviant worship center of the tribe of Dan? The grandson of Moses. When did things get this bad? When Moses's grandson was still young—the term for "youth" (*na'ar*) is repeated five times (17:7, 11, 12; 18:3, 15)—that is, shortly after Israel entered the land.

The second epilogue unfolds in three panels: the Sodom-like people of Gibeah of Benjamin gang-rape a guest's concubine; all Israel battle against Benjamin; and the other tribes help the remnant of Benjamin steal virgin girls to survive.

The episode begins with the refrain "In those days there was no king," and the opening formula "There was a Levite" (19:1 AT). After getting a late start to return home from Bethlehem with his concubine, the Levite's servant suggested they spend the night in Jebus (later renamed Jerusalem). The Levite replied, "We will not stop at a foreign city where there are no Israelites. Let's move on to Gibeah" (v. 12). This seems to make sense. Unfortunately, it is a grave mistake in the backward distortions of the days when everyone does what was right in their own eyes.

The story overflows with echoes of Lot's visitors in Genesis 19.[30] The arrival of the Levite and his small entourage in the city square of Gibeah already sounds like the two visitors Lot took home with him in Sodom. An old man persuades the Levite to come to his house as a guest. On cue, the men of Gibeah form a mob at the old man's house, asking for the Levite (emphases added).

> They called out to Lot and said, "Where are the men who came to you tonight? **Send** them **out** to us **so we can have sex with** them!" (Gen 19:5)

> While they were enjoying themselves, all of a sudden, wicked men of the city surrounded the house and beat on the door. They said to the old man who was the owner of the house, "**Bring out** the man who came to your house **so we can have sex with** him!" (Judg 19:22)

In a very Lot-like way, the old man suggests that the men of Gibeah were welcome to gang-rape his virgin daughter or the Levite's concubine. Unlike Genesis there are no delegates of Yahweh to blind the men of the city and shut the door. Either the old man or the Levite—the text leaves the identity of the culprit up in the air—throw the Levite's concubine out to the mob. Then they go to bed! This is worse than Sodom in the days of Lot (cf. Ezek 16:48–50).

---

[30] For a list of more than a dozen parallels between Genesis 19 and Judges 19, see C. F. Burney, *The Book of Judges* (London: Rivingtons, 1918), 444–45.

In the morning the Levite took home the body of his concubine who had been gang-raped. He dismembered her and sent the pieces throughout Israel. All the tribes gathered to go to war against Benjamin, who was protecting Gibeah. This is the only event in Judges that includes all Israel.

Judges begins with Yahweh calling Judah to lead the way against the Canaanites. The last battle in Judges reveals the deeper problem as Yahweh calls on Judah to go up first against Benjamin (20:18; cf.1:1–2). Yahweh communicated his will at the tabernacle where Phinehas the grandson of Aaron served (v. 28). The appearance of Phinehas here indicates this episode is set in the earliest days of Israel in the land of promise. The tribes had some trouble at first because of an ultra-elite troop of left-handed slingers of the tribe named Benjamin ("Son-of-the-right-hand"; 20:16).

After slaughtering most of the Benjaminites, the other tribes seek a way to help the remnant repopulate. However, their oath not to give their daughters to Benjamin creates a problem. Where can the Benjaminite remnant find wives? The problem is solved when they advise the remaining Benjaminites to ambush the virgin girls who went out dancing from Shiloh. Kidnapping girls seems dangerously close to the original outrage of Gibeah that sparked the civil conflict. And dancing virgins sounds a lot like Jephthah's daughter. The reason this stunning hypocrisy seems like a good idea to the tribal leaders is spelled out one more time: "In those days there was no king in Israel; all the people did what was right in their own eyes" (17:6//21:25 NRSVue).

No part of Judges sinks to lower depths than the two epilogues. But this moral disintegration characterized the tribes of Israel from their first days in the land. That is the point. There is no such thing as the good old days in Dan or in the hill country of Benjamin and Ephraim. Exile is assured from the beginning.

Biblical Connections

The fourfold refrain "In those days Israel had no king" invites comparison to the days when Israel does have a king.

The Benjaminite troop of expert left-handed slingers provides a key element of a deep irony in the days of Saul (20:16). King Saul of the tribe of Benjamin is a giant. He stood head and shoulders above everyone else (1 Sam 9:2; 10:23). The large Philistine champion from Gath—one of the last cities with Anakites (Josh 11:22)—taunted Israel every day for forty days while Saul the giant of Benjamin did nothing (1 Sam 17:16).

David of Judah came from Bethlehem, the town near where Rachel died giving birth to Benjamin. He showed up and immediately took the challenge to fight the champion from Gath. Previously, David had killed a lion and a bear. In the next scene David would kill 200 Philistine men (1 Sam 18:27). All of this suggests that David could have fought the champion from Gath with any number of weapons. But none would be more humiliating for the Benjaminite giant Saul—who came from a tribe known for its expert left-handed slingers—than a sling.

The refrain "In those days everyone did what was right in their own eyes" alludes to Deuteronomy 12. That context looks ahead to when Yahweh would bring his people into the land of promise (emphasis added).

> You shall not act as we do today, **all the people doing what is right in their own eyes,** because you have not yet come to the resting place and to the inheritance that Yahweh your God is giving to you. (Deut 12:8–9 AT)

> In those days there was no king in Israel; **all the people did what was right in their own eyes**. (Judg 17:6//21:25 NRSVue)

The author of Judges brilliantly adopts the phrase from Deuteronomy 12 to use as the refrain of the days of the judges. Deuteronomy 12 is known as "the place legislation" because it requires Israel to worship exclusively at the place Yahweh chose for his name to dwell (cf. Deut 12:5, 11, 14). In Judges 17–18, Micah of Ephraim and the tribe of Dan continue to worship wherever they want. And worse, they perform false worship and bless themselves in the name of Yahweh.

In Judges 19–21 the phrase is used more broadly. What seems right in the eyes of the Sodom-like men of Saul's hometown, Gibeah, eventually is transferred to all the tribal leaders who help Benjamin kidnap unsuspecting virgins.

The allusion to the place legislation of Deuteronomy 12 provides evidence to interpret negatively the days when there was no king. Unfortunately, after Yahweh gave the people their inheritance, they continue to do what is right in their own eyes.

Gospel Connections

No scroll of Scripture reveals the human problem more vividly than the book of Judges. The prophetic author of Judges does not say directly but rather shows the depth of the human problem. The purpose of loading the narrative with satire, irony, and dark humor is to urge readers to knowingly shake their heads at Israel's immorality. That impulse needs to be followed by recognizing the sinful condition common to all of us (Rom 3:9–11).

Judges excels at showing its readers the need for deliverance not merely from mortal enemies but from our own sinfulness. This is critical since the gospel begins with repentance. That is exactly where the Messiah began: "Repent and believe the good news!" (Mark 1:15). The next thing he said as he walked by the Sea of Galilee is "Follow me" (v. 17).

Judges prepares us for the gospel. It prepares us for repentance.

Life Connections

The days of the judges can be characterized by the formula that closes the book: "In those days there was no king in Israel; all the people did what was right in their own eyes" (17:6//21:25 NRSVue). Though that refers to lawless times in ancient Israel, it sounds very modern.

Today's culture celebrates doing what one sees as right as long as it does not hurt anyone else. People bristle at being told what is right and wrong. No one is surprised when matters of morality—sin and righteousness—are treated as personal preferences. But morality has nothing to do with personal preferences. Yahweh declares what is sinful and what is righteous by his sovereign will.

Judges teaches the dangers of doing what is right in our own eyes. We need to measure our lives by what is right in the eyes of Yahweh.

Interactive Questions

What is the purpose of pervasive literary humor in Judges?

What is the date of the authorship of Judges? What are the implications of that date for interpreting Judges?

How does Judges use dischronological narrative for its surprise ending?

How should the chronological interpretive difficulties in Judges be handled?

What are the leading functions of women in Judges?

What is the purpose of the formulaic structure of the cycles of the major judges?

What are the implications of the ironic elements in the account of Deborah?

How does Gideon function as a turning point in Judges?

What are the leading ironies in the accounts of Jephthah and Samson?

What is the significance of the use of Yahweh's name in the first epilogue (Judges 17–18)?

What is the importance of echoes of Genesis 19 in the account of the outrage of Gibeah?

Study Resources

Block, Daniel I. *Judges, Ruth*. NAC. Nashville: B&H, 1999.

Chisholm, Robert B., Jr. *A Commentary on Judges and Ruth*. KEL. Grand Rapids: Kregel Academic, 2013.

Evans, Mary J. *Judges and Ruth*. TOTC. Downers Grove, IL: IVP Academic, 2017.

Kuruvilla, Abraham. *Judges: A Theological Commentary for Preachers*. Eugene, OR: Cascade Books, 2017.

Way, Kenneth C. *Judges and Ruth*. TT. Grand Rapids: Baker, 2016.

3

Samuel

Outline

The last days before a Hebrew kingdom (1 Samuel 1–12)
    Hannah's son and Eli's sons (1–4)
        Prayer of Hannah (2:1–10)
    The ark among the Philistines (5–6)
    Finding a king in the closing days of Samuel's judgeship (7–12)
Coronation and failure of Saul's kingship (13–15)
Anointing a new king and the decline of Saul's kingship (16–31)
Rise of the Davidic kingdom (2 Samuel 1–10)
    David made king of Judah, which causes an extended civil war (1–4)
        Song of the Bow (1:17–27)
    David becomes king of all Israel (5–6)
    The Davidic promise (7)
    David defeats regional nations (8–11:1; see also 12:26–31)
The troubles of David's kingship (11:2–12:25; 13–20)[a]
Scenes from David's kingship (21–24)
    Impaling Saul's seven sons at Gibeon (21:1–14)

Defeating large-sized Philistines (21:15–22:22)

Song of David (22)

David's last words (23:1–7)

David's mighty warriors (23:8–39)

David's sin with the census (24)

ᵃ See figure 3.3 for a detailed outline of 2 Samuel 11–20.

Author, Date, and Message

The author of Samuel is unknown. The author writes from a prophetic, covenantal perspective.

Samuel could not have been written until after the time of David, who died c. 970 BCE, because the book includes an important poem framed as David's last words (2 Sam 23:1). And the narrative's pivotal role within the Deuteronomistic narrative—Joshua, Judges, Samuel, Kings—suggests it was composed before that serial narrative took its final shape in the early exilic period. The book of Kings, the last scroll in the great serial, may have been finished about 561 or 560 BCE (see chapter 4). This evidence suggests the anonymous scroll of Samuel was likely written during the 400-year period between David's death and the early days of Judah's exile.

The Samuel narrative stands as the third part of the Deuteronomistic serial narrative of the rise and fall of the Hebrew kingdoms. The scroll overlaps the Judges narrative by presenting Samuel as the last judge, and it overlaps Kings because David passes away in 1 Kings 2.

Yahweh's promise to David in 2 Samuel 7 is the high point and theological center of Samuel and the Deuteronomistic narrative. But it is more than this. The Davidic promise set in motion elements of Yahweh's redemptive will spoken by the prophets, sung by the psalmists, and preached by the apostles. It is easy to step back and see how much of Israel's Scriptures moves to and from David and the promise of Yahweh to him. The centrality of the Davidic promise within Scripture begins to explain how all of Scripture bears witness to the gospel of the Messiah, the son of David.

The Davidic promise does not simply drop out of the sky. It starts long before the days of David with two leading expectations of Torah: the coming Judah-king and the place of worship that Yahweh would choose where his name would dwell.

When Jacob blessed his fourth son in Gen 49:8–12, he expected a Judah-king to rule over his family and over the nations with a rulership that would never end. When Nathan delivered Yahweh's promise to David he used the language of the blessing of Judah to present the expectation of a kingship that would rule forever.

At the beginning of the torah collection of Deuteronomy 12–26, Moses spelled out Yahweh's intentions to select a place of worship for his name to dwell—a section known as the place legislation (Deut 12:5–27). Jerusalem was not named. The expectation did not even include building a permanent structure for worship. The oracle of Nathan to David uses the language of the place legislation to advance revelation by promising that David's own son would build a temple for Yahweh's name.

The Davidic promise brings together these two ancient Torah expectations (see Biblical Connections, page 107): the son of David would rule forever, and he would be the one who builds a house for the name of Yahweh. The redemptive plan of Yahweh reaches a high point with David's desire to build a temple in Jerusalem and Yahweh's promise to adopt David's son as his own son.

The promise to David is buried in the middle of a complicated narrative. The Samuel narrative surprises readers again and again with many wrong turns and dead ends that lead to David of Bethlehem. Samuel did not want a kingdom. Saul was from the tribe of Benjamin, not Judah. After David was anointed he repeatedly decided not to kill Saul, who hunted him as a fugitive. And even after Saul died it took seven and a half years and a civil war before David became king of all Israel. After David conquered Jerusalem and received the promise from Nathan, he raped his neighbor's wife and then murdered his neighbor. This sent rape and murder and revolution through David's own household. David's life is riddled with failures and disappointments and a few moments of hope and joy.

For all of this, David's own last words tell us the message of the narrative. David affirms the enduring covenant Yahweh made with him through Nathan. David said, "For he has established a permanent covenant with me, ordered and secured in every detail" (2 Sam 23:5). David's words point readers back to the message of the promise of Yahweh to take David's son as his own (7:14). The son of David is the son of God who would build a temple so Yahweh's name may dwell with his people.

Interpretive Overview

The purpose here is not to summarize the surprising and messy Samuel narrative with all its turns and twists. The story is told in episodes—usually one or two per chapter—each one connecting with the one before and leading to new obstacles that need to be overcome in later episodes. These episodes do not need to be summarized here. They need to be read with delight.

The reader may wish to use the outline at the beginning of this chapter (as well as figure 3.3) as a reading guide. Also take note of the bottom part of figure 3.1

that shows how the stories of the major characters overlap. Saul's story begins amid Samuel's story. And David's story begins a couple of episodes into Saul's story, which starts with his own complete failure.

The purpose of this overview is to focus on leading interpretive elements of Samuel: (1) the function of the three great poems at the beginning, middle, and end; (2) key literary devices; (3) ironic uses of physical characteristics at major turning points; and (4) Yahweh's promise to David. The Davidic promise makes the many twists and complications of the story much more important than the individual troubles episode by episode. Israel and the redemptive will of Yahweh hinge on the outcomes of the promise to David.

First, the author organized the overall Samuel scroll by placing major theologically pregnant poems at the beginning, middle, and end (see figure 3.1). These poems offer theological interpretation of the entire narrative. The common denominator of the three poems is kingship. These poems interact with the narrative context that precedes and that follows them.

The first major poem is the prayer of Hannah in 1 Sam 2:1–10. Earlier, in a rare case of silent prayer in the Bible, Eli thought she was drunken and babbling to herself (1:12–14). After Yahweh granted her a son that she gave back to Yahweh for tabernacle service, she prayed using poetic language.

Figure 3.1: Three Major Poems of Kingship in Samuel

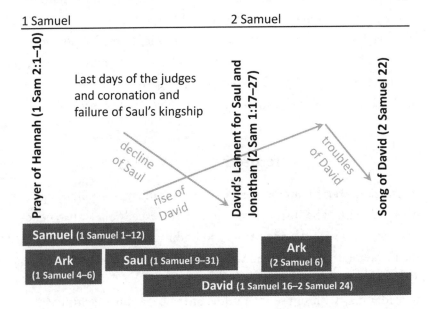

The theme of Hannah's prayer is reversal. She prayed acknowledging that things do not work out the way humans expect them to. Yahweh humbles the proud and exalts the humble. The strong, wealthy, and fertile end up broken, hungry, and dried out. Meanwhile, the weak are strengthened, the hungry are filled, and the childless have many children (2:4–5). Many years later, when Mary was pregnant with the Messiah, her song echoed Hannah's prayer (Luke 1:52; cf. 1 Sam 2:6–7).

Unlike much of the narrative of Samuel, which speaks of human events without disclosing the interventions of Yahweh like the authors of Joshua and Judges, Hannah spelled it out. Yahweh kills and grants life. He humbles and he exalts (1 Sam 2:6).

Hannah closed by saying Yahweh "will give power to *his king;* he will lift up the horn of *his anointed*" (v. 10, emphasis added). But Hannah lived in the days when there was no king in Israel, as the author of Judges stated repeatedly (Judg 17:6; 18:1; 19:1; 21:25). Hannah was the first in the Bible to speak of anointing a king. Anointing refers to rubbing or pouring oil on the one Yahweh chooses (see Ancient Connections 3.1). Anointing Saul and David (three times) plays a significant role in Samuel. Did Hannah speak better than she knew? Her expectation for Yahweh to raise up his king to set things right looked ahead to the second king that her own son Samuel would anoint.

Many years later, when Hannah's son Samuel was old, he tried to persuade Yahweh that having a human king was a bad idea (1 Sam 8:6–8). Yahweh partially agreed. Yes, the people had rejected Yahweh, but he had always intended to raise up a human king (Gen 17:16; 49:8–12; Num 24:7, 17; Deut 17:14–20; 1 Chr 28:4–5). Hannah got it right.

ANCIENT CONNECTIONS 3.1: ANOINTING KINGS

In a letter Hattusili III of Hatti complains to Adad-nirari I of Assyria (both ruled in early thirteenth century BCE) that though he had been ruling for some time, he had not received proper treatment including anointing.

> But when I assumed kingship, [then] you did not send a messenger to me. It is the custom that when kings assume kingship, the kings, his equals in rank, send him appropriate [gifts of greeting], clothing befitting kingship, and fine [oil] for his anointing. But you did not do this today. (*HDT*, 149 [II 24B §4]; cf. RINAP 3.2:205 [150.i.8])

Appearing in the middle of the book, David's lament for Saul and Jonathan is extraordinary at several levels (2 Sam 1:17–27). Though David had been anointed privately to rule over Israel many years earlier, he mourned the loss of Yahweh's anointed Saul and his own close friend Jonathan. Readers are amazed at David's lament, for if Saul or Jonathan had lived, David would never become king of Israel. But David meant it. His commitment to Saul and Jonathan was so strong that he had the messenger killed who claimed to have finished Saul off and brought what he thought was good news to David (vv. 15–16).[1]

Among many pairs and juxtapositions of the lament, the threefold refrain stands out—"How the mighty have fallen!" (vv. 19, 25, 27). David's lament for Saul and Jonathan was more than personal. He required the people of Judah to learn it (v. 18). It would be a mistake to see the lament as a shrewd political move to win over loyalists to Saul. David's long commitment to Jonathan showed that he would gladly set aside the throne to serve Saul's son. Yet, it seems Jonathan would have set aside the kingship to serve David. In any case, the lament did not stop a long civil war from breaking out between the tribes of Judah and Benjamin (2 Samuel 2–4).

David's lament epitomizes his longstanding commitment to allow God to bring down and raise up rulers. David had previously said he would not raise his hand against Yahweh's anointed (1 Sam 24:6, 10; 26:9). Many mistakenly think this means to take a passive attitude. David was not passive and did not do what the king said (26:21). To not raise a hand against Yahweh's anointed means to not kill the person.[2]

David's lament underlines that he was not involved in the battle against Saul. The women's song, "Saul has killed his thousands, but David his tens of thousands," had previously gotten David into trouble with Saul and the Philistines (18:7; 21:11). This time it caused David to be discharged from the Philistine militia (29:6). When the Philistines were defeating Saul, David was down south attacking the Amalekites and bringing home his family and others of Ziklag who were taken captive (30:1–31).

David closed the lament with a strong statement that has caused much debate: "I grieve for you, Jonathan, my brother. You were such a friend to me. *Your love for me was more wondrous than the love of women*" (2 Sam 1:26, emphasis added). Some modern interpreters mistakenly detect a homoerotic relationship in David's words.[3] This confusion comes from reading into the text modern romantic connotations of

---

[1] Cf. 1 Sam 31:4; 2 Sam 1:10.

[2] See David A. Croteau and Gary Yates, *Urban Legends of the Old Testament: 40 Common Misconceptions* (Nashville: B&H Academic, 2019), 119.

[3] For citations and refutation, see David G. Firth, *1 & 2 Samuel*, AOTC (Downers Grove, IL: InterVarsity, 2009), 208.

love instead of appreciating the ancient political and brotherhood sense of the imagery. David and Jonathan made numerous covenants (1 Sam 18:3; 20:8; cf. 20:17, 23, 42).[4] The term *love* commonly referred to political loyalties in ancient contexts (see Ancient Connections 3.2). Besides this, David and Jonathan shared a brotherly bond ("my brother," 2 Sam 1:26). Some have compared the deep friendship of David and Jonathan to that of Gilgamesh and Enkidu—whose love for each other is also compared to the love of a woman in the ancient legend known as the *Epic of Gilgamesh*.[5] While there is some merit to ancients being aware of deep friendships between men, the attention to the covenants between David and Jonathan suggests seeing the love in the poem as brotherly affection as well as political loyalty. Notice the connection between these elements earlier in the narrative: "The soul of Jonathan was bound to the soul of David, and Jonathan loved him as himself. . . . So Jonathan *made a covenant* with David *because he loved him as himself*" (1 Sam 18:1, 3 AT, emphasis added).

ANCIENT CONNECTIONS 3.2: POLITICAL ALLEGIANCE SIGNIFIED BY "LOVE"

Ancients commonly used the word *love* to speak of political loyalty rather than romantic feelings. Notice the way the Amarna letters in the fourteenth century BCE speak of the city of Byblos's loyalty to its ruler as a political commitment of heart.

> Behold, many are the people who *love*[a] me in the city [of Byblos]; few are the rebels in it. . . . Let my lord know that I would die for him. When I am in the city, I will protect it for my lord, and *my heart is fixed* on the king, my lord; I will not give the city to the sons of 'Abdu-Ashirta. (*ANET*, 483 [no. 137, 47–56], emphasis added).

[a] This translation uses "love" (*râmu*) while a less wooden translation uses "loyal" to get at its sense: "As there are many that *are loyal* to me in the city" (*AL*, 218, emphasis added). For many examples of "love" (*râmu*) as political loyalty, see *CAD* 14:140–41 (3'.c). Thank you to Nancy Erickson for help with the Akkadian phrasing here.

The heading of the song of David generalizes the occasion for the poem: "David addressed to Yahweh the words of this song on the day Yahweh delivered him from

---

[4] See Firth, *1 & 2 Samuel*, 326. Firth says 1 Sam 23:20 but must mean 20:23.
[5] See Paul S. Evans, *1–2 Samuel*, SGBC (Grand Rapids: Zondervan, 2018), 310.

the hand of all his enemies and from the hand of Saul" (2 Sam 22:1 AT). The heading praises Yahweh for salvation of David in general by naming alongside of Saul (1 Samuel 18–31) all his other enemies, which included Benjamin (2 Samuel 2–4), Jebus (5:6–9), the Philistines (5:17–25), foreign enemies (8:1–14; 12:26–31), Absalom (14–17), and Bichri (20).

The song of David uses powerful theophanic imagery. Theophany refers to self-revelation of God. Theophanies in poetic contexts tend to share certain traits. They present natural phenomena like storms, thunder, and lightning, and present Yahweh as a mighty warrior.[6] These biblical theophanic poems share some similarities with other traditions such as those of ancient Ugarit (see Ancient Connections 3.3).[7]

The song refers to the past redemptive acts of God using the imagery of dramatic cosmic forces. Chisholm explains that the song of David uses language from the exodus and Yahweh's revelation on Mount Sinai: "God's saving acts, which were accompanied by actual divine appearance, naturally provided the inspiration for later poetic descriptions of providential deliverance."[8] The song of David memorably praises God for deliverance by using the dramatic language of Yahweh's great acts of redemption.

David's claims of his own righteousness as the basis for Yahweh's rewarding him often incites questions from modern readers (22:21–28). How could David speak of his righteousness and cleanness after the way he treated Bathsheba and Uriah?

Commentators use two related lines of interpretation to make sense of David's claims. One, the heading of the song explains the context against which to read David's claims—namely, in the day Yahweh rescued him from his enemies and from Saul (v. 1). When David passed up an opportunity to kill Saul, he said he has "done nothing evil or rebellious" (1 Sam 24:11 NJPS). Saul asserted the same thing: "You are more righteous than I, for you have done what is good to me though I have done what is evil to you" (v. 17; cf. v. 19; 26:23).[9]

Two, the song of David is generalizing and speaking in a categorical manner. This corresponds to many psalms that speak of two kinds of people: the righteous and the wicked (cf. 2 Sam 22:25–28). In the same way, the Deuteronomistic narrator referred

---

[6] See Theodore Hiebert, "Theophany in the OT," *ABD* 6:505–11.

[7] Chisholm draws attention to parallels between the song of David and ancient Mesopotamian, Ugaritic, and Egyptian imagery. See Robert B. Chisholm Jr., "An Exegetical and Theological Study of Psalm 18/2 Samuel 22" (ThD diss., Dallas Theological Seminary, 1983), 313–47.

[8] Robert B. Chisholm Jr., "An Exegetical Study of Psalm 18/2 Samuel 22" (ThM thesis, Grace Theological Seminary, 1978), 117.

[9] See Evans, *1–2 Samuel*, 495.

ANCIENT CONNECTIONS 3.3: ANCIENT GOD OF THE STORM

The powerful imagery in the song of David needs to be quoted at length and can be compared to the Baal myth (emphases added).

"Listen, Baal the Conqueror, pay attention, Rider on the Clouds: I should put an opening in the house, a window in the palace." . . . *He opened a window in the house, an opening in the palace.* Then Baal opened a break in the clouds, **Baal sounded his holy voice, Baal thundered from his lips.** . . . the earth's high places shook; **Baal's enemies fled to the woods.** ("Palace of Baal," 4 v 59–62; 4 vii 25–30, 35–36 in *SFAC*, 134, 137)

For the waves of death engulfed me; the torrents of destruction terrified me. The ropes of Sheol entangled me; the snares of death confronted me.

In my distress I called upon Yahweh, and called out to my God. *From his temple he heard my voice,* my cry entered his ears. Then the earth shook and quaked; the foundations of the heavens trembled; they shook because he burned with anger. Smoke rose from his nostrils, and consuming fire came from his mouth; coals were set ablaze by it. He bent the heavens and came down, total darkness beneath his feet. He rode on a cherub and flew, soaring on the wings of the wind. He made darkness a canopy around him, a gathering of water and thick clouds. From the radiance of his presence, blazing coals were ignited. **Yahweh thundered from heaven, and the Most High sent out his voice. He shot arrows and scattered them; he hurled lightning bolts and routed them.** The valleys of the sea were exposed, and the foundations of the world were uncovered by Yahweh's rebuke, by the blast of breath from his nostrils.

He reached down from on high and took hold of me; he pulled me out of deep water. He rescued me from my powerful enemy and from those who hated me, for they were too strong for me. (2 Sam 22:5–18; vv. 7, 14, 16 AT)

The song of David is one of the places where Yahweh the God of Israel outdid the storm god of the ancient Canaanites. Baal created storms to celebrate his power over his own enemies. Yahweh used storms as weapons to deliver his servant David.

to David as a model of faithfulness to God by which to measure later kings (1 Kgs 3:3, 6, 14; 9:4; 11:4, 6, 33–34, 38; 14:8; 15:3, 5, 11; 2 Kgs 14:3; 16:2; 18:3; 22:2).[10]

In summary of this issue, both lines of interpretation recognize that David was not claiming to be perfect (without sin). Instead, David and the biblical narrator focused narrowly on David's trust in God for the kingship and deliverance from his enemies. David was righteous in that sense.

Several specific elements connect Hannah's prayer, David's lament for Saul, and the song of David, such as Yahweh's thundering (1 Sam 2:10; 2 Sam 22:14) and the use of bow imagery (1 Sam 2:4; 2 Sam 1:18, 22; 22:35). The most important connection is kingship in Israel. Hannah acknowledged that Yahweh raised up his king (1 Sam 2:10). David called on Israel to weep for the death of the king (2 Sam 1:24). David praised Yahweh for deliverance and covenantal faithfulness to his messiah, David (22:51).[11]

The three great poems give voice to the theological meaning of the Samuel narrative. Yahweh humbles the proud and lifts up the humble. Yahweh turned against the self-aggrandizing of Saul and raised up David, who repented in humility.[12]

A second interpretive element in Samuel is the use of literary devices. The author of Samuel used formulas as well as minor poems, repeated ironic questions, and repeated imagery to interconnect the narrative. Samuel opens using formulas that link it with the flashback episodes at the end of Judges (emphases added).

There was a man from the hill country of Ephraim named Micah. (Judg 17:1)

There was a young man, a Levite from Bethlehem in Judah, who was staying within the clan of Judah. (17:7)

In those days, there was no king in Israel; *there was a man*, a Levite, staying in an out-of-the-way part of the highlands of Ephraim. (19:1 AT)

There was a man from Ramathaim-zophim in the hill country of Ephraim. His name was Elkanah. (1 Sam 1:1)

---

[10] These Scriptures and this point are indebted to Robert B. Chisholm Jr., *1 & 2 Samuel*, TT (Grand Rapids: Baker Books, 2013), 299.

[11] The term *messiah* means "anointed one" and refers to those chosen by God, such as a king. The divine selection was confirmed by a ceremony of anointing with oil (see figure 3.2). For more on messiah, see the discussion of Daniel 9 in the chapter on Daniel.

[12] On Saul's "repentance" in 1 Sam 15:24–25, see Life Connections on p. 110.

There was a prominent man of Benjamin named Kish son of Abiel, son of Zeror, son of Becorath, son of Aphiah, son of a Benjaminite. He had a son named Saul. (9:1–2a)

The headings at the beginning of Samuel effectively show the continuation of the days of the judges. Things changed when Saul became king. Though it is unusual because the author left Saul's age blank, notice the chronological opening of Saul's story in the style of Kings (emphases added; see Ancient Connections 3.4).[13]

Saul was . . . *years old when he began to reign, and he reigned* . . . and *two years* over Israel. (1 Sam 13:1 NRSVue)

Ahaz *was* twenty *years old when he became king, and he reigned* sixteen *years* in Jerusalem. (2 Kgs 16:2a; see also 18:2a; 21:1, et al.)

Thus, in a real sense the structure of the beginning of Samuel transitions between the formulaic structures of Judges and Kings.

ANCIENT CONNECTIONS 3.4: LEAVING A CHRONOLOGICAL BLANK

In the Bible it is very unusual that the author left a blank for the age of Saul and another blank for how long he ruled. In all likelihood the author did not know the information and left the blank for a later scribe to fill in if the scribe acquired chronological records. The same phenomenon of leaving chronological blanks when it was unknown can be found in Assyrian royal annals.

Saul was . . . **[blank]** *years old when he began to reign, and he reigned* . . . **[blank]** and *two years* over Israel. (1 Sam 13:1 NRSVue)

The second year: Tiglath-pileser (III) died in the month Tebet. For . . . **[blank]** years Tiglath-pileser (III) ruled Akkad and Assyria. For two of these years he ruled in Akkad. On the twenty-fifth day of the month Tebet Shalmaneser (V) ascended the throne in Assyria . . . He ravaged *Samaria.* (*ABC* 1 i 25–28; cf. note pp. 72–73)

---

[13] On the lack of chronological data, see text note in NET of 1 Sam 13:1; Samuel R. Driver, *Notes on the Hebrew Text and Topography of the Books of Samuel*, 2nd ed. (Oxford: Clarendon, 1913), 97. Acts 13:21 uses the round number of forty years for Saul's rule.

It is worth pausing to note that the lack of dating for Saul's rule was one of several challenges that prevented firm chronological conclusions in the period before David's rule (cf. figure 2.1 in chapter 2). David was anointed three times in Samuel: privately, over Judah, and over all Israel. Figure 3.2 shows how precise chronological alignment begins with David's second anointing.

Figure 3.2: Chronological Details and David's Three Anointings

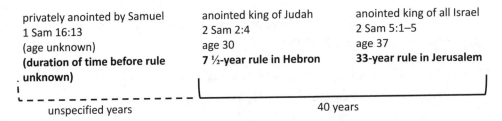

privately anointed by Samuel	anointed king of Judah	anointed king of all Israel
1 Sam 16:13	2 Sam 2:4	2 Sam 5:1–5
(age unknown)	age 30	age 37
(duration of time before rule unknown)	**7 ½-year rule in Hebron**	**33-year rule in Jerusalem**

unspecified years   40 years

The author of Samuel uses repeated questions and short poems to make connections. Notice how the same question asked positively, "Is Saul also among the prophets?," can get flipped over to a negative question (1 Sam 10:12; 19:24). As noted earlier, the several appearances of "Saul has killed his thousands, but David his tens of thousands" got David into or out of mortal danger (18:7; 21:11; 29:5). David's entire exile from Jerusalem is framed by his repeated question to his loyal associate Abishai: "What have I to do with you, you sons of Zeruiah?" (2 Sam 16:10; 19:22 AT; see figure 3.3).

Sometimes the author used other kinds of similarities to make connections within the narrative. Absalom's sexual relations with David's concubines on the palace roof links back not too subtly with David's lustful gazing on Bathsheba (2 Sam 11:2; 16:22; see figure 3.3). This helps readers see the fulfillment of Nathan's prediction of trouble entering David's household because of his great sin (12:11–12). Yet, the trouble in David's household that led to Absalom's revolution included Amnon's rape of Tamar spelled out explicitly (13:14). These connections invite readers to reconsider David's sin against Bathsheba (11:2–4).[14] David's silence when Amnon raped Tamar suggests David had no moral standing from which to rebuke his son.[15]

---

[14] The context of 2 Samuel 11–12 does not explicitly accuse David of rape. Yet, arguments from silence (David, not Bathsheba, was on a roof, 2 Sam 11:2; Nathan did not rebuke Bathsheba, 12:7–10) and circumstantial evidence (David sent for Bathsheba, 11:4; Bathsheba had no voice in the story except to say she was pregnant, 11:5) suggest it was rape. Thank you to Carmen Joy Imes for these observations.

[15] Thank you to Brian Luther for this observation.

In sum, these examples of connections begin to show the care by which the narrator drew together and juxtaposed elements between the episodes.

Figure 3.3: The Trouble of David's Kingship (2 Samuel 11–20)

Joab attacks Rabbah of Ammon (11:1)
    David and Bathsheba and Uriah in Jerusalem (11:2–12:24)
        David sees Bathsheba from the palace roof (11:2) - - - - - - - - - - - -
David finishes off Rabbah (12:26–31)
Amnon rapes Tamar (13:1–22)
Absalom kills Amnon (13:23–39)
Absalom returns to Jerusalem (14)
Absalom's revolution (15:1–12)
David flees Jerusalem (15:13–16:14)
    "What have I to do with you, you sons of Zeruiah?" (16:10 lit.) - - - - - - - -
Absalom enters Jerusalem and David's concubines (16:15–23)
      Absalom goes into David's concubines on the palace roof (16:22) - - - -
Plotting against David (17)
Death of Absalom (18:1–19:8)
Return of the king to Jerusalem (19:9–20:3)
    "What have I to do with you, you sons of Zeruiah?" (19:22 lit.) - - - - - - - -
      David banishes his concubines (20:3) - - - - - - - - - - - - - - - - - -
Hunting down the rebel Sheba son of Bichri (20:4–25)

A third interpretive element is how the author of Samuel frequently used the physical appearances of characters in highly ironic ways. Three examples appear at major turning points of the story: Eli's death, David fighting the champion from Gath, and the death of Absalom.

The death of Eli resulted from the rebellion of his family. The sins of his sons Phinehas and Hophni included having illicit relations with the women who served at the tabernacle (1 Sam 2:22) and taking the fat of the sacrifices (vv. 12–17). This latter sin was particularly reprehensible because Yahweh insisted the fat of sacrifices belonged to him alone.[16] This sin stood behind the condemnation of Eli and his sons by the unnamed man of God: "Why, then, do all of you despise my sacrifices and offerings that I require at the place of worship? You *have honored* [*kbd*] your sons more than me, by *making yourselves fat* with the best part of all of the offerings of my people Israel" (v. 29, emphasis added). The root of the term *honor* (*kbd*) can also mean "heavy." That is what killed Eli. Notice: "When he mentioned the ark of God, Eli fell

---

[16] See, e.g., Lev 3:16–17; and see Schnittjer, *Torah Story*, 2nd ed., 261–62 (see intro., n. 10).

backward off the chair by the city gate, and since he was old and *heavy [kbd]*, his neck broke and he died. Eli had judged Israel forty years" (4:18, emphasis added).

Eli did not fall over and die from being heavy when he heard about the death of his sons (v. 17). That was the problem. When he heard about the loss of the ark he fell over (v. 18).[17] Though this shows that Eli cared deeply for the ark of the covenant, the man of God got it right: by not stopping his sons, Eli honored *(kbd)* his sons over Yahweh (2:29).[18]

The scene ends with pregnant Mrs. Phinehas hearing of the loss of the ark, the death of her husband, and the death of her father-in-law. She went into labor and died. As she was dying she named her son Ichabod, a name meaning "Where is the glory (*'iy-kbd*)?" (4:21): "And she said, 'The glory (*kbd*) has been exiled from Israel, for the ark of God has been taken'" (v. 22 AT).[19] In this way, the naming of Eli's grandson symbolizes the tragic failure of priestly leadership even while it foreshadows the inevitable exile of the people.

The next turning point pivots on the primary physical characteristic of Saul, the giant of Israel (9:2; 10:23). He sat for forty days listening to the champion from Gath taunt Israel twice a day (17:16). David of Judah came from Bethlehem, the town associated with the birth of Benjamin, the namesake of Saul's tribe (v. 12). David used a sling to kill the Philistine champion, the weapon of choice for the tribe of Benjamin (v. 49; Judg 20:16). These ironic details heap up scorn on Saul.[20] David's triumph inspired the women's song that signaled the people already turning from Saul to David: "Saul has killed his thousands, but David his tens of thousands" (1 Sam 18:7).

Just as there was no one like Saul, there was no one like Absalom—whose death signaled another turning point (9:2; 2 Sam 14:25). Absalom's distinctive physical feature was his magnificent hair. Getting it cut was an event. They weighed the hair they cut off—about five pounds! (2 Sam 14:26). This relates directly to what led to his death in his revolution against his father: "Absalom was riding on his mule when he happened to meet David's soldiers. When the mule went under the tangled branches of a large oak tree, *Absalom's head was caught fast in the tree*. The mule under him kept going, so he was suspended in midair" (18:9, emphasis added). When the news of

---

[17] See Jaime A. Myers, "The Wicked 'Sons of Eli' and the Composition of 1 Samuel 1–4," *VT* 72 (2022): 241 [237–56].

[18] See *OTUOT*, 177–78.

[19] The use of "exiled" (*glh*) here follows Everett Fox, *The Early Prophets: Joshua, Judges, Samuel, and Kings* (New York: Schocken Books, 2014), 299.

[20] For more detail, see Biblical Connections in chapter 2.

his death reached David in exile, many literary patterns converge in one of the most dramatic scenes in the Bible.

The runner who brought the news did not know what readers know: sometimes David killed the bearer of (good) news of his enemy's death (vv. 31–32; cf. 1:15–16). Eli, who did not react when he heard the runner report the death of his sons, could not be more different than David. "The king was deeply moved and went up to the chamber above the city gate and wept. As he walked, he cried, '*My son Absalom! My son, my son Absalom!* If only I had died instead of you, *Absalom, my son, my son!*' . . . The king covered his face and cried loudly, '*My son Absalom! Absalom, my son, my son!*'" (2 Sam 18:33; 19:4, emphasis added). Readers are stunned. David would rather his rebel son had lived even if it meant his own demise. But readers may also make other deductions.

David's response to the death of Absalom should erase any doubts readers may have had about the genuineness of his lament for Saul and Jonathan. David grieved for the loss of his mortal enemies. But the setting of David's mourning above the gates of the city may trigger another connection. There seems to be a series of causes and effects, from David atop his palace watching a woman bathe to weeping for his son atop the city gates in exile.

In sum, the narrator of Samuel masterfully uses physical features and settings to overturn ironically the story's colorful characters. This fits exactly what readers hear Yahweh say to Samuel when David's oldest brother stood before him: "Do not look at his appearance or his height, for I have rejected him because *Yahweh does not look at things the way humans do.* People look at the outer appearance, but Yahweh looks at the heart" (1 Sam 16:7 AT, emphasis added).

A fourth interpretive element is the Davidic promise. Yahweh's promise to David through Nathan in 2 Samuel 7 stands as the centerpiece of the Samuel story and the entire Deuteronomistic narrative. The prophets and psalmists repeatedly return to this oracle, rediscovering new reasons to trust in Yahweh and place hope in his promise for redemption.

The key wordplay in Nathan's oracle turns on the dual function of the term *house*. David desired to build a house (temple) for Yahweh. But Nathan brought an oracle to David that he would not build a house for Yahweh. Instead, Yahweh would build a house (royal dynasty) for David. And David's house would build a house for Yahweh.

The term *covenant* does not appear in 2 Samuel 7. But that was exactly how David understood this promise. In his last words David said, "Is it not true my house is with God? For he has established a permanent *covenant* with me, ordered and secured in every detail" (2 Sam 23:5a, emphasis added).

Covenants operated according to the symbolic idea of making non-kin, kin. When ancient parents adopted a son, the previously unrelated persons now together formed a family. Covenants triggered legal changes. In a patriarchal system, an adopted son now stood to inherit the estate of the father (see discussion of covenants in the introduction).

The heart of the promise to David was when Yahweh said of David's son, "I will be his father, and he will be my son" (7:14a). That the son of David was adopted as the son of Yahweh changes everything.[21] The divine sonship of the Davidic heir is what undergirds the permanence of the Davidic promise.

Many interpreters have imposed a modern binary category on biblical covenants, debating whether each one is "conditional" or "unconditional." These interpreters awkwardly try to explain how biblical covenants with conditions should be seen as unconditional: "But *this dichotomy is false:* they [biblical covenants] *all* exhibit signs of *both irrevocability and contingency.*"[22] In the case of the Davidic covenant, its conditions were what demonstrated its permanence. "I will be his father, and he will be my son. When he does wrong, *I will discipline him* with a rod of men and blows from mortals. *But my faithful love will never leave him* as it did when I removed it from Saul, whom I removed from before you" (vv. 14–15, emphasis added). Outside of Israel, ancient covenants likewise featured both conditions and permanence (see Ancient Connections 3.5).

ANCIENT CONNECTIONS 3.5: PERMANENT HITTITE COVENANT WITH CONDITIONS

The Hittite treaty of Tudhaliya IV with Ulmi-Teshup (Kurunta) (thirteenth century BCE) included severe punishment for disobedience even though the covenant endures.

> And even if some son or grandson of yours commits treason . . . they shall do to him whatever the king of the land of Ḫatti decides. . . . *But they may not take from him his "house"* (i.e., his dynasty). (*COS* 2.18:104)

---

[21] See Schnittjer, "Your House" (see intro., n. 3).

[22] Block, *Covenant*, 2, emphasis added (see chap. 1, n. 6). Also see Chisholm, *1 & 2 Samuel*, 218–19, 224–25; Schnittjer, "Your House"; and references to Johnston's seminal work in Gary Edward Schnittjer, "The Blessing of Judah as Generative Expectation," *BSac* 177 (2020): 25–26, n. 22 [15–39].

The obligations of the covenant come into sharp focus when the prophets repeatedly threatened the Davidic kingdom with exile if the people did not submit to God's will set out in the Torah. This is exactly what David told Solomon (1 Kgs 2:3–4).

Yet, the very same prophets could assure their constituents of Yahweh's faithfulness to his promises to David on the eve of exile (Jeremiah) or even after the people had been taken into captivity (Ezekiel).

> "See the days are coming," says Yahweh, "when *I will raise up for David a righteous branch*, a king who will rule with wisdom and do what is just and right in the land. In his days Judah and Israel will live in safety. This is the name by which he will be called: 'Yahweh is our righteousness.'" (Jer 23:5–6 AT, emphasis added)

> I will save them [Israel and Judah] from all their apostasies by which they sinned, and I will cleanse them. Then they will be my people, and I will be their God. *My servant David will be king over them*, and there will be one shepherd for all of them. They will follow my ordinances, and keep my statutes and obey them. (Ezek 37:23b–24, emphasis added)

In sum, Yahweh established with David an irrevocable covenant that included obligations. The Davidic covenant continued to provide sure hope for God's people, even during the exile, when a Davidic ruler no longer sat enthroned in Jerusalem.

Biblical Connections

This section focuses on two biblical connections within the Davidic promise. The focal points of the Davidic promise are each based on an expectation from the Torah. Building a house for David fulfilled the expectation for the coming Judah-king of Genesis 49. Building the house of Yahweh in Jerusalem fulfilled God's promise to select a place for his name to dwell in Deuteronomy 12, known as the place legislation.[23] Both of these were proximate fulfillments in the days of Solomon that point forward to greater fulfillments.

Moses explained that Yahweh would not select a place for his name to dwell until the people enjoyed peace from their enemies. Notice how the Davidic promise alludes to the place legislation.

---

[23] These observations come from Schnittjer, "Your House," forthcoming.

[Moses:] He [Yahweh] **will give you rest from all your** surrounding **enemies** so that you live in safety. Then the place that Yahweh your God chooses to place his name . . . (Deut 12:10b–11a AT, emphasis added)

[Nathan:] "I **will give you rest from all your enemies**. Thus Yahweh declares to you that Yahweh will make a house for you. . . . He [David's seed] will build a house for my name." (2 Sam 7:11, 13a AT, emphasis added)

This is ironic. David went to war to defeat the surrounding enemies. For this reason he could not build the temple. He had blood on his hands (1 Chr 22:8; 28:3). In David's view a temple-building king needed to be a person of rest, not warfare (22:9–10; 28:2). David needed to defeat the enemies so that Solomon could build the temple in a time of peace. Building the temple for Yahweh was necessarily a multigenerational project. One king subdued the enemies, and the next king built the temple.[24]

Nathan used the term for "scepter/rod of iron" (*shebet*), and three times he used the term for "turn aside" *(sur)* from the blessing of Judah.[25]

[Jacob said:] <u>The scepter</u> (*shebet*) shall **not turn aside** (*sur*) from Judah. (Gen 49:10a AT, emphasis added)

[Nathan said:] I will be a father to him and he will be a son to me. When he does wrong I will punish him with <u>the rod</u> (*shebet*) of mortals and with wounds inflicted by humans. But my covenantal loyalty **shall not depart** (*sur*) from him, as **I removed it** (*sur*) from Saul whom **I removed** (*sur*) before you. (2 Sam 7:14–15 AT, emphases added).

The use of ironic reversals fits well with the major running wordplay of the Davidic promise—house as temple and house as dynastic line. The punishment of the son of David adopted as the son of Yahweh did not signal that the promise ended. Yahweh showed his covenantal loyalty to the Davidic son by punishing him for his sin (v. 15). This was the way Yahweh treated Israel and followers of Messiah as his own children (Deut 8:5; Heb 12:5–6). Despite the ironic reversals in Nathan's oracle, both Jacob and Nathan says the same thing: the Judah-king shall rule forever.

To summarize these biblical connections, the Davidic promise brought together two ancient Torah expectations, namely, the blessing of Judah and the place legislation. In this way Yahweh built a house for David, and the house of David built a house for Yahweh.

---

[24] This set of observations is from Schnittjer, "Your House."

[25] These comparisons are based on Schnittjer, "Blessing of Judah," 24–26.

Gospel Connections

The Davidic promise plays a pivotal role in the progressive revelation of God's redemptive will. Yahweh's declaration of the son of David as the son of Yahweh points the way toward greater fulfillment in Jesus the Messiah as the son of David and the son of God.

All humans are sons or daughters of God in the sense of being created in his own image (Gen 5:1–2). This became more focused when Yahweh elected Israel and redeemed the nation as his own son (Exod 4:23; Deut 1:31). He took the next step by choosing the son of David to sit on the throne of the kingdom of Yahweh (1 Chr 28:5; 29:23).

The game-changing advancement of revelation appears in Nathan's oracle to David. Yahweh spoke in third person of taking David's son as his own. The psalmists poetically unfolded the importance of David's son as Yahweh's son by reframing the Davidic covenant as direct discourse from Yahweh in Psalm 2 and to Yahweh in Psalm 89 (emphases added).

> *I will be his father, and he will be my son.* . . . . Your house and kingdom will endure before me forever, and your throne will be established forever. (2 Sam 7:14a, 16)

> I shall recount Yahweh's decree: he said to me, "*You're my son; today I myself have fathered you.*" (Ps 2:7 FT)

> I [Yahweh] have found David my servant; I have anointed him with my sacred oil. . . . He will call to me, "*You are my Father,* my God, the rock of my salvation." I will also make him my firstborn, greatest of the kings of the earth. (Ps 89:20, 26–27)

The incarnation of God in Messiah dramatically fulfilled the prophetic expectations for the coming of the expected Davidic king. The sonship of the Davidic heir became "literalized" in the virgin birth of the Messiah (Matt 1:21–22).

The initial and later anointings of David set a precedent for the Messiah (see figure 3.2). The Spirit came upon David at his first anointing (1 Sam 16:13) as the Spirit came upon Jesus at his baptism (Luke 3:22). Both David and Jesus became designated as messiah at the first anointing and baptism but did not rule as messiah until later. In this way the baptism of Jesus establishes him as the Messiah, anointed by the Spirit, in preparation for his death, resurrection, and exaltation-enthronement.[26]

---

[26] See Mark Strauss, *The Davidic Messiah in Luke-Acts*, JSNTSup 110 (Sheffield, UK: Sheffield Academic Press, 1995), 202–3; cf. 60, n. 1, 164–65.

The revelation of God in Jesus the Messiah stems from his identity as the son of David and the Son of God in the fullest sense. "[Paul says] concerning his Son, Jesus Christ our Lord, who was *a descendant of David according to the flesh* and was appointed to be the powerful *Son of God according to the Spirit* of holiness by the resurrection of the dead . . ." (Rom 1:3–4, emphasis added). Notice the way Paul identified Jesus as the son of David by his birth and the Son of God by his resurrection. The birth and resurrection of the Lord reveals who he is and why "everyone who calls on the name of the Lord will be saved" (10:13).

Life Connections

The central contrast of the book of Samuel is between Saul and David. Samuel told Saul, "Now your kingdom shall not endure. Yahweh has sought out for himself *a man after his own heart*" (1 Sam 13:14 AT, emphasis added). When the expression "after God's own heart" is taken on its own, it can lead to confusion. It cannot mean righteous, because Saul and David were both sinners. The expression speaks to Yahweh's choice of David.[27]

The major sins of Saul in 1 Samuel 15 and of David in 2 Samuel 11–12 reveal what was different between the two kings.

When Samuel confronted Saul for his disobedience, Saul began with denial. He blamed the people. He said they saved the spoils of Amalek to worship Yahweh. Samuel blasted Saul: "Does Yahweh delight in burnt offerings and sacrifices as much as obedience to the voice of Yahweh? See, to obey is better than sacrifice. . . . Because you have rejected the word of Yahweh, *he has rejected you as king*" (1 Sam 15:22–23 AT, emphasis added). By itself Saul's confession sounds genuine (vv. 24–25). But then Saul revealed that he was worried Samuel would dishonor him, so he confessed again: "I have sinned. *Please honor me* now before the elders of my people and before Israel" (v. 30, emphasis added). Earlier in the episode Saul was caught in the act of setting up a monument to himself (v. 12). Saul's anxiety over his own honor makes his confessions seem fake. It is reminiscent of Pharaoh's phony confessions of his sin to stop the plagues, only for his heart to reharden (Exod 9:27; 10:16).

David famously sinned against Bathsheba. When she became pregnant David murdered her husband to cover up his sin. So far David is exactly like Saul. They are both brazen sinners.

---

[27] See V. Philips Long, *1 and 2 Samuel*, TOTC (Downers Grove, IL: IVP Academic, 2020), 147–48.

When the prophet Nathan confronts David, readers see something very different. Nathan baits David by telling a story of grave injustice, making David angry at the oppressor. Nathan's response: "You are the man!" (2 Sam 12:7). David responded by confessing his sin (v. 13). David's repentance seems to be genuine, because Nathan said that Yahweh forgives him.

Yahweh did not choose David because of sinless perfection. David was as much a sinner as Saul. The difference is seen in the way Saul and David responded when being confronted by the prophet. At issue was how David responds to his own sin.

The heading of Psalm 51 invites reading the psalm in the context of David's great sin with Bathsheba and Uriah. This psalm of confession in many respects embodies how David differs from Saul. It is worth noting how the psalmist and David, in the narrative, responds. Both of these can be compared to how Joseph responds to a similar temptation (emphases added):

[Joseph:] "So how could I do this immense evil, and how could I *sin against God?*" (Gen 39:9b)

David said to Nathan, "*I have sinned against Yahweh.*" (2 Sam 12:13a AT)

"*Against you—you alone—I have sinned* and done this evil in your sight." (Ps 51:4a)

Directly before the last episode of the book is a list of David's mighty men. The last person on the list, in a place he cannot be missed, is Uriah the Hittite (2 Sam 23:39). The author points readers back to David's great sin and makes it even worse. Uriah is on a list of the men who devoted their lives to protecting and serving David. He was one of David's closest associates. Increasing the horrendousness of David's sin helps make sense of the last episode. David sins again with the census. But this time there is no cover-up. David confesses his sin even before the prophet arrives (24:10–11). The sin comes with consequences. Just as Bathsheba's baby died, so too the people are punished for David's sin with the census (12:15–18; 24:15). This fits with other cases when God forgives the repentant even while he brings judgment for their sin (cf. Num 14:20–23).

The book of Samuel ends showing that David has grown stronger in the characteristic that set him apart from Saul. Readers of Samuel need to pause at this very point to examine themselves and how they respond to sin. David points the way.

Interactive Questions

What is the central theme of Hannah's prayer? How does this provide interpretive commentary for events in the book of Samuel?

What does it mean not to lift a hand against the Lord's anointed?

What did David mean when he said he shared a love with Jonathan that was better than the love of women?

How does the song of David use imagery of God's great redemptive acts?

What is the importance of the "and there was a man" episodes at the end of Judges and beginning of Samuel?

Compare and contrast the twofold repetition of the question: "Is Saul also among the prophets?" (1 Sam 10:12; 19:24).

Compare and contrast the effects of the threefold repetition of the song of the women (1 Sam 18:7; 21:11; 29:5).

How did the author of Samuel use the appearances of Eli, Saul, and Absalom in ironic ways at key turning points in the narrative?

What is the problem with the conditional/unconditional debate about the Davidic covenant? How do irrevocability and obligations both fit together within the Davidic covenant?

What two great Torah expectations connect within the Davidic covenant? How does the Davidic promise build on these ancient expectations?

What is the role of the Davidic covenant in advancing revelation concerning salvation by the Son of God?

Study Resources

Chisholm, Robert B., Jr. *1 & 2 Samuel*. TT. Grand Rapids: Baker Books, 2013.

Firth, David G. *1 & 2 Samuel*. AOTC. Downers Grove, IL: InterVarsity, 2009.

Kim, Koowon. *1 Samuel: A Pastoral and Contextual Commentary*. Asia Bible Commentary. Carlisle, UK: Langham Global Library, 2018.

Long, V. Philips. *1 and 2 Samuel*. TOTC. Downers Grove, IL: IVP Academic, 2020.

Schnittjer, Gary Edward. "Your House Is My House: Exegetical Intersection within the Davidic Promise." *BSac* (forthcoming).

4

Kings

Outline

Solomon king of all Israel (1 Kings 1–11)

 Solomon's kingship established (1–2)

  Rule established (2:12)

  Kingdom established (2:46, resumptive repetition)

 Solomon's accomplishments (3:1–10:25)

  Vision at Gibeon (3:3–15)

  Second vision (9:1–9)

 Solomon's downfall (10:26–11:43)

Two Hebrew kingdoms: Israel in the north and Judah in the south (1 Kings 12–2 Kings 17)

 Kingdom divided (1 Kgs 12:1–24)

[Southern kingdom of Judah]	**[Northern kingdom of Israel]**	**[Northern prophets]**
	Jeroboam (928–907) (12:25–14:20)	

[Southern kingdom of Judah]	[Northern kingdom of Israel]	[Northern prophets]
		Man of God (13:1–32)
		Ahijah (14:1–18)
Rehoboam (928–911) (14:21–31)		
Abijam (911–908) (15:1–8)		
Asa (908–867) (15:9–24)		
	Nadab (907–906) (15:25–32)	
	Basha (906–883) (15:33–16:7)	
		Jehu, son of Hani (16:1–4, 12)
	Elah (883–882) (16:8–14)	
	Zimri (882) (16:15–20)	
	Omri (16:21–28)	
	[rebellion of Tibni (882–878) (16:21–22)]	
	Ahab (873–852) (16:29–22:40)	
		Elijah (17:1–19:21; 21:17–29)
		Micaiah (22:8–28)
Jehoshaphat (870–846) (22:41–50)		
	Ahaziah (852–851) (22:51–2 Kgs 1:18)	
		Elijah (2 Kgs 1:1–17; 2:1–12)
		Elisha (2:1–25)
	Joram (851–842) (3:1–3; 9:14–24; see figure 4.1)	
	[Battle against Mesha of Moab (3:4–27)]	Elisha (3:11–19)

[Southern kingdom of Judah]	[Northern kingdom of Israel]	[Northern prophets]
		Elisha (4:1–8:15)
Jehoram (851–843) (2 Kgs 8:16–24)		
Ahaziah (843–842) (8:25–29; 9:16–26; see figure 4.1)		
	Jehu (842–814) (9–10)	Elisha (9:1–3)
Queen Athaliah (842–836) (11)		
Joash (836–798) (12)		
	Jehoahaz (817–800) (13:1–9)	
	Jehoash (800–784) (13:10–13)	
		Elisha (13:14–21, 22–24)
Amaziah (798–769) (14:1–22)		
	Jeroboam (II) (788–747) (14:23–29)	Jonah (14:25)
Azariah/Uzziah (785–733) (15:1–7)		
	Zechariah (747) (15:8–12)	
	Shallum (747) (15:13–15)	
	Menahem (747–737) (15:16–22)	
	Pekahiah (737–735) (15:23–26)	
	Pekah (735–732) (15:27–31)	
Jotham (759–743) (15:32–38)		
Ahaz (743–727) (16)		
	Hoshea (732–724) (17:1–6)	
	Explanation of the fall of Israel (2 Kgs 17:7–41)	

The last days of the kingdom of Judah (18–25)

    Hezekiah (727–698) (18–20)[1]

    Manasseh (698–642) (21:1–18)

    Amon (641–640) (21:19–26)

    Josiah (639–609) (22:1–23:30)

    Jehoahaz (609) (23:31–35)

    Jehoiakim (609–598) (23:36–24:7; see figure 4.2)

    Jehoiachin and exile of prominent citizens (597) (24:8–17; see figure 4.2)

    Zedekiah (596–586) (24:18–25:7; see figure 4.2)

    Fall of Jerusalem and exile of prominent citizens (586) (25:8–21)

    Governor Gedaliah (25:22–26)

    Elevation of Jehoiachin in Babylon (25:27–30)

---

[1] Dates of the kings are based on Mordechai Cogan, "Chronology," *ABD* 1:1005–11. For a survey of failed attempts to explain the fourteenth year in 2 Kgs 18:13, including his own proposal that does not acknowledge the dischronological note in 20:6, see Gershon Galil, *The Chronology of the Kings of Judah* (Leiden: E. J. Brill, 1996), 102–3. Archer correctly diagnoses the problem with Thiele's view that reads against the sense of the text of 2 Kgs 18:1, 9, 10. Archer's solution—emending a single Hebrew letter of 18:13 to make it Hezekiah's twenty-fourth year—is very attractive except for lack of supporting evidence. See Gleason L. Archer, review of *The Mysterious Numbers of the Hebrew Kings*, rev. ed. by Edwin R. Thiele, *Christianity Today* 10, no. 14 (April 15, 1966): 34–36. McFall does well to suggest that 2 Kgs 18:1, 9 are dated to one thing and 18:13 to something else—the view taken here agrees with this point. However, McFall does not account for the dischronological note in 2 Kgs 20:6 that undermines his coregency suggestion. See Leslie McFall, "Did Thiele Overlook Hezekiah's Coregency?" *BSac* 146 (1989): 393–404. The view here follows a modified version of the logic of Cogan and Tadmor. Namely, 18:13 is not the fourteenth year of his rule to introduce the story of Hezekiah's illness (so Cogan and Tadmor), but (against Cogan and Tadmor) it may be the fourteenth of his extra fifteen years granted in 20:6 (on the dischronological placement of Hezekiah's illness, see figure 4.5). See Mordechai Cogan and Hayim Tadmor, *II Kings*, AB (New York: Doubleday, 1988), 228. That is, while 2 Kgs 18:1, 9, 10 are dated from the start of Hezekiah's rule (727 BCE), 18:13 is dated from the start of his fifteen-year extension of life (20:6//Isa 38:5). Please note that 2 Kgs 18:13–16 refers to the tribute Hezekiah sent Sennacherib *after* the failed campaign of 701. Sennacherib's royal inscription made in c. 700 says that Hezekiah's tribute was sent to Nineveh "*after* my [Sennacherib's] departure to Nineveh" (*RT*, 115, emphasis added; cf. *COS* 2.119B:303, lines 55–58) from the military campaign against Jerusalem in 701. The Akkadian logogram EGIR signifies *arkû*, meaning "after" or "later" (*CAD* 1.2:286; for the transliteration see RINAP 3.1:66 [4.58]). (Thank you to Nancy Erickson for help with the Akkadian here.) The relevant passage of Sennacherib's royal inscription appears below in Ancient Connections 4.4. The chronological interpretation of 2 Kgs 18:13 here accepts the Hebrew text without emendation and resolves the chronological tensions of this thorny issue. A lingering difficulty is caused by Isa 36:1 carrying over the date of the tribute but excluding the details of the tribute (i.e., 2 Kgs 18:14–16 not carried over). Perhaps Isa 36:1 serves to date the conclusion of the Assyrian debacle. For the evidence of the dependence of Isaiah 36–39 on 2 Kgs 18–20, see *OTUOT*, 232–34; cf. 815–16. On the chronological relationship of 2 Kgs 18:13–16, 17–19:35; and 20:1–11, 12–19, see figure 4.5 below.

Figure 4.1: Families of Ahab and Jezebel of Israel and Jehoshaphat of Judah‡

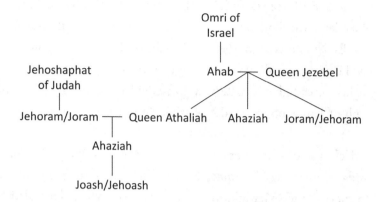

‡The narratives of Israel and Judah in Kings in the latter days of Omri's dynasty often seem complicated to readers new to Old Testament studies. One challenge is that Joram of Israel is also known as Jehoram (851–842 BCE) and Jehoram of Judah is also known as Joram (851–843)— both ruling at the same time. These two kings with the same names from two kingdoms at about the same time likely sprang from the joining of their families by marriage. Another challenge is Jehu's uprising in which he killed in quick succession Joram of Israel (2 Kgs 9:22–24), Ahaziah of Judah (9:27), and Jezebel, wife of Ahab of Israel (9:30–37).

Figure 4.2: The Last Kings of Judah†

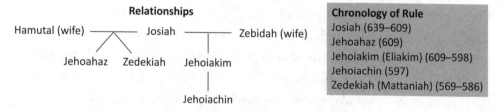

†On many significant events at the end of the kingdom of Judah, see figure I.9 in Introduction.

Author, Date, and Message

The author of Kings is unknown.

Kings stands as the final installment of the four-part serial known as the Deuteronomistic narrative (see discussion in the introduction). The authorship of Kings and compilation of the Deuteronomistic narrative in their received form including their use of many older literary artifacts, such as the "Historical Record of

Israel's Kings" (e.g., 1 Kgs 14:19), can be dated to the early part of the Judean exile (major exiles in 597 and 586 BC; see table I.5 in the introduction). The final episode of Kings narrates the release from prison of Jehoiachin, former king of Jerusalem, by the ruler of Babylon, Evil-merodach in 562 (2 Kgs 25:27–30). This event not only connects to the Davidic promise but may have triggered the completion of the great serial narrative that had already been underway to explain the exile. The evidence in the final paragraph of Kings points to the possible completion of authorship in c. 561 or 560.

First, Evil-merodach is so obscure that he can be called "Mr. Nobody." The biblical name Evil-merodach, meaning "Marduk's Stooge," seems to be an intentional scribal distortion to mock Amel-Marduk, meaning "Marduk's Man." He ruled for about twenty-two months (October 562 to sometime between May and August 560), leaving behind no records and doing nothing that anyone knows about besides releasing Jehoiachin. Serge Frolov says, "Evil-Merodach was one of the most obscure, insignificant, and ephemeral rulers Babylon and the ancient Near East in general have ever known." The point is that Jehoiachin's release from prison by Evil-merodach would seem of significance only at that very time. Second, and more importantly, the testimony of Jehoiachin eating with the king and receiving provisions from the king for the rest of his life (vv. 29–30) only fits before Evil-merodach's rule ended.[2]

The books of Joshua, Judges, Samuel, and Kings contain substantial literary artifacts written nearly contemporary with the events they narrate, though each book of the serial reflects a much later outlook.[3] Kings itself spans over 400 years from David's final days (c. 970) to Jehoiachin's release from prison in Babylon (562). The major goal of the Deuteronomistic narrative is explaining the destruction of Jerusalem and the Judean exile. The final paragraph of Kings contains an account that makes the most sense within the rule of Evil-merodach. This closing paragraph may be contemporary with the completion of the composition of Kings, the final installment of Deuteronomistic narrative in the early part of the exile.

The message of Kings and the Deuteronomistic narrative it concludes is that the exile was inevitable. The urgent need for this message and how it comes out of the complex book of Kings call for brief attention.

---

[2] This paragraph is indebted to Serge Frolov, "Evil-Merodach and the Deuteronomist: The Sociohistorical Setting of Dtr in the Light of 2 Kgs 25:27–30," *Biblica* 88 (2007): 179–85 [174–90]; the quotations are from 179, 180. My disagreements with Frolov's highly speculative account of scribal mechanics on pages 186–90 cannot be taken up here. In spite of these problems, Frolov's basic argument on 2 Kgs 25:27–30 on pages 179–85 holds much merit.

[3] See discussions of date of Joshua, Judges, and Samuel in their respective chapters.

The exile created a crisis by seeming to contradict the Abrahamic and Davidic covenants. The Abrahamic covenant promised to give the land to Israel forever. The Davidic covenant assured that a descendant of David would rule from Jerusalem forever. The destruction of the temple, dethronement of the king, and exile of the people did not seem to fit with these cherished promises.

The conflict between these permanent covenants and reality required explanation. The burden of the Deuteronomistic serial narrative is showing that God's people have been on their way to exile from the beginning. Within the generation of the grandchildren of Moses, Aaron, and the former slaves who came out of Egypt with them, things were already worse than any of the days of the judges as shown in the two flashbacks at the end of Judges (Judges 17–18; 19–21). Though the covenant to David came with obligations, many had blindly assured themselves it made them immune from exile.[4] An excellent example is the near-death experience of Jeremiah when he was accused of being a false prophet for predicting the destruction of the temple (Jer 26:8–9). The exile verified the message of prophets like Jeremiah and Ezekiel as well as earlier prophets like Isaiah and even Moses, who all had expected exile.[5]

The narrative interpretation of history in Kings grounds the inevitability of the fall of Jerusalem on the prayer of Solomon and the word of the prophets.[6] During the dedication of the temple Solomon looked ahead to inevitable exile based on the sinfulness common to all humans. Solomon prayed: "When they sin against you—*for there is no one who does not sin*—and you are angry with them and hand them over to the enemy, *and their captors deport them to the enemy's country*—whether distant or nearby . . ." (1 Kgs 8:46, emphasis added). In the next generation the kingdom was broken into the northern kingdom of Israel and the southern kingdom of Judah. The narrator's own interpretive commentary on the fall of Israel, which anticipated the fall of Judah, rests on the prophets, who likewise rest on the Torah (see Ancient Connections 4.1).

Yahweh warned Israel and Judah by the hand of *all his prophets and seers*, saying: "Turn from your evil ways and keep my commandments and my decrees, *according to all the torah* that I have commanded your ancestors and that I sent

---

[4] See 2 Sam 7:14; 1 Kgs 2:2–4. On the obligations of the Abrahamic covenant, see Gen 17:2–3. For a detailed explanation of the permanence and obligations of biblical covenants, see Schnittjer, "Your House," forthcoming (see intro., n. 3).

[5] See Lev 18:27; 26:31–33; Deut 29:23–30:1; Isa 39:5–7; Jer 7:11–15; 15:1–4; Ezek 24:21; Mic 4:10.

[6] On 1 Kings 8 and 2 Kings 17, see *OTUOT*, 206–7.

to you *by my servants the prophets.*" . . . *Even Judah* did not obey the commands of Yahweh their God. *They followed the customs of Israel.* . . . Finally, Yahweh removed Israel from his presence as he had warned them *by all his servants the prophets.* So Israel was exiled from their land to Assyria until this day. (2 Kgs 17:13, 19, 23 AT, emphasis added).

ANCIENT CONNECTIONS 4.1: FALL OF SAMARIA IN ASSYRIAN ROYAL INSCRIPTIONS

The description of the fall of Samaria to Sargon II in 722 BCE appears in many royal inscriptions, including one found at Calah. It can be compared to the biblical version.

> [The Sa]marians, who had come to an agreement with a [*hostile?*] king not to do service or to render tribute to me, did battle. In the strength of the great gods, my lords, I fought with them; 27,280 people . . . I counted as spoil . . . [and] I settled in Assyria. I resettled Samaria more (densely) than before and I brought there people from the lands of my conquest. I appointed my eunuch over them as governor and counted them as Assyrians. (*RT*, 89).

> In the ninth year of Hoshea, the king of Assyria captured Samaria. He deported the Israelites to Assyria and settled them in Halah, along the Habor (Gozan's river), and in the cities of the Medes. . . . Then the king of Assyria brought people from Babylon, Cuthah, Avva, Hamath, and Sepharvaim and settled them in place of the Israelites in the cities of Samaria. (2 Kgs 17:6, 24a)

In addition to the narrator of Kings' own interpretation of the prophetic word as guaranteeing exile, he also embedded the words of the prophets in the narrative. More than a century before the exile of Judah, Isaiah spelled it out to King Hezekiah, and the narrator cited an unnamed prophet against his son, King Manasseh:

[Isaiah said:] "There, days are going to come when everything that's in your house, and that your ancestors have stored up until this day, *will be carried to Babylon. Not a thing will be left,*" Yahweh has said. "Some of your descendants who will issue from you, whom you will father, *will be taken and will be court- iers in the palace of the king of Babylon."* (20:17–18 FT, emphasis added)

Yahweh spoke *by means of his servant the prophet,* "Since King Manasseh of Judah has committed all these detestable acts—worse evil than the Amorites who preceded him had done—and by means of his idols has also caused Judah to sin, . . . *I will wipe Jerusalem clean as one wipes a bowl*—wiping it and turning it upside down. I will abandon the remnant of my inheritance *and hand them over to their enemies. They will become plunder and spoil* to all their enemies." (21:10–11, 13b–14, v. 10 FT, emphasis added)[7]

The message of Kings is not new. But it is unwelcome. In spite of repeated warn- ings from Moses and the prophets, the exile still came as a surprise to God's people who interpreted the Abrahamic and Davidic covenants the way they wanted to. But these covenants offered enduring hope—through exile, not without exile. This makes the message of Kings critical.

Interpretive Overview

The opening of this chapter features a special reading outline to assist readers un- familiar with Kings. The outline helps readers navigate the three kinds of historical narrative interwoven in the middle section of Kings (more on this later).

This section surveys five major turning points in Kings. Understanding how these five turning points work helps to make sense of each major section of Kings.

Readers who are not familiar with the ancient Near Eastern historical context of the period of the Hebrew kingdoms will do well to review the section on ancient context in the introduction of this study.

Two of the five turning points appear at the transitions between the book's three major sections (see outline at the beginning of the chapter). Kings opens with Solomon and closes with the last kings of Judah from Hezekiah to Zedekiah (1 Kings 1–11; 2 Kings 18–25). The downfall of Solomon led to the competing kingdoms of Israel and Judah. The narrative of Hezekiah's pride follows the deliverance of Jerusalem from the Assyrians. Both of these turning points operate by dischronological narration (rearranged from their chronological sequence; see the introduction). These events set in motion new bad directions (see figure 4.3).

---

[7] Cf. 2 Kgs 23:26–27; 24:3–4; Jer 15:4.

Figure 4.3: Overview of the Hebrew Kingdoms

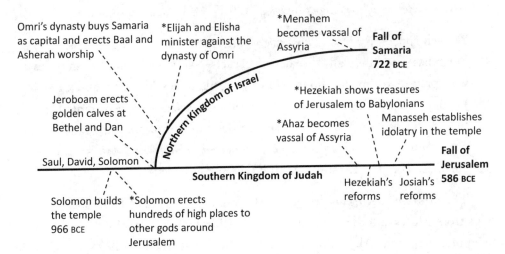

* Asterisks signify the five turning points.

The other three of the five turning points appear within the complex middle section of Kings (1 Kings 12–2 Kings 17; see figure 4.3 and the outline at the beginning of the chapter). Elijah ushered in the beginning of the end of the dynasty of Omri. His famous public contest with the prophets of Baal on Mount Carmel and the private revelatory experience on Mount Horeb set in motion the decline of this unprecedented rule of wickedness (1 Kings 18–19). King Menahem of Israel and King Ahaz of Judah independently put themselves under vassalage to Tiglath-pileser III of Assyria (2 Kgs 15:19–20; 16:7–9). These three turning points stand within the three different kinds of stories the author of Kings uses to build the middle part of the historical narrative.

The middle section of Kings interweaves stories of the kings of the northern kingdom of Israel with stories of the kings of Judah—the kings of each are dated in relation to the rival kingdom. The narration moves along back and forth from the next episode of the one kingdom to the other. This way both kingdom stories move forward incrementally and in relation to each other. Then interspersed among the interwoven episodes of the two kingdoms is a series of colorful northern prophet stories. These undated stories usually do not name the king, instead simply call him the king.

Scholars often refer to this middle period of Kings as the "divided kingdom." This reminds readers that both kingdoms were part of the people of Israel. But this approach does not consider the viewpoint of the individual kingdoms. It might be like treating the United States as a history of independent British colonies. Though beginning as thirteen British colonies needs to be kept in mind, it does not provide the best framework to explain civil rights, the hippies of the sexual revolution, or the destruction of the Twin Towers. Yes, both Hebrew kingdoms looked back to the same ancestors and the same Torah, and both disobeyed the same God. But they were two independent rival kingdoms.

In sum, close attention to five key turning points can help readers make the most of their study of the Kings narrative.

The first turning point is Solomon's downfall and its aftermath. The narrator took advantage of dischronological narration to readjust the entire Solomon story. A close reading shows that Solomon's problems actually begin in the last years of David. The narrator uses several allusions to the Torah to explain Solomon's devastating downfall.

After establishing his rule, during a vision Solomon asks for discernment. He then demonstrates his gift of discernment by saying to chop the baby in half (1 Kgs 3:9, 16–28).[8] The narrator recounts Solomon's vast, peaceful, and prosperous kingdom; the building of the temple and other projects; and his fame and wealth (1 Kings 4–10).

But in the middle of describing Solomon's wealth the narrator seems to wink at readers in the know.[9] Notice how the seeming praise of Solomon's wealth disguises a terrible fault line of disobedience by alluding to the law of the king (emphases added).

> Solomon accumulated 1,400 chariots and **12,000 horsemen** and stationed them in the chariot cities and with the king in Jerusalem. The king made silver as common in Jerusalem as stones . . . Solomon's **horses were imported from Egypt** and Kue. . . . In the same way, they exported them to all the kings of the Hittites and to the kings of Aram through their agents. (1 Kgs 10:26–29)

> Surely, he [the king] must **not acquire many horses** for himself or cause the people to **return to Egypt in order to acquire more horses,** for Yahweh has said to you, "You must not go back that way again. He must not marry many wives, or else his heart will turn away. He must not amass large amounts of silver and gold. (Deut 17:16–17 AT)

---

[8] For a detailed explanation of how the realistic depiction of ancient Near Eastern legal procedures of 1 Kgs 3:16–28 showcases Solomon's wisdom, see Raymond Westbrook, "Law in Kings," in *The Books of Kings: Sources, Composition, Historiography, and Reception,* ed. André Lemaire and Baruch Halpern (Atlanta: SBL Press, 2010), 446–50 [445–66].

[9] See J. Daniel Hays, "Has the Narrator Come to Praise Solomon or Bury Him?: Narrative Subtlety in 1 Kings 1–11," *JSOT* 28, no. 2 (2003): 156–57 [149–74]. My use of "wink" here comes from Hays's comments on page 154.

The horse-trading and excessive silver served as an on-ramp to Solomon's problem with women. How many wives were too many? (See v. 17 above.) Deuteronomy does not specify, but sixty queens and eighty concubines (Song 6:8) or eventually 700 wives and 300 concubines (1 Kgs 11:3) were too many.[10]

The narrator shifts from subtleties to open condemnation of Solomon's violation of several Torah standards against apostasy marriages (emphases added).[11]

[Solomon's downfall]	[Torah standards]
Now, king Solomon loved many foreign women along with **the daughter of pharaoh**, **Moabites**, **Ammonites**, **Edomites**, Sidonians, and **Hittites**, from the nations *of which Yahweh had said* to the Israelites, "You shall not come into them, and they shall not come into you, otherwise they will turn your heart after their gods." Solomon clung to them in love. He had 700 royal wives and 300 concubines. And his wives turned his heart away. When Solomon grew old his wives turned his heart away after other gods and his heart was not wholly devoted to Yahweh his God like the heart of his father David. (1 Kgs 11:1–4 AT)	And when you take from their daughters for your sons, and their daughters whore after their gods, then they will cause your sons to whore after their gods. (Exod 34:16 AT) When Yahweh your God brings you into the land you are entering to possess and he drives out before you many nations—**Hittites**, Girgashites, Amorites, Canaanites, Perizzites, and Jebusites . . . You shall not intermarry with them. . . . For they will turn your sons from following after me and they will serve other gods. (Deut 7:1a, 3a–4a AT) He [the king] shall not acquire many wives for himself so that his heart will not turn away. (Deut 17:17a AT) **Ammonites** and **Moabites** shall not come into the assembly of Yahweh. . . . You shall not despise **Edomites**, for they are your relatives. You shall not despise **Egyptians**, for you were residing foreigners in their land. (Deut 23:3a, 7 AT)

---

[10] On even larger ancient harems, see James A. Montgomery, *The Book of Kings*, International Critical Commentary (Edinburgh: T&T Clark, 1951), 234–35; and see Isaac Kalimi, *Writing and Rewriting the Story of Solomon in Ancient Israel* (Cambridge: Cambridge University Press, 2019), 89–90. It was common for later Persian rulers to have 300 or 360 concubines (see *PE*, 589–90, 595).

[11] Treatment of Solomon's fall is based on Gary Edward Schnittjer, "An Overview of Composite Citations in the Hebrew Bible with a Case Study from 1 Kings 11:1–4," in *Composite Allusions in Antiquity*, ed. Sean Adams and Seth Ehorn (New York: Bloomsbury, forthcoming); *OTUOT*, 200–202.

The italicized phrase in 1 Kgs 11:2 shows that the narrator was alluding to the Torah. It is not a quotation but rather a blended paraphrase of several laws. The use of "many . . . women" in verse 1 alludes to the law of the king in Deuteronomy 17. But the threefold use of "turned" his heart in verses 2–4 matches the grammatical sense of "cause to whore" and "turn" in the two laws against intermarriage (Exod 34:16; Deut 7:4).[12] The upshot is that they turned him away from Yahweh. More subtly, the grammatically masculine pronoun "them" in "Solomon clung to *them* in love" in verse 2 more naturally refers to the grammatically masculine "gods" (1 Kgs 11:2) than the feminine "wives" (v. 1). In addition, Solomon went after these gods by building high places (worship centers) for them (vv. 5–8). That his treaty wives worshiped the gods of their homelands and not the God of Israel demonstrates that these were apostasy marriages.

The first four ethnicities in verse 1 match the same four in the law of the assembly in Deuteronomy 23—two excluded (Amon, Moab) and two included (Egypt, Edom). But for Solomon all four are excluded because they did not turn to Yahweh's covenant but worshiped the gods of their homelands. Of the seven nations listed in Deuteronomy 7, only the Hittites were far enough away to still have royal daughters to marry since Solomon had already enslaved the other six nations as well as any Hittites in Israel (1 Kgs 9:20–21). The mention of the wives from Sidon shows that the narrator understood the lists from Deuteronomy 7 and 23 not as comprehensive or ethnic but representative of any spouse who did not trust in the true God of Israel.

The reader may be relieved that Solomon did not turn away until he was "old" (1 Kgs 11:4). But how old is old? Solomon was young when he began ruling. In the fourth year he built the temple for seven years and then his palace for thirteen years (6:1, 38; 7:1). When he finished these projects in the twenty-fourth year of his forty-year rule (9:10), his building supervisor, Jeroboam, built a retreat for Solomon's Egyptian wife in Gezer and the terraces for the supporting wall in Jerusalem (9:15–16, 24). By that time Solomon had already built hundreds of worship centers for his treaty wives all around Jerusalem. We know this because that was when God's prophet Ahijah predicted that Jeroboam would take most of Solomon's former kingdom rather than Solomon's heir because of the false worship sites (11:27, 33). Since Solomon was building hundreds of worship centers for the wives of his apostasy marriages while building the temple and his palace, he was old early in his life. In other

---

[12] The term *turn* (*nth*, causative stem) in 1 Kgs 11:2, 3, 4 is different than "turn" (*sur*) in Deut 17:17 but matches the grammatical stem of "cause to whore" (*znh*, causative stem) in Exod 34:16 and "turn" (*sur*, causative stem) in Deut 7:4.

words, the narrator used a flexible term *old* to invite readers to learn how far back the rebellion of Solomon went.

The narrator also revealed by flashbacks that Solomon had perpetual military conflicts with Hadad the Edomite from the time of David's death (vv. 14, 21) and with Rezin, king of Damascus, "all the days of Solomon" (v. 25 AT).[13] The narrator of Kings used these two dischronological problems—military troubles from the beginning and Solomon's apostasy marriages during the first half of his rule—to invite a review of Solomon's rule (see figure 4.4). The narrator organized Solomon's rule thematically: first telling of peace and prosperity (3:1–10:25; esp. 4:20, 25), then of horse-trading with the nations, apostasy marriages that turned him away from God, and lifelong military troubles (10:26–29; 11:1–8, 22, 23–25). The organization of the narrative around the good days of Solomon and Solomon's fall functions similarly to the flashbacks to the terrible early days of the judges at the end of the story (Judg 18:30; 20:28).

Figure 4.4: Thematic versus Chronological Arrangement of the Solomon Story

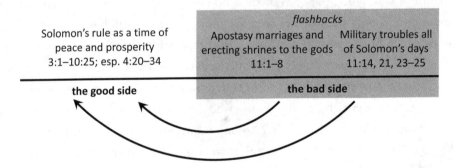

One outcome of Solomon's sin was Jeroboam's revolution to break off the northern kingdom of Israel. From the beginning Jeroboam established golden calves after the manner of the golden calf Israel worshiped in the wilderness (emphases added).

He [Aaron] took the gold from them, fashioned it with an engraving tool, and made it into an image of a calf. Then they said, "*Israel, these are your gods, who brought you up from the land of Egypt!*" (Exod 32:4)

Then he [Jeroboam] made two golden calves, and he said to the people, "Going to Jerusalem is too difficult for you. *Israel, here are your gods who brought you up from the land of Egypt.*" (1 Kgs 12:28)

---

[13] See Hayim Tadmor and Mordechai Cogan, "Ahaz and Tiglath-Pileser in the Book of Kings: Historiographic Considerations," *Biblica* 60, no. 4 (1979): 498–99 [491–508].

Israel's original sin of making an image of God and thereby breaking the second of the Ten Commandments became the northern kingdom of Israel's original and ongoing sin. All of the northern kings did evil in Yahweh's sight by giving royal support for these shrines of idolatry to the God of Israel in Bethel and Dan (see figure I.4 in the introduction). The narrator accused all of them as following the sin of Jeroboam, son of Nebat: Nadab (15:26); Baasha (15:34; 16:2, 7); Elah (16:13); Zimri (v. 19); Tibni (n/a, splinter faction not able to sponsor the shrine); Omri (vv. 25–26); Ahab (v. 31); Ahaziah (22:52); Joram/Jehoram (2 Kgs 3:3); Jehu (10:29, 31); Jehoahaz (13:2); Jehoash/Joash (v. 11); Jeroboam II (14:24); Zechariah (15:9); Shallum (n/a, too brief to sponsor shrines); Menahem (v. 18); Pekahiah (v. 24); and Pekah (v. 28). This sin was the cornerstone of the narrator's explanation of the fall of Israel (17:16, 21–23). And the narrator was quick to add that Judah did all the same things (v. 19).

In sum, Solomon's downfall is a major turning point of Kings. His apostasy marriages directly resulted in building around Jerusalem hundreds of shrines dedicated to false worship. This commitment to promoting the worship of false gods caused the division of the kingdom, which naturally led the northern kingdom to establish their own rival idolatry to the God of Israel. All of this points toward exile.

The next turning point comes in Elijah's contest against Ahab and Jezebel's prophets of Baal and its aftermath. The economic high point of the northern kingdom of Israel in the dynasty of Omri was widely recognized by ancient Near Eastern rivals.[14] A treaty marriage between Omri's son Ahab and Jezebel of the coastal trade city of Sidon established lucrative relations. This treaty marriage also led to building a temple to Baal and setting up an Asherah pole in the new capital city of Samaria. This prompted the narrator to say, "Ahab made an Asherah and he did more to provoke Yahweh, the God of Israel, than all of the kings of Israel who were before him" (1 Kgs 16:33 AT; cf. 21:25–26).

The Elijah and Elisha stories are the most expansive of the undated northern prophet stories interspersed through the middle part of Kings (see the right-hand column in the outline at the beginning of the chapter). Many of these stories focus on the mundane daily lives of common folks, such as a widow facing poverty, a couple struggling with infertility, a man who lost a borrowed tool, and the like (17:14; 2 Kgs 4:3, 16; 6:6). The effect of these northern prophet stories overall is to show that Yahweh's interests go beyond kings and nations. He cares for the disadvantaged protected classes who cry out to him as he said he would (Exod 22:23).

---

[14] See Daniel M. Master, "Institutions of Trade in 1 and 2 Kings," in Lemaire and Halpern, *The Books of Kings*, 509 [501–16].

Elijah became an enemy sought by Ahab when he proclaimed a drought (1 Kgs 17:1). The irony of causing a drought upon the royal couple who introduced worship of the storm god Baal into Samaria makes readers smile (see Ancient Connections 2.2 and 2.3 in chapter 2). The contest on Mount Carmel pits Elijah singularly against hundreds of false prophets—he taunts them until God answered him with fire (18:38).[15] When the people acknowledged God and slaughtered the prophets of Baal, Elijah fled from Jezebel to Mount Horeb.

The revelatory experience of Elijah in a cave resembles Moses's experience on the same mountain.[16] While God covered Moses's face and put him in the cleft when the glory came, the "still small voice" (KJV) or "a soft whisper" (CSB) caused Elijah to cover his own face and return to the cave (Exod 33:22; 1 Kgs 19:12–13).[17] Yahweh commissioned Elijah to anoint Elisha, who later anointed Hazael and Jehu (1 Kgs 19:15–17).[18] They incited war and revolution that would end the line of Omri (see figure 4.1). This revelation on Mount Horeb was the beginning of the end of Omri's wicked dynasty.

The next turning point stems from King Menahem of Israel selling Israel into vassalage—surrendering the nation's sovereignty and wealth—to Tiglath-pileser III in order to enjoy his own personal place of privilege.[19] Vassalage means that Israel lost their sovereignty as a nation to Assyria as well as incurring excessively high taxes. The narrator goes out of his way to heap up blame upon Menahem. To illustrate the narrator's interpretive moves requires first observing the repeated frame narrative for all the kings (table 4.1). (The reader can look for these formulas to interpret the accounts of other rulers in Kings.)

The narrator opens and closes the account of Menahem with the standard formulas noted in table 4.1 (signified by italics). The narrator uses the standard theological evaluation (good/evil in the eyes of Yahweh) and the northern kingdom comparison to Jeroboam (signified by bold). The narrator added "throughout his reign" or "all of his days" (AT) to the theological evaluation to emphasize a negative judgment against

---

[15] For explanation of Elijah's taunting, see David T. Lamb, *1–2 Kings*, SGBC (Grand Rapids: Zondervan Academic, 2021), 240.

[16] See Carmen Joy Imes, *Bearing God's Name: Why Sinai Still Matters* (Downers Grove, IL: IVP Academic, 2019), 120–21.

[17] The parallels between the two revelations on Mount Horeb anticipate the appearance of Moses and Elijah at the Lord's transfiguration (Matt 17:3; Mark 9:4; Luke 9:30).

[18] See Robert L. Cohn, "The Literary Structure of Kings," in Lemaire and Halpern, *The Books of Kings*, 115 [107–22].

[19] For Assyrian records of Menahem's vassalage, see RINAP 1:46 (14.10), 77 (32.2), 87 (35.iii.5); cf. *ARAB* 1:276.

Table 4.1: Royal Formulas of Frame Narratives of the Kings of Israel and Judah[‡]

Opening frame	• Synchronism with northern/southern counterpart[a] • Age at accession (Judah only) • Length of reign • Name of mother of king (Judah only)
Evaluation	• Editorial on king's fidelity (did what was evil/good in the eyes of Yahweh) • Comparison to David (Judah) or Jeroboam (Israel)
Closing frame	• Summation along with source citation • Sometimes a supplementary notation • King's death and description of burial • Notice of successor

[‡] Table adapted from *OTUOT*, 717 (see sources cited there).

[a] For an example of ancient Assyrian historical accounts synchronized with Babylonian accounts, see *ABC* 21 (pp. 157–70); cf. explanatory overview pp. 51–56.

Menahem (signified by underlining).[20] Notice the details of Menahem's rule in verses 19–20 with a purpose clause, giving the narrator's commentary on the king's self-serving motive for putting Israel under vassalage (signified by underlining). This cost Menaham himself nothing because the nobles paid for it. Pul's throne name is Tiglath-pileser.

In the thirty-ninth year of Judah's King Azariah, Menahem son of Gadi became king over Israel, and *he reigned ten years* in Samaria.

> [18] **He did evil in the eyes of Yahweh.** <u>All of his days,</u> **he did not turn from the sins of Jeroboam son of Nebat caused Israel to commit.** [19] King Pul of Assyria invaded the land, so Menahem gave Pul seventy-five thousand pounds of silver <u>so that Pul would support him to strengthen his grasp on the kingdom.</u> [20] Then Menahem exacted twenty ounces of silver from each of the prominent men of Israel to give to the king of Assyria. So the king of Assyria withdrew and did not stay there in the land.

[21] *The rest of the events of* Menahem's reign, along with all his accomplishments, *are written in the Historical Record of Israel's Kings.* [22] Menahem *rested with his fathers, and his son Pekahiah became king in his place.* (2 Kgs 15:17–22, v. 18 AT)

---

[20] This observation and others here are indebted to Nadav Na'aman, "The Deuteronomist and Voluntary Servitude to Foreign Powers," *JSOT* 65 (1995): 38–40 [37–53].

The narrator made an unusual addition to the account of Menahem outside of the frame narrative to put his immoral character in its worst light. Before the opening frame the narrator added the atrocities committed by Menahem—likely when he served in the military before his kingship.

> At that time, starting from Tirzah, Menahem attacked Tiphsah, all who were in it, and its territory because they wouldn't surrender. *He ripped open all the pregnant women*. (15:16, emphasis added)

Ripping open pregnant women of defeated enemies is a particularly vile act. Though some of Israel's prophets accused foreigners of this act (2 Kgs 8:12; Hos 13:16; Amos 1:13), the Assyrians rarely celebrate this practice (see Ancient Connections 4.2). No Hebrew king besides Menahem committed such an act. The narrator went out of his way to recount this unprecedented evil of Menahem to heap up condemnation upon him for trading Israel's sovereignty for his own gain.

ANCIENT CONNECTIONS 4.2: RIPPING OPEN PREGNANT WOMEN

The ancient Assyrians reveled in depicting torture, maiming, and killing of rebellious enemies (see figure I.8 in introduction). Yet even they have only one known poetic record of ripping open pregnant women by Tiglath-pileser I (1114–1076 BCE). No Assyrian royal inscriptions refer to this practice.[a]

> Even before the sun rose, its earth was aglow (?). He slits the wombs of pregnant women; he blinds infants.[b]

The rareness of this evidence makes the actions of Menahem of Israel all the more reprehensible (2 Kgs 15:16).

[a] The version of this battle in the royal annals merely says, "I butchered their troops like sheep. . . . I burnt, razed, (and) destroyed that city" (*ARI* 2:11).

[b] Cited in Mordechai Cogan, "'Ripping Open Pregnant Women' in Light of Assyrian Analogue," *Journal of the American Oriental Society* 103, no. 4 (1983): 756 [755–57]. For a rare sculptural relief of an Assyrian soldier ripping open a pregnant woman (now in the British Museum), see Peter Dubovský, "Ripping Open Pregnant Arab Women: Reliefs in Room L of Ashurbanipal's North Palace," *Orientalia*, Nova series, 78, no. 3 (2009): 397, 413–15, 418 [394–419].

The next turning point is when Ahaz, king of Judah, turned to Tiglath-pileser III, king of Assyria, for help with military pressures from Damascus and Israel. Notice the son/father covenantal language Ahaz uses to place himself as a vassal under his suzerain Tiglath-pileser III.

> So Ahaz sent messengers to King Tiglath-pileser of Assyria, saying, "*I am your servant and your son.* March up and save me from the grasp of the king of Aram and of the king of Israel, who are rising up against me." (2 Kgs 16:7, emphasis added)

In Ahaz's mind he made a politically expedient maneuver to deliver Jerusalem from its immediate troubles. He may have rationalized that sacrificing temple treasures to pay tribute to Assyria and losing sovereignty as a nation were the tough choices he made to save the day. The narrator of Kings takes the opposite view. Ahaz willingly initiated Judah's servitude to Assyria.[21]

The author adds elements (italics) to Ahaz's evaluation formula (bold) to pile condemnation on him (cf. table 4.1).

He did not do what is right in the eyes of Yahweh like his ancestor David. *He followed the way of the kings of Israel and even sacrificed his son in fire in the fashion of detestable practices of the nations whom Yahweh had driven out before Israel. He offered sacrifices and burned incense at the high places, on the hills, and under every green tree.* (16:2b–4 AT)

The phrase in verse 3—he "even sacrificed his son in fire" (AT)—could be translated as "[He] even made his son to pass through the fire" (cf. KJV). Many interpreters see this as some kind of ritual but not child sacrifice. This lesser interpretation fails to notice how the Chronicler clarifies that Ahaz performed child sacrifice, by adding the verb "he burned" as well as a phrase from Jeremiah about the Valley of Ben Hinnom where Jeremiah accused the people of sacrificing their children (2 Chr 28:3; cf. Jer 7:31; 19:5–6).[22] Only two kings of Judah were accused of child sacrifice in Scripture: Ahaz and Manasseh, the father and son of Hezekiah (cf. 2 Chr 33:6).

In summary of the turning points during the rules of Menaham and Ahaz, the narrator of Kings goes out of his way to heap up guilt on the kings of Israel and Judah who gave up national sovereignty by placing their people in vassalage under Assyria.

---

[21] See Tadmor and Cogan, "Ahaz and Tiglath-Pileser," 505.
[22] See *OTUOT*, 809–10.

The last turning point of Kings comes in the rule of Hezekiah of Judah about two decades after the Assyrians had taken the northern kingdom of Israel in 722 BCE. The Assyrians came up against Judah and Jerusalem in 701. The narrator opens the account of Hezekiah by demonstrating that no king trusted Yahweh more than Hezekiah (2 Kgs 18:5). The unmatched faithfulness of Hezekiah makes the turning point that comes from his pride tragic as well as ironic.

The narrator's use of the verb *trusted* (NIV) in v. 5 in connection with Hezekiah is correct even though its source is ironic. The royal spokesperson for Sennacherib, the Assyrian king, taunted the people of Jerusalem for blindly following Hezekiah, who was trusting Yahweh for no good reason (see Ancient Connections 4.3). Eight times the royal spokesperson accused Hezekiah of trusting his God (18:19, 20, 21 [2x], 22, 24, 30; 19:10).[23] The narrator includes the scornful words of the royal spokesperson because Hezekiah had good reasons to trust in Yahweh.

ANCIENT CONNECTIONS 4.3: AUTHORIZED DELEGATE SPEAKS TO PEOPLE AT THE GATE

The "royal spokesman" (CSB) or "field commander" (NIV) or "Rabshakeh" (KJV) who came to Jerusalem to offer terms of surrender to those listening on the city walls in 2 Kings 18–19 was a high-ranking authorized delegate who spoke on behalf of the Assyrian king. Compare an example from an archival letter during the rule of Tiglath-pileser III (744–722 BCE).

> On the 28th day (of the month), *we went to Babylon, took our stand in front of the Marduk Gate, and spoke to the citizens of Babylon.* (Z)asin(u), a servant of Mukin-zeri, (and?) some(?) Chaldeans(s) (who) were with him, came out (too), standing with the citizens of Babylon in front of the gate. We ourselves spoke to the citizens of Babylon as follows: "The king has sent us to you, saying: '[Let me speak(?)] with the citizens [of Babylon].'" . . . We had a long discussion with them, (but some) ten powerful men did not agree to come out and speak with us, sending messages (instead). ("A Letter from the Reign of Tiglath-pileser III" in *COS* 4.43:219–20, emphasis added)

---

[23] This observation is indebted to Brevard S. Childs, *Isaiah and the Assyrian Crisis* (London: SCM Press, 1967), 85.

A further observation relates to the source of the royal spokesperson's ridicule. The royal spokesperson's taunts share many parallels with the messages of Isaiah (see table 4.2). This suggests the royal spokesperson and his people studied the local culture in order to turn the words of their own prophets against them. Hezekiah had every reason to be afraid, for Sennacherib had already destroyed dozens of Judean cities and fortresses and had exiled thousands (see Ancient Connections 4.4). Hezekiah trusted in God and prayed. In response, Yahweh's delegate of death killed the Assyrian army while they slept (19:35).

Table 4.2: Thematic Parallels in the Royal Spokesperson's Taunts and Isaiah's Messages[‡]

	Royal spokesperson	Isaiah
Worthlessness of Egypt as ally	2 Kgs 18:21//Isa 36:6	30:2
Futility of Judah trusting horses	2 Kgs 18:23–24//Isa 36:8–9	31:3
Assyrian domination over peoples and gods	2 Kgs 18:34–35//Isa 36:19–20	10:9–11
Yahweh shall deliver Jerusalem	2 Kgs 18:30, 32–33, 35//Isa 36:15, 18, 20	29:5–8; 31:4–5, 8–9; cf. 37:35

[‡] Adapted from *OTUOT*, 231 (see citations there).

ANCIENT CONNECTIONS 4.4: SENNACHERIB'S EXILE OF JUDEANS AND SIEGE OF JERUSALEM

The biblical accounts and Sennacherib's accounts of his attacks against Judah and Jerusalem agree on many historical details even while they were written with their own agendas. The earliest of Sennacherib's many records of his exile of Judeans and the siege of Jerusalem in 701 BCE are inscribed on the Rassam Cylinder composed in c. 700.

As for Hezekiah, the Judean, I besieged 46 of his fortified walled cities and surrounding smaller towns, which were without number.[a] Using packed-down ramps and applying battering rams, infantry attacks by mines, breeches, and siege machines (or perhaps: storm ladders), I conquered (them). I took out 200,150 people,[b] young and old, male and female, horses, mules, donkeys, camels, cattle, and sheep, without number, and I counted them as spoil. He himself, I locked up within Jerusalem, his royal city, *like a bird in a cage*. I surrounded him with armed posts, and made it unthinkable (literally, "taboo") for him to exit by the city gate.[c] . . . I imposed dues and gifts for my lordship upon him. . . . He, Hezekiah, was overwhelmed by the awesome splendor of my lordship, and he sent me *after my departure to Nineveh*[d] . . . 30 talents of gold, 800 talents of silver [and many other treasures and many persons].[e] (*RT*, 114–15, emphasis added)

[a] "Assyria's King Sennacherib attacked all the fortified cities of Judah and captured them" (2 Kgs 18:13b).

[b] This exaggeration is likely hyperbole common in royal propaganda since the number is too high for population estimates. It may have been more like 120,000 captives (see *RT*, 120).

[c] The famous phrase "locked up . . . *like a bird in a cage*" reflects Sennacherib's failure to take Jerusalem even while cutting them off from the outside world for a time (see *RT*, 120).

[d] On the chronological significance of this phrase, see the first footnote in this chapter.

[e] A talent was about seventy-five pounds: "So King Hezekiah of Judah sent word to the king of Assyria at Lachish: 'I have done wrong; withdraw from me. Whatever you demand from me, I will pay.' The king of Assyria demanded *eleven tons of silver* [or 300 talents, CSB text note] *and one ton of gold* [or 30 talents, CSB text note] from King Hezekiah of Judah. *So Hezekiah gave him all the silver in the house of Yahweh and in the treasury of the royal palace*." (18:14–15, v. 15 AT, emphasis added).

The narrative of Hezekiah presents the events of his rule in reverse order (see figure 4.5; see introduction for dischronological narration). In narrative sequence after Yahweh delivered Hezekiah and Jerusalem from the Assyrian threat, Hezekiah got sick. But it is a flashback. Isaiah's pronouncement that God would heal Hezekiah includes a future expectation that he would also deliver him from the Assyrian threat (2 Kgs 20:6). The reason for narrating these events dischronologically is to present Hezekiah's pride and its consequences after presenting the mighty deliverance from Assyria. Readers learn that the fate of Jerusalem rests entirely on Yahweh's will before needing to appreciate the gravity of Hezekiah's failure.

Figure 4.5: Narrative versus Chronological Sequence of Hezekiah's Rule‡

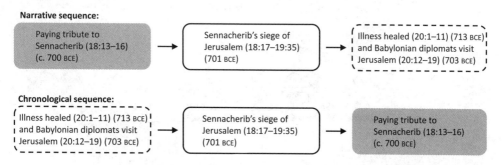

‡ Hezekiah ruled 727–698 BCE. On the date of Hezekiah's tribute see the first footnote of this chapter. The date for his healing from illness is deduced from the date of the tribute. The other dates are widely accepted.

After Hezekiah was healed, he received diplomatic delegates from Merodach-baladan (see figure 4.6). Both based on 2 Kgs 20:6 and historical records of Merodach-baladan's rule, this diplomatic visit could have occurred in c. 711 or more likely 703 BCE, in either case before Sennacherib's attack on Judah.[24] Hezekiah showed his guests from Babylon all of the treasures of Jerusalem.

The author of Kings uses omniscient narration to show readers Hezekiah's inner thoughts when Isaiah confronted him. Isaiah told Hezekiah that the treasures of Jerusalem and Hezekiah's royal descendants would be taken by force to Babylon. Notice what Hezekiah said and what Hezekiah thought.

> Hezekiah said to Isaiah, "*The word of Yahweh that you have spoken is good.*" He said [in his heart], "Isn't it so, *if there'll be well-being and truthfulness in my days?*" (20:19 FT, emphasis added)[25]

The word of Isaiah to Hezekiah that exile was assured for Judah is a major turning point in Kings. Though the fall of Jerusalem did not occur for more than a century, the word of Yahweh through his prophet Isaiah guaranteed the doom of Jerusalem. But the importance of Hezekiah should not be missed.

The narrator arranges Hezekiah's story so readers first learn of his unmatched trust in God (see figure 4.5). The narrator shows that Yahweh is worthy of that

---

[24] See A. L. Oppenheim, "Merodach-baladan," *IDB* 3:355; cf. RINAP 3.1:32–34 (1.5–7, 16, 25–26).

[25] On internal dialogue, see *OTUOT*, xxxii, n. 37.

Figure 4.6: Suzerain-Vassal Treaty between an
Assyrian Ruler and Merodach-baladan‡

Sketch by Gary Edward Schnittjer

‡ This sculptural relief housed in the Royal Museum at Berlin depicts an Assyrian ruler (Sargon or Sennacherib, left) making a suzerain-vassal treaty with Merodach-baladan (right), who ruled as king of Babylon 722–710 and 703 BCE. Merodach-baladan may have been shorter than the Asyrian king, or the artisans may have depicted him as shorter to show his inferiority. Merodach-baladan was a nuisance to the Assyrian rulers. He fled from Sargon in 710 until he again assumed the throne in Babylon for less than a year. In 703 he sent diplomatic delegates to Hezekiah to stir up unrest against Sennacherib. When Sennacherib marched on Babylon in 703, Merodach-baladan fled into the marshes in disgrace. See RINAP 3.1:42 (2.5–6) (written 702 BCE); cf. 3.2:296 (213.34).

trust by delivering Hezekiah and Jerusalem from a previously undefeated opponent (18:33–35).

No one had more faith than Hezekiah (18:5). But even a king with more faith in God than any other king had too much pride (20:13).

The turning point toward exile is born of the prideful acts of the most faithful of kings. In this way the author demonstrates the inevitability of the exile. It could not be stopped by Josiah's unmatched devotion to Yahweh any more than Hezekiah's unmatched faith (23:27). It had to happen.

Biblical Connections

Later authors of the Old Testament connect Kings to the Prophets and postexilic restoration narratives. The Hezekiah stories of 2 Kings 18–20 are spliced into Isaiah with only a few important edits (Isaiah 36–39). The sacking of Jerusalem in 2 Kings 25 is spliced onto the end of Jeremiah chapter 52.[26] These synoptic (to see together) parallels strengthen the importance of reading Kings with the Prophets and vice versa. Kings in narrative and Isaiah and Jeremiah in prophetic oracles explain why Judah had to be taken into exile.

The opening sections of the return and restoration narrative housed in Ezra-Nehemiah interpret the identity of the assembly of Yahweh in relation to the exile (cf. Ezra 4:1; 6:21). But after several generations grew up within their ancestors' homeland the exile was no longer adequate to explain their identity. About ninety-two years after the original return from exile, the Levitical intercessors prayed before the restoration assembly (returned exiles and their descendants) and made a solemn oath to serve God. The prayer folds the exile into the larger reality of vassalage to the empire that began in the days of Tiglath-pileser III—narrated in Kings and extended to their own day. They said, "So now, our God—the great, mighty, and awe-inspiring God who keeps his gracious covenant—do not view lightly all the hardships that have afflicted us, our kings and leaders, our priests and prophets, our ancestors and all your people, *from the days of the Assyrian kings until today*" (Neh 9:32, emphasis added). The restoration assembly failed to keep their solemn oath (10:30–39). When Nehemiah returned to Jerusalem twelve years later he learned that the leaders and the people had broken every part of their promise (13:4–31). They were exactly like their ancestors. In frustration Nehemiah came upon men of Judah who had rebelled by marrying those who would not accept the covenant. The problem was not the ethnicity of their spouses—that was never the problem—but rather not raising their children according to the covenant (v. 24; cf. Deut 6:7; 7:4). He beat them and tore the beards from the faces of the hapless rebels and then connected their failures to those of King Solomon. The Hebrew syntax shows that Nehemiah used a shrill tone when he said:[27]

---

[26] On the dependence of Isaiah 36–39 on 2 Kings 18–20 and Jeremiah 52 on 2 Kings 25, see *OTUOT*, 232–34, 299.

[27] See *OTUOT*, 691, n. 114.

Didn't King Solomon of Israel sin in matters like this? There was not a king like him among many nations. He was loved by his God, and God made him king over all Israel, yet foreign women drew him into sin. Why then should we hear about you doing all this terrible evil and acting unfaithfully against our God by marrying foreign women? (Neh 13:26–27, emphasis added)

Nehemiah's wrath did not help matters. But it underlines the failure of the restoration. Long gone were the days of collective repentance and attempts of renewal (see Ezra 9–10; Nehemiah 8–10). Nehemiah alone vented his anger in a futile attempt to stop a backslidden people.

In sum, the rebellion of the Hebrew kings remains an important measurement for the ongoing troubles and failures of God's people.

Gospel Connections

When Jesus read from the Isaiah scroll in the synagogue of Nazareth, he claimed that his own reading was fulfilled in their own hearing. The congregation made initial praise or sarcastic remarks about this son of Joseph (Luke 4:16–22). But then the Messiah pushed them past their snarky comments by how he interpreted the stories of Elijah and Elisha from Kings. As noted earlier, the northern prophet stories frequently include acts of God's mercy for the mundane concerns of the disadvantaged and foreigners.

Jesus asked the annoyed congregation why Elijah was sent to help a Gentile widow or why Elisha would help a Gentile official with a skin disease (4:25–27; cf. 1 Kgs 17:8–16; 2 Kgs 5:1–19). This enraged the congregation to the point of trying to kill Jesus on the spot.

God's concern to reach all people is not new to the New Testament. The grace of God for outsiders in the days of the kings of Israel was the same grace preached by the Messiah.

Life Connections

Apostasy marriage refers to persons in the community of faith who married those who will not turn to the one true God but continue to worship other gods. In spite of laws against apostasy marriage in Torah and in warnings by Joshua, the people of ancient Israel often wanted to help their children by arranging advantageous marital matches to those who did not commit to Yahweh's covenant (Exod 34:15–16; Deut 7:3–4; Josh 23:12–13).

David was no exception. Solomon said David was not able to build the temple because of his constant warfare (1 Kgs 5:3). Solomon began his practice of apostasy marriages during David's lifetime. Notice how Solomon's son Rehoboam, born to Naamah the Ammonite, was forty-one years of age when he began to rule after Solomon's forty-year rule (11:41–43; 14:21). This means Solomon married Naamah the Ammonite at least one year and nine months before David died.[28] In an environment of arranged marriages, this was most likely David's doing or at least with his blessing.

It makes sense. If David could not build the temple because of warfare, then Solomon could keep the peace by entering into hundreds of treaty marriages, beginning with an Ammonite. Unfortunately, treaty marriages to keep the peace required building worship centers to many gods and goddesses, including one to Milcom the detestable god of the Ammonites (11:5).

The marriage covenant is as important as any decision a person makes in this life. The temptation to apostasy marriages remains as high as it was in ancient Israel. There is no shortage of "good reasons" to do the wrong thing in our own day. As noted in the section on Biblical Connections, Nehemiah was shocked that the restoration assembly had not learned anything from Solomon's disastrous apostasy marriages. Incredibly, many Christians today fail to learn from Solomon's downfall.

Interactive Questions

Why did the permanent promise to David make it essential for the author of Kings to explain the inevitability of the exile?

According to Kings, why did the northern kingdom of Israel go into exile?

According to Kings, why did the southern kingdom of Judah go into exile?

How can praising Solomon also function as an indictment against him in 1 Kgs 10:26–29?

---

[28] The two coronations of Solomon suggests that he and David may have had a short coregency (1 Chr 29:22). In this case, he married Naamah the Ammonitess at least two years before David's death. For the observation on Solomon's second coronation, see Brian Peterson, "Did the Vassal Treaties of Esarhaddon Influence the Chronicler's Succession Narrative of Solomon?" *BBR* 28, no. 4 (2018): 557, 560–61 [554–74]. For the observation on Solomon's treaty marriage to Naamah during David's lifetime, see *OTUOT*, 202; Abraham Malamat, "Naamah, the Ammonite Princess, King Solomon's Wife," *Revue Biblique* (1999): 36 [35–40].

Why do some people misinterpret the laws against intermarriage as based on ethnicity or race? What evidence from Kings demonstrates that these laws speak against apostasy marriages?

What is the importance of the blended allusion to Torah in 1 Kgs 11:2?

When did Solomon begin to build high places (worship centers) for his treaty wives?

What are some of the ironies of Elijah's prophetic work against Ahab and Jezebel?

How did the narrator heap up condemnation on Menahem?

What evidence suggests that "pass through . . . fire" (KJV) in 2 Kgs 16:3 refers to child sacrifice?

What are some examples of Sennacherib's royal spokesperson's allusions to the prophecies of Isaiah? What is their significance?

Why did the author of Kings emphasize the faith of Hezekiah before focusing on his pride?

Why did the restoration assembly's identity shift from being based on exile to being based on vassalage to the empire?

Study Resources

Israel, Alex. *I Kings: Torn in Two*. Jerusalem: Maggid Books, 2013.
———. *II Kings: In a Whirlwind*. Jerusalem: Maggid Books, 2019.
Lamb, David T. *1–2 Kings*. SGBC. Grand Rapids: Zondervan Academic, 2021.
Wray Beal, Lissa M. *1 & 2 Kings*. AOTC. Downers Grove, IL: InterVarsity, 2014.

PART 2

Narratives of Exile and Restoration

5

Ruth

Outline

Prologue: Leaving Bethlehem (1:1–5)
A widow returns home with her widowed daughter-in-law (1:6–22)
Gleaning in the fields of Boaz in the daytime (2:1–23)
Courting Boaz in the nighttime (3:1–18)
Acquiring Ruth at the city gate (4:1–17)
Epilogue: The family line of David (4:18–22)

Author, Date, and Message

The narrator of Ruth is female. Pronouns in biblical Hebrew align with either masculine or feminine grammatical gender. The narrator uses the grammatically feminine "they" of the women of Bethlehem and refers to the women as the "whole town" (1:19). No ancient male would refer to the women as the whole town. For this reason the present study regards the author of Ruth as a woman.[1] The author of Ruth is

---

[1] Though not the norm, female scribes are known throughout the ancient Near East. See, e.g., Brigitte Lion, "Literacy and Gender," in *The Oxford Handbook of Cuneiform Culture*, ed. Karen Radner and Eleanor Robson (New York: Oxford University Press, 2011), 96–104.

among the most gifted storytellers in Scripture. She is especially well versed in theology and biblical legal instruction. Since we do not know the author's identity, it will help to consider when she wrote.

The storyline of Ruth is set about a century before David in the days of his great-grandparents. Though twenty years is often used to count each generation, David as the youngest son of at least seven sons adds a few years. The late eleventh and early tenth centuries BCE are better known as the days of the judges. Since the story ends by mentioning David, it dates at least a century after the events took place. Though a few interpreters think the book may have been written in the days of David or Solomon, they have not presented evidence to support this proposal. The evidence suggests it was written at a much later time. Three kinds of evidence suggesting an exilic or postexilic date can be mentioned here.

First, and most importantly, near the end of the story the author talks directly to readers and says that these events occurred long ago. She realizes her readers will not understand the odd custom with the sandal and so explains, "*At an earlier period* in Israel, a man removed his sandal and gave it to the other party to make any matter legally binding concerning the right of redemption or the exchange of property. This was the method of legally binding a transaction in Israel" (4:7, emphasis added). The need to explain this custom provides strong evidence that it was set in ancient times from the author's perspective. Advocating for an early date requires reading against the sense of the text.

Second, the Ruth story includes linguistic evidence of a later period, such as "Aramaisms" and the syntax of Late Biblical Hebrew.[2] The captivity of Judah triggered massive changes including a shift from Hebrew to Aramaic as the spoken language. Even the educated class of Hebrew authors, like the author of Ruth, tend to have an Aramaic flavoring on occasion.

Third, a leading concern of Ruth is identical to that of the restoration assembly (those who returned from exile)—namely, the identity of Israel with respect to assimilations of outsiders. When the Judean captives returned to their homeland during a period of protracted economic depression, the people faced great ongoing temptation

---

[2] For Aramaisms, see Edward Allen Jones III, *Reading Ruth in the Restoration Period: A Call for Inclusion*, LHBOTS 604 (New York: T&T Clark, 2016), 124–26 (e.g., cf. Ruth 1:13 "*gn*," "*sbr*," *HALOT* 1:785; 2:1304–5; 2:16 "*tsevet*," *HALOT* 1:1000). Late Biblical Hebrew (LBH) expressions appear, for example, in 1:4 ("*ns*'," *CLLBH* 185–86). LBH syntax includes cases of a finite verb with an attached article: "the one who returned" (*hashavah*; Ruth 1:22; 2:6; 4:3). See GKC §138i, k; *IBHS* §19.7c; Joüon §145d (against conjectural emendations from perfect to participle without evidence in *IBHS* §19.7d; Joüon §145e). For a discussion of other features of LBH in Ruth, see Robert B. Chisholm Jr., *A Commentary of Judges and Ruth*, KEL (Grand Rapids: Kregel Academic, 2013), 577–80.

to intermarry with foreigners. Ancient people wanted to help their children with crushing economic and social difficulties. The hardships became so bad that many people had to sell their children into slavery to avoid starvation (Neh 5:1–5). In the face of these challenges many Judeans who worshiped Yahweh helped their children by arranging for them to "marry up" by "marrying out."[3] Marriages to spouses who refused to submit to Yahweh's covenant with his people represent apostasy. Nehemiah brutally confronted those males of Jerusalem who had gotten into apostasy marriages with women of Ammon, Moab, and Ashdod. Nehemiah could see that these young families were turning away because their children spoke the languages of the spouses but not the language of Judah (13:23–27). In spite of several spectacular mass divorces from apostasy marriages to try to get right with God, the returned exiles continued to turn away from God by intermarriages with outsiders (Ezra 10; Neh 9:2; 13:1–3; Mal 2:11).

In sum, several lines of evidence suggest that the Ruth story dates from the postexilic period when many people from the former kingdom of Judah returned to their ancestral homeland. These impoverished Judeans faced great economic hardship and persistent temptation to marry out. These readers badly needed a story of another kind of marriage wherein a righteous outsider "married in." During ancient days of economic hardship and civil unrest, one of David's own matriarchs provides a counterpoint. The Ruth story offers meaningful hope for the people of God facing hard times. This leads us to the point of Ruth.

The message of Ruth pivots on the mercy of Yahweh to outsiders who cling to him. Outsiders who turn to Yahweh and his covenantal people have an enduring hope. Even the most excluded others, such as the Moabites, can find refuge in the faithfulness of Yahweh's covenant.

Interpretive Overview

Ruth tells the story of an outsider who finds refuge in Yahweh. In the days of the judges everyone did what was right in their own eyes. Almost everyone. This is a story of an unlikely marriage of an excellent woman from Moab to an excellent man of Bethlehem. The surprise ending is that they became the great-grandparents of Israel's most celebrated king.

A modern person who comes across the book of Ruth could regard it along the lines of a script for a sentimental holiday special. Perhaps ancients would look at it the same way. After a widow loses everything, she returns to her homeland with her

---

[3] For these terms, see Daniel L. Smith-Christopher, *A Biblical Theology of Exile*, Overtures to Biblical Theology (Minneapolis: Fortress Press, 2002), 158–61.

daughter-in-law, at once available and unavailable. But the narrative's surprise ending changes everything.

The surprise comes in the very last word of the story, "David." What had seemed like a quaint romantic story of an older gentleman falling in love with a young Moabite suddenly becomes a big deal because of their great-grandson David. The law of the assembly in Deut 23:3–6 forbids Moabites from ever assimilating into the assembly of Israel. This does not merely create a personal problem for David and his family. If David is excluded from Israel, it creates a problem for anyone who relies on the promises of Yahweh found in the Davidic covenant. To be blunt: if David is excluded from Israel because of a forbidden Moabite matriarch, it would nullify the messianic hopes grounded in the Davidic covenant. The central importance of a Davidic messiah for the gospel requires close attention to the Ruth story.

The literary symmetry of Ruth includes everything. Every word of this remarkable short narrative bears witness to a gifted storyteller. For example, some of the book's key terms appear seven or fourteen times, a numerical literary symbol of completeness in Scripture based on the creation week of Genesis 1. "Moab" and "Moabite" each appear seven times. The word *name* appears fourteen times including the explicit comments of Ruth's mother-in-law.[4] She said her given name Naomi, meaning "pleasant" or the like, should be Mara, meaning "bitter" (Ruth 1:20). All of this helps readers pay attention to the names of people and places in the story.

The ironic setup of the story is what happens to a man named Elimelech ("My-God-is-king") when he leaves Bethlehem ("House-of-bread") to find food. His family moves to Moab (figure 5.1). Elimelech dies. His sons each marry Moabite women. The sons both die, which makes sense with their names being Mahlon ("sick") and Chilion ("frail") (1:2 NET note). Ten years go by in five verses, and the widow Naomi decides to return home with her two widowed daughters-in-law. But along the way she changes her mind.

Naomi shows her heart when she tries to get her daughters-in-law to go back to their people and to their gods (v. 15). At the point when her mother-in-law says to go back to her own people and her own gods, Ruth proclaims one of the most poignant statements of faith in Scripture. She says, "Do not urge me to leave you or turn back from you. For where you go, I go. Wherever you live, I live. *Your people, my people. Your God, my God.* Wherever you die, I die, and there I shall be buried. Thus may Yahweh do to me and more if even death separates me and you" (vv. 16–17 AT, emphasis added).

---

[4] See Ruth 1:2 [3x], 4 [2x]; 2:1, 19; 4:5, 10 [2x], 11, 14, 17 [2x] ("*shem*," Even-Shoshan, 1161–64 [nos. 25–26, 153–57, 241–44, 606, 694, 728]). Also see "*mo'av*," 629 (nos. 5–10, 15).

Figure 5.1: Moab

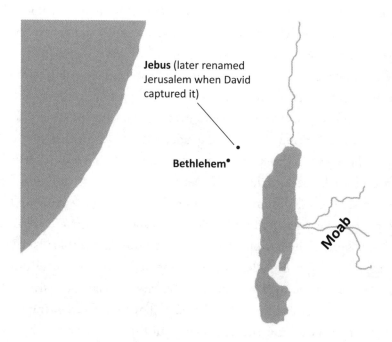

Two remarkable elements can be observed about Ruth's oath in reverse order. First, Ruth claims that even in death she shall be with Naomi. Her commitment extends beyond this life. If we think of the sayings in Genesis that in death the Hebrews are gathered to their people, then Ruth determines to join Naomi's people in this life and beyond (Gen 25:8; 35:29; 49:33). Second, Ruth not only "clung" to Naomi with her hands, she places herself under Yahweh's protection with her words (Ruth 1:14, 16–17). At a later time a man of Bethlehem interprets Ruth's oath as placing herself under Yahweh's protection (2:12). The journey of the two widows from the heights of Moab down through the Jordan Valley and up to Bethlehem in the Judean hills is impressive (figure 5.2). More impressive is Ruth's commitment to Yahweh and his people. Ruth places herself under Yahweh's covenant.

Figure 5.2: Elevation of Moab and Bethlehem

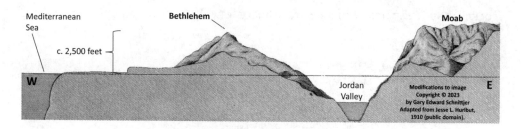

Ruth 2 tells of Ruth gleaning in the fields of Bethlehem. Gleaning is an ancient practice in which the needy gather up what the harvesters leave behind. Ruth just happens to glean in the fields belonging to a relative of her mother-in-law. The narrator says Boaz ("Strong") was an "excellent man" (2:1 AT), and later Boaz says that everyone in Bethlehem knows that Ruth was an "excellent woman" (3:11 AT).

The first meeting of the two provides Boaz an opportunity to interpret two scriptural laws that press against one another. There are two kinds of "others" in Scripture: excluded others and included others. Excluded others are enemies of God's people and those who reject Yahweh's covenant. Included others seek to serve Yahweh.[5] Included others who seek asylum in Israel are referred to as "residing foreigners," while excluded others are often referred to as "foreigners" or "enemies." The law of gleaning provides help for residing foreigners, widows, and orphans (Deut 24:19; cf. Lev 19:9–10; 23:22). The law of the assembly in Deut 23:6 forbids Israel from ever seeking the well-being of excluded others represented by the ancient Ammonites and Moabites: "Never pursue their welfare or prosperity as long as you live." The grammatical structure is identical to the Ten Commandments and can be translated: "*Thou shalt not* seek their peace nor their prosperity all thy days for ever" (KJV, emphasis added). The law of the assembly bases the exclusion on the ancient actions of the Moabites, who refused to provide for Israel in the wilderness and hired a wicked prophet to condemn Israel by Israel's own God (Deut 23:4). Boaz needs to decide if he could extend gleaning rights to Ruth. Should Ruth be denied gleaning rights based on her status as a Moabite or granted gleaning rights open to residing foreigners? Boaz's work supervisor overemphasizes that she is a Moabite from Moab (Ruth 2:6). Ruth refers to herself as a "foreigner" unlike the other female gleaners (vv. 10, 13). However, Boaz decides she should be granted gleaning rights like any of the protected classes based on Ruth's tending to Naomi and her commitment to Yahweh (vv. 11–12).[6] Though Ruth came from Moab, she does not follow the treacheries of her ancestors against Israel. Boaz treats her as an included other of Yahweh's covenant (for more see Biblical Connections, page 154).

Ruth 3 transitions to nighttime during harvest. At Naomi's bidding Ruth goes to Boaz on the threshing floor. When he wakes up in the night to find Ruth at his feet she proposes marriage in an extraordinary way. When Ruth tells Boaz to "spread

---

[5] See *OTUOT*, 240, 341 (tables I4 and Ezk6).

[6] See *OTUOT*, 581–84; Nicoletta Gatti, "From Alien to Neighbor: The Journey of Ruth," *BBR* 32, no. 1 (2022): 12–13.

your wing over me" (3:9 AT) it has at least three senses. First, she is simply asking him to cover her with the corner of his robes. Men like Boaz wore robes, the sides of which could be called "wings" since that is what they looked like if lifted. Second, to uncover or cover a person's "wing"/"robe" could be used euphemistically to refer to marital relations (Deut 22:30; Ezek 16:8). Thus, for Ruth to say "cover me with your wing" was a proposal of marriage by means of a figure of speech. Third, earlier Boaz had prayed that Yahweh would care for Ruth since she had put herself under Yahweh's wings (Ruth 2:12). Ruth repeats the same language to Boaz, inviting him to be Yahweh's instrument to care for her. Notice the shift from the covenantal imagery of adoption in v. 12, as though Yahweh is a mother bird protecting Ruth, to the covenantal imagery of marriage in 3:9.

> [Boaz said:] "May Yahweh repay your work and may it be to your full reward from Yahweh the God of Israel whom you have come to seek refuge **under his wings**" (2:12 AT, emphasis added).

> He asked, "Who are you?" She said, "I am Ruth your servant. Would you **spread out your wing** upon your servant for you are a financially responsible next of kin?" (3:9 AT, emphasis added).[7]

Ruth uses language in her proposal of marriage that connects back to Boaz's prayer, which, in turn, connects back to her covenantal commitment (see table 5.1).

Table 5.1: Covenantal Connections in Ruth[‡]

"Your God, my God" (1:16)	Under Yahweh's wings (2:12)	Under Boaz's wing (3:9)
Commitment to God's people	Adoptive parental protection	Marital relationship
Ruth to Yahweh	Yahweh to Ruth	Ruth to Boaz and Boaz to Ruth

[‡] Table adapted from Schnittjer, *Torah Story*, 2nd ed., 437 (see intro., n. 10).

---

[7] Unfortunately, many laypersons and a few scholars use the expression "kinsman redeemer" to extrapolate wild typological and allegorical interpretations. For example, see Mitchell L. Chase, *40 Questions about Typology and Allegory* (Grand Rapids: Kregel Academic, 2020), 157; cf. 262. Since the expression "kinsman redeemer" means "financially responsible near relative" (see, e.g., Lev 25:25), this study will use that kind of language.

Boaz responds to Ruth by explaining that he needs to speak to an even nearer financially responsible relative of Naomi's family before he could accept Ruth's marriage proposal. This sets up the climax of the story at the city gate.

Ruth 4 tells of Boaz's ingenuity with legal interpretation to acquire Ruth. In a classroom each law in the Torah can be discussed one a time. Messy life situations attract overlapping laws to handle competing challenges. The situation facing Boaz includes at least three legal issues that overlapped like circles in a Venn diagram, plus a twist. These legal standards need to be observed to make sense of what Boaz accomplishes in the dramatic confrontation at the city gate.

First, the laws associated with Jubilee provide relief for landowning families who fall into poverty. The preferred method of help comes in the form of a financially responsible near relative repurchasing the property. The relative holds the property until the original landowner could afford to buy it back or until the Jubilee—once every fifty years—automatically restored the property to the original family, whichever came first (Lev 25:25–29). This may be called the "law of redemption" for short. The basis of this law is that Yahweh is the true landowner: "The land must not be sold permanently, *because the land is mine* and you reside in my land as foreigners and strangers. Throughout the land that you hold as a possession, you must provide for the redemption of the land" (vv. 23–24 NIV, emphasis added).

Second, the law of female inheritance stipulates that in the event there were no male heirs the land went to the daughters (Num 27:7). However, when there are no daughters the land passed to the nearest relative (vv. 8–11). In the case of Elimelech, the land would have gone to Naomi, then to the next legal heir, her son now represented by his widow. A clue for understanding Ruth is knowing that the female heir retained the property in order to prevent the loss of "the name" of the landowner (v. 4). The many uses of the word *name* in Ruth help make the connection.

Third, the law of levirate marriage is also directed to inheritance and keeping "the name" of a married person who dies without children (Ancient Connections 5.1). In this case, the brother of the deceased is encouraged, but not required, to marry his brother's widow, in addition to his own wife, and raise children with her to preserve his brother's estate and his name (Deut 25:5–7). If the brother refused, he participates instead in a shame ceremony involving his sandal at the city gate (vv. 8–10).

Fourth, the twist is a key connection in the way the law of female inheritance connects to Jubilee. The tribe of Manasseh complained to Moses that if a female

ANCIENT CONNECTIONS 5.1: LEVIRATE MARRIAGE

Hittite Laws (c. 1500 BCE) say:

> If a man has a wife, and the man dies, his brother shall take his widow as wife. (If the brother dies,) his father shall take her. When afterwards his father dies, his (i.e., the father's) brother shall take the woman whom he had (§193 in Roth, 236).

Middle Assyrian Law (c. 1200 BCE) says:

> If a man either pours oil on her head or brings (dishes for) the banquet, (after which) the son to whom he assigned the wife either dies or flees, he shall give her in marriage to whichever of his remaining sons he wishes, from the oldest to the youngest of at least ten years of age (§43 in Roth, 169).

inherited the land and married outside her tribe, it would diminish the land Yahweh had granted to the tribe and place it into the ownership of the tribe of the female heir's husband. Yahweh agreed and made a legal amendment that females could only inherit if they married within the tribe of their father (Num 36:1–12). This causes the law of female inheritance to connect to the law of redemption (v. 4). The female heir must marry before a financially responsible near relative could temporarily purchase the land according to Jubilee regulations.[8]

In sum, real-life circumstances can be messy, relating to several overlapping laws at the same time. The laws of female inheritance and levirate marriage both focus on retaining the name of the deceased. The law of redemption of land for the impoverished landowner hinge on the marriage of the female heiress. Boaz could not deal with these laws individually but needed to work out the difficult set of entanglements of a real-life situation where these laws pressed on Ruth's situation in several ways. All of these things are on Boaz's mind as he headed to the city gate (Ancient Connections 5.2; figure 5.3).

---

[8] Brad Embry, "Legalities in the Book of Ruth: A Renewed Look," *JSOT* 41, no. 1 (2016): 41.

ANCIENT CONNECTIONS 5.2: CITY GATE

In ancient Canaan, like Israel, the city gate was a place where people settled legal and civil matters. A traditional Canaanite story from c. 1400 BCE (about three centuries before the time of Boaz) mentions the city gate.

> Danel . . . "got up and sat at the entrance to the gate, among the leaders on the threshing floor. He judged the cases of the widows, presided over orphans' hearings" (Aqhat 1 v 6–8 in *SFAC*, 39).

Figure 5.3: City Gate at Tel Dan (Eighteenth Century BCE)

Sketch by Gary Edward Schnittjer

At the city gate Boaz legally confront the financially responsible near relative in front of witnesses. At first the financially responsible near relative says he will buy Naomi's land. But then Boaz says something else in Ruth 4:5, and the financially responsible next of kin backs out of the purchase and Boaz acquires Ruth. Because v. 5 is so important, it requires a close look.

The language of Ruth 4:5 is very tricky in Hebrew. The entire Ruth narrative seems to be written in an old-fashioned way like a period piece. The narrator uses the old term "fields of Moab" and many other touches to help readers think back to the days of the judges. She even seems to present the two older citizens of Bethlehem, Naomi and Boaz, as using an old dialect or speaking with an accent. When we see a quaint sign that says "Ye Olde Shoppe" we probably realize that the extra *e*'s are silent and merely add a sense of antiquity. Because Boaz speaks with an old accent (which we can infer based on the way it is spelled in Hebrew), it is not clear if Boaz says, "I acquire Ruth" or "You acquire Ruth."[9] Thus, after comparing both possibilities in modern translations, we can think through potential reasons why the financially responsible near relative backs out.

> Boaz continued: "On the day you take over the field from Naomi, *I take over the widow, Ruth the Moabite,* so as to perpetuate the name of the dead man on his holding." (Ruth 4:5 REB, emphasis added)

> Then Boaz said, "On the day you buy the land from Naomi, *you also acquire Ruth the Moabite, the dead man's widow,* in order to maintain the name of the dead with his property." (v. 5 NIV, emphasis added)

These two different ways of understanding what Boaz said (based on the difficulty of him speaking with an old accent) can lead to at least three ways of thinking through why the unnamed near relative backed out. First, if Boaz tells him that Boaz himself is marrying Ruth, then the near relative may realize that if Boaz and Ruth had children, he would need to give the land back to the family. Second, if the near relative hears Boaz say, "When you buy the land you must marry Ruth *the widow,*" he may realize he cannot afford to take two needy widows into his household. Third, if the unnamed financially responsible near relative hears Boaz say, "When you buy the land you must marry Ruth *the Moabite,*" he may refuse because the law of the assembly prohibited good treatment to Moabites (Deut 23:6). All three of these possibilities work. Since we do not have enough evidence to know what the unnamed financially responsible near relative was thinking, it is enough to realize that any of these three scenarios shines a light on Boaz's legal prowess.

Once Boaz acquires the legal right to marry Ruth, they have a son within a few verses. The women of Bethlehem celebrate with Naomi and said, "May his name be declared in Israel" (Ruth 4:14 AT). This statement by the women in a story that uses the word *name* fourteen times, including many wordplays on the names, highlights the one person with no name. Instead of including his name, the narrator paraphrases Boaz as calling him "So-and-so" (4:1, note in CSB; cf. NET; NJPS). The narrator blots out his name. We can call him "So-and-so," like Boaz did, or "the unnamed financially responsible near relative." But whoever he is, when he decides not to buy Naomi's field in a time of financial difficulty, his name is not remembered.

---

[9] See *OTUOT,* 587–88.

The very last verse of the story proper covers five generations, from Naomi to her grandson Obed, great-grandson Jesse, and great-great-grandson David. Only then does the narrator include the genealogy of Judah's ancestors that runs down ten generations to David, with Boaz in the middle. Normally genealogies go at the front of stories (e.g., Gen 11:10–26; Ezra 7:1–5). The author of Ruth waits until the end of the story so she could keep the ending a surprise. Ruth committed herself to Naomi's people and their God. By placing herself under Yahweh's covenant, Ruth comes to be the great-grandmother of the royal messiah, King David.

Biblical Connections

The book of Ruth connects with the days of the judges, the wisdom of Proverbs, and the law of the assembly.

The first verse in Ruth situates the story line in the days of the judges. This helps explain why Ruth follows Judges in the Old Testament. Judges ends with two stories of moral degeneration in Israel. One tells of "a man," while the other tells of "a Levite" (Judg 17:1; 19:1). One episode concerns a Levite from Bethlehem and the other a concubine from Bethlehem (17:7; 19:1). Ruth likewise begins with "a man" of Bethlehem (Ruth 1:1). These narrative vignettes at the end of Judges go to great lengths to display the depths of Israel's wickedness. The narrator uses two taglines to characterize these immoral days: "In those days there was no king in Israel" repeated four times (Judg 17:6; 18:1; 21:25; see also 19:1) and "everyone did whatever seemed right in their own eyes" repeated twice (17:6; 21:25 AT). All these connections show Ruth as a counterpoint. During the days of the judges, when immorality ran rampant, two exceptions stand out: Ruth and Boaz.

The Scriptures only use the expression "excellent woman" three times (AT): in Prov 12:4; 31:10; and Ruth 3:11.[10] The use in Prov 31:10 stands at the opening of an acrostic poem of the excellent woman, with each line starting with the next letter of the Hebrew alphabet. This woman has it all—she is excellent from A to Z. Most interpreters consider the excellent woman an ideal, not a real, woman. This makes the question rhetorical: "An excellent woman who can find?" (Prov 31:10 AT). But in the traditional arrangement of the Hebrew Bible, the book of Ruth immediately follows Proverbs (see table I.1 in the introduction). This answers the question.

An excellent woman who can find? Boaz, of course. The most important connection stems from the excellent woman being praised in the city gates (Prov 31:31).

---

[10] See "*ḥayil*," Even-Shoshan, 365 (nos. 34, 35, 38; cf. second set of collocations).

That is exactly what Boaz says to Ruth: "All of my people in the gate know that you are an excellent woman" (Ruth 3:11 AT). Boaz is the excellent man of Bethlehem, and he finds the excellent woman from Moab.

The law of the assembly forbids Moabites from ever entering the assembly of Yahweh (Deut 23:3–6). If this law were interpreted literally—that is, racially or ethnically—it would exclude Ruth's family from being a part of Israel, including her great-grandson David. This would erase the Davidic covenant and its hopes for a son of God to rule forever. Though the Scriptures use the law of the assembly many times, it is never interpreted racially. Instead, the Scriptures show that it is not about ethnic Moabites and Ammonites, but people who act treacherously, like the ancient Moabites when they refused to provide food for Israel and hired Balaam to damn them (vv. 4–5). The law of the assembly is applied to the Babylonians who destroyed the temple of Yahweh (Lam 1:10; Isa 52:1). The law is applied to any foreigner who rejected God's covenant (Neh 13:1–3). Paul said that not all Israel is Israel (Rom 9:6). In like manner, not all Moabites are Moabites.[11] Not only did Ruth act with hospitality providing grain for Naomi, she placed herself under Yahweh's covenant (Ruth 1:16–17; 2:18). Ruth was born in Moab, but she assimilated into Yahweh's people by embracing his covenant. In this way Ruth became a matriarch of David.

Gospel Connections

The New Testament opens with a genealogy of the Messiah (Matt 1:1–17). A remarkable feature of the list of the Messiah's ancestors are the several women therein—Tamar the Canaanite, Rahab the Canaanite prostitute, Ruth the Moabite, and Bathsheba the wife of Uriah the Hittite (1:3, 5–6). Messiah came for the kind of people in his own ancestry. Messiah brings salvation to outsiders. Ruth started her life among the excluded people of Moab. Her faith and devotion to Yahweh placed her in the family of the Messiah.

Life Connections

Ruth's extraordinary confession of commitment to Naomi's God and her people frequently is read at weddings. This makes sense because the prophets often use marriage as an analogy to speak of the covenantal relationship between Yahweh and his people.[12] Ruth proclaimed:

---

[11] See Schnittjer, *Torah Story*, 2nd ed., 437 (see intro., n. 10).
[12] Cf., e.g., Isa 62:5; Jer 2:2; Hos 2:19-20.

Where you go I go, and where you sleep I sleep.
Your people my people, and your God my God.
Where you die I die, and there I shall be buried.
Thus may Yahweh do to me and more if death separates you and me.
    (Ruth 1:16–17, AT)

It is worth asking ourselves how this kind of commitment relates to marriages. But we also need to consider if this confession fits with our own devotion to the Lord and his kingdom. It might be one thing to dare to say it. But what would it look like to live up to it? Will we reach out to the needy as Ruth did for Naomi and as Boaz did for Ruth?

Interactive Questions

What evidence suggests that Ruth was written during the exilic or postexilic period?

In light of the law of the assembly in Deut 23:3–6, what evidence in Ruth shows that a Moabite could rightfully assimilate into Israel?

What were the legal complications Boaz needed to solve at the city gate, and how did he do it?

In what ways does the book of Ruth offer a counterpoint to the days of the judges when everyone did what was right in their own eyes?

What evidence in Ruth supports Boaz's claim that Ruth was an excellent woman?

Study Resources

Eskenazi, Tamara Cohn, and Tikva Frymer-Kensky. *Ruth*. JPSBC. Philadelphia: Jewish Publication Society, 2011.

Embry, Brad. "Legalities in the Book of Ruth: A Renewed Look." *JSOT* 41, no. 1 (2016): 31–44.

Matheny, Jennifer M. "Ruth in Recent Research." *Currents in Biblical Research* 19, no. 1 (2020): 8–35.

Schnittjer, Gary Edward. "Ruth." In *Old Testament Use of Old Testament*, 578–90. Grand Rapids: Zondervan Academic, 2021.

Ziegler, Yael. *Ruth*. Jerusalem: Maggid Books, 2015.

6

Daniel

Outline

Author, Date, and Message

The author of Daniel is unknown.

Dating the authorship of Daniel is complex and disputed. But it is important to work through the details to know how to interpret the book. Is it predictive or fictional?

The book was composed sometime after the time of Daniel. In addition to writing about Daniel in the first half of the book, the author makes use of some first-person accounts of Daniel's visions in the second half of the book. Notice how the author uses a third-person frame for the first-person vision accounts in Dan 7:1 and 10:1. Dating Daniel's life will give the earliest possible date the book could have been written. Consider the difficulty in identifying Darius the Mede (table 6.1).

Based on the dating within the book, it must have been written sometime after 537 BCE. However, the book speaks of sealing up its visions until the right time, which means it would not be produced (or better, released) as a book until much later (Dan 8:26; 12:4, 9).

The royal court stories of Daniel 1–6 are mentioned in a Second Temple narrative known as 1 Maccabees (cf. 1 Macc 2:59–60; on the Second Temple see the introduction). Thus, the royal court stories were already well known by the latter half of the second century BCE when 1 Maccabees was written.

The prayers in the first two chapters of a Second Temple Judaic fictional work known as Baruch make many allusions to the prayer that precedes the vision in Daniel 9.[1] The author of Baruch makes allusions to Daniel in the same way he alludes to many other authoritative writings of Israel's Scriptures such as Leviticus, Deuteronomy, and Jeremiah.[2] The author of Baruch also referred to Belshazzar as "son" of Nebuchadnezzar (Bar 1:11, 12). But Belshazzar was the biological son of Nabonidus, a usurper not from the line of Nebuchadnezzar.[3] The only known place Belshazzar is referred to as Nebuchadnezzar's "son" is in Daniel's royal court stories (Dan 5:2, 11, 13, 18, 22). This makes it likely that the author of Baruch knew of

---

[1] E.g., see Bar 1:15, cf. Dan 9:7; Bar 1:18, cf. Dan 9:6, 10; Bar 2:1–2, cf. Dan 9:12–13; Bar 2:9, cf. Dan 9:14; and many more. For a list, see Emanuel Tov, *The Book of Baruch* (Missoula, MT: Scholars Press, 1975), 15–23; Carey A. Moore, "Toward the Dating of the Book of Baruch," *CBQ* 36 (1974): 312, n. 3; 313, n. 7 [312–20].

[2] See, e.g., Bar 2:3, cf. Lev 26:29; Bar 2:13, cf. Deut 4:27; Bar 2:16, cf. Deut 26:15; Bar 2:18, cf. Deut 28:65; Bar 2:23, cf. Jer 7:34; Bar 3:29–30, cf. Deut 30:12–13; Bar 5:7, cf. Isa 40:4–5.

[3] For dates and relations, see table I.3 in the introduction. On "father" as predecessor, see NET note on Dan 5:2.

Table 6.1: Dates within the Book of Daniel

1:1	605 BCE	Daniel and his three associates were taken captive from Jerusalem by King Nebuchadnezzar in the third year of Jehoiakim king of Judah[a,b] to serve as administrators in the royal court of Babylon. There is no other record of this event.
2:1	604	Second year of Nebuchadnezzar[b,c]
5:30	539	Death of Belshazzar[c]
7:1	549	First year of Belshazzar[c]
8:1	547	Third year of Belshazzar[c]
9:1	? (views 2, 3, and 4 date to 538)	The identity of Darius the Mede is sharply contested (cf. 5:31; 6:28; 9:1; 11:1). Competing views include the following: (1) Darius the Mede was a mistaken allusion to Darius the Great (522–486). (2) Darius was Gubaru, the governor of Babylon under Cyrus. (3) Darius was Cyrus based on translating 6:28 as "during the rule of Darius, namely, during the rule of Cyrus the Persian" (AT). This view notes that Cyrus's mother was a royal Mede. (4) Darius was another regional ruler named Darius mentioned by two ancients: Berossus (third century BCE) and Valerius Harpocration (late second century CE).[d]
10:1	537	Third year of Cyrus's rule over Babylon[c]

[a] See dates in outline in chapter 4.

[b] See dates in figure I.9 in the introduction.

[c] See dates in table I.3 in the introduction.

[d] For views 1, 2, 3, see NET note on Dan 9:1. For the *explanatory* function of the Hebrew letter *vav* as "namely" instead of "and" in Dan 6:28 in view 3, see GKC §154a, n. 1(b); *IBHS* §39.2.4c. The same construct appears in 1 Chr 5:26: "King Pul of Assyria (that is, King Tiglath-pileser of Assyria)" (NET); cf. D. J. Wiseman, "Some Historical Problems in the Book of Daniel," in *Notes on Some Problems in the Book of Daniel*, ed. D. J. Wiseman (London: Tyndale, 1965), 12–13. I became aware of Wiseman's study from Wendy L. Widder, *Daniel*, SGBC (Grand Rapids: Zondervan, 2016), 118, n. 38. On Cyrus's mother from Media, see Xenophon, *Cyropaedia* VIII, 5.17–20 (370 BCE) in *PE*, 60. For view 4, see Steven D. Anderson and Rodger C. Young, "The Remembrance of Daniel's Darius the Mede in Berossus and Harpocration," *BSac* 173 (2016): 315–23.

Daniel 9 as part of the same book as Daniel 5. This evidence suggests that by the time of the authorship of Bar 1:1–3:8 (if the rest of Baruch is dated later), Daniel, including its vision accounts like those in Daniel 9, was already old and held in esteem like other Scriptures. The date of Bar 1:1–3:8 must be a long time before 117–116 BCE (when the grandson of Ben Sira consulted a written copy in translating Sirach).[4] And the evidence of Baruch's use of Daniel 9 akin to other esteemed, authoritative Scriptures (see footnotes 1 and 2) suggests Daniel 9 was already very old when Bar 1:1–3:8 was written. Readers can confirm the evidence in footnotes 1 and 2 by looking up Baruch in the NRSVue at BibleGateway.com.

The evidence in the previous paragraph and its footnotes calls into question the use of Daniel 9 in Baruch 1–2 as a basis to date Baruch after 165 BCE. A commonplace set of views sees the vision accounts of Daniel as written in 165 BCE, the time of the latest events in Daniel 11 involving Antiochus IV Epiphanes, the Seleucid ruler

---

[4] The present study can only get at the difficulties of dating in broad terms. Six steps need to be taken into account to approximate the latest date the visions of Daniel could have been written. These include evidence in the Second Temple Judaic writings known as Baruch and Sirach presented in Emanuel Tov, *The Septuagint Translation of Jeremiah and Baruch* (Missoula, MT: Scholars Press, 1976), and in Armin Lange, "The Book of Jeremiah in the Hebrew and Greek Texts of Ben Sira," in *Making the Biblical Text: Textual Studies in the Hebrew and Greek Bible*, ed. Innocent Himbaza (Göttingen: Vandenhoeck & Ruprecht, 2015), 118–61. Here are the six steps: (1) Daniel 9 was composed. (2) Canonical esteem was granted to Daniel 9 akin to the esteem of Torah and the Prophets. (3) Baruch 1:1–3:8 was composed in Hebrew and used Daniel 9 as it used other scriptures (see footnotes 1 and 2). (4) Hebrew-Baruch 1:1–3:8 was affixed to the Hebrew parent text (*Vorlage*) of Septuagintal Jeremiah (Jer-LXX; Tov, 6). Baruch 1:1–3:8 was translated into Greek as part of the initial translation of the Hebrew parent text of Jer-LXX—this initial translation is called Old Greek Jeremiah (Jer-OG). Michael suggests Baruch was translated into Greek in the early second century BCE. See Tony Michael, "1 Baruch (Greek)," in *Textual History of the Bible*, vol. 2B, *The Deuterocanonical Scriptures*, ed. Frank Feder and Matthias Henze (Leiden: Brill, 2019), 2B:11 [11–15]. (Note that two Hebrew versions of Jeremiah circulated in antiquity: the Hebrew parent text of Jer-LXX and proto-Masoretic Text of Jeremiah [Jer-proto-MT]. Jeremiah-proto-MT is the ancestor of the Hebrew version behind Jeremiah in the English Bible. See *OTUOT*, 263–67.) (5) A scribe revised Jer-OG 29–52 and Bar-OG 1:1–38 to correspond more woodenly to the Hebrew parent text of Jer-LXX plus the Hebrew parent text of Bar 1:1–3:8 affixed to it (Tov, 111–26). Jeremiah-LXX, therefore, refers to Jer-OG 1–28 plus the revised version of Jer-OG 29–52-plus-Bar-OG 1:1–3:8. (6) The grandson of Ben Sira translated Hebrew Sirach into Greek. The evidence shows that the grandson's translational efforts included his consultation of a written copy of the Jer-proto-MT that he compared to a written copy of Jer-LXX (Lange, 159–60). The grandson of Ben Sira did this translation in c. 117–116 BCE (a fairly precise date because of the details he mentioned of his visit to Egypt) (Lange, 160; Tov, 165). Every step needed considerable time between them. The longest period is step 2. It would have taken a very long time for Daniel 9 to be given the same esteem as the other Scriptures with which it is used by the author of Baruch. Once Bar 1:1–3:8 was written in Hebrew, it needed to be affixed to Jeremiah, then translated (perhaps early second century BCE, see step 4), then revised, and then this translated and revised version (Jer-LXX) needed to be disseminated widely enough to be consulted in 117–116 by the grandson of Ben Sira.

who troubled Jerusalem (see later discussion). These views regard the accounts as past historical events cast as though they were predictive visions of Daniel, an exilic Jewish administrator of the long-gone Neo-Babylonian royal court. However, the evidence points in the opposite direction and suggests that Bar 1:1–3:8 was composed many years before 117–116 BCE, perhaps as early as the fourth century BCE,[5] and that at the time it was composed Daniel 9 was already old, esteemed, authoritative, and part of the same book as Daniel 5. This evidence makes the view that Daniel's visions were not written until 165 BCE highly improbable and almost implausible.

In sum, the evidence suggests that Daniel was released long after the rise of the Persian Empire in 539 BCE because the visions were sealed for many years. But it was released long before—long enough for Daniel 9 to be esteemed as Scripture—the composition of Bar 1:1–3:8 (itself written a long time before 117–116 BCE, maybe as early as the fourth century BCE). Taken at face value the evidence implies that Daniel (royal court stories and visions together) was already old and esteemed by the time of the Seleucid rule (198–167 BCE). The present study will follow the natural outcomes of this evidence and regard the visions of Daniel as predictive and written before the events to which they refer.

The message of Daniel is that Yahweh the Most High God rules over all nations and will be faithful to his word to his people Israel. The focus on the Most High as the sovereign ruler of all nations serves as the leading emphasis of the three pairs of stories in Daniel 2–7 (see the outline at the beginning of the chapter and table 6.2). Emphasis on God's care for his people when they are in trouble appears in Daniel 1 and in the visions of 7–12. Daniel 7 plays an important role in connecting both parts of the narrative's message.

Interpretive Overview

Almost every aspect of the interpretation of Daniel is highly contested. The present purpose is not to sort these out. This interpretive overview focuses on the structure of Daniel and the genre of its revelatory visions, as well as briefly introducing leading interpretive issues in the six royal court stories and the accounts of Daniel's four visions.

Literary indicators in Daniel naturally invite two viewpoints on its structure—Daniel 1, 2–7, 8–12 and 1–6, 7–12. These literary indicators include language and genre.

---

[5] So Moore, "Toward the Dating of Baruch," 317. Moore is only focusing on Bar 1:1–2:9 here.

The authorship and expected readership of Daniel are bilingual. Daniel 1:1–2:4 and chapters 8–12 are written in Hebrew, while 2:5–7:28 is written in Aramaic. The shift in language corresponds to a shift in emphasis. Daniel 1 and 8–12 emphasize God's providential care for his people. Daniel 2–7 demonstrates again and again the Most High's sovereign rule over nations and empires. The designation of Yahweh as the Most High is very old, going back to when God divided the nations and even to the priest of Salem (Jerusalem), Melchizedek, who was known by Abraham (Gen 14:18–19; Deut 32:8).

Daniel 1–6 features third-person narration about Daniel, while 7–12 presents Daniel's visions in first-person accounts. In 1–6 Daniel is an interpreter of the visons of others. In 7–12 Daniel needs help from celestial delegates to interpret his own visions.

Both approaches show much merit as ways to approach the structure of the book. In some ways it seems as though they should not be treated as binary choices. Daniel 7 connects both structural elements. Daniel 7 closes out the third of three pairs of stories in 2–7 (2 and 7, visions of four kingdoms; 3 and 6, salvation from horrific public executions; 4 and 5, divine humbling of arrogant rulers), even while it dramatically offers the first of four visions of Daniel in 7–12. The vision of the creatures representing kingdoms in Daniel 7 shows how the visions of kingdoms in Daniel 2 and 8 correspond. Both the outline at the beginning of this chapter and table 6.2 summarize these structural elements in different ways.

Table 6.2: Structural Elements of Daniel

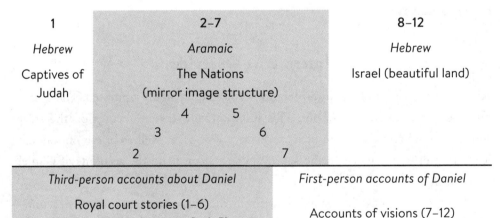

1	2–7	8–12
Hebrew	*Aramaic*	*Hebrew*
Captives of Judah	The Nations (mirror image structure)	Israel (beautiful land)
	4 5	
	3 6	
	2 7	
Third-person accounts about Daniel		*First-person accounts of Daniel*
Royal court stories (1–6) (with embedded visions: 2, 4, 5)		Accounts of visions (7–12)

The revelatory visions appearing in Daniel are often called *apocalyptic*, from the Greek word meaning "revelation."[6] In the Bible some of Zechariah's night visions and the visions of John in Revelation share similar revelatory characteristics.

Biblical revelatory visions place terrible evils in scenarios building to dramatic salvation for Israel effected by God or his delegates. Besides the biblical revelatory visions this genre became very popular during the Second Temple period. This makes sense, with many Judeans studying the Scriptures of their ancestors with its covenants, promises, and prophecies pushing up against the hard realities of the empire.[7]

The genres of revelatory visions and so-called pessimistic wisdom—both of which wrestle with misery—had a similar function in the exilic captivity and the subsequent return to Judah. They helped strengthen belief in a good and all-powerful God in the face of terrible evils (sometimes called *theodicy*). Books like Job and Ecclesiastes wrangle with the challenges of evil through wisdom. Revelatory visions in Daniel, Zechariah, and Revelation use scenarios filled with symbolic imagery to face that same evil.

Daniel 1 opens with Daniel and his three Judean captive friends Hananiah (Shadrach), Mishael (Meshach), and Azariah (Abednego) facing the challenge of not defiling themselves in captivity. Before they ate one royal meal, readers are informed that Daniel "purposed in his heart" (KJV), or more conventionally, "resolved" (NIV), that he would not defile himself (v. 8). This decision to do the right thing before getting into a tempting situation sets Daniel apart from others such as Samson and David (Judg 16:4–20; 2 Sam 11:2). Daniel's success was not because of a better situation than Samson or David. Far from it. The difference was his commitment of the heart to do God's will before it was too late.

Daniel 2 features Nebuchadnezzar's vision of a four-part composite image (cf. Ancient Connections 6.1). The interpretive correlation of the four parts of the image to historical kingdoms will be discussed in relation to Daniel 7 later. The discussion here focuses on the chapter's similarity to Genesis 41 in its setting as well as its similarity to Isaiah in its imagery—imagery that no Babylonian would understand.

---

[6] The discussion of revelatory visions, although he does not use that expression, is indebted to Tremper Longman III, *How to Read Daniel* (Downers Grove, IL: IVP Academic, 2020), 8–12.

[7] Popular extrabiblical narratives using fictional revelatory visions in the Second Temple period include *Jubilees* and *1 Enoch*.

ANCIENT CONNECTIONS 6.1: INTERPRETING DREAMS

The following excerpts are from an ancient Egyptian guide for interpreting dreams from c. 1300 BCE. The principle of interpretation is often similarities, such as similar sounds of words in the original language or similar situations. This inscription was written in two columns with the words "good" or "bad" written in red (here signified by bold).

If a man see himself in a dream:

white bread being given to him—   **good:** it means things at which his face will light up.

seeing a large cat—   **good:** it means a large harvest will come [to him].

plunging into a river—   **good:** it means cleansing from all evil spirits.

seeing the catching of birds—   **bad:** it means taking away his property.

looking into a deep well—   **bad:** putting him into prison. (*ANET*, 495)

Daniel contains many echoes of Joseph decoding Pharaoh's dreams in Genesis 41.[8] Anyone who reads the two stories can see the similarities. The point of this extended echo effect is less about similarities and more about differences (on extended echo effect, see the introduction). Nebuchadnezzar baffled his court wizards and sages by refusing to tell them the dream but demanding an interpretation on the threat of death. This was very un-pharaoh-like (Dan 2:5; cf. Gen 41:8). Daniel proceeded to be more Joseph-like than Joseph himself by giving the dream and its meaning. For now, brief attention can be given to two details in the vision that seem to come from Isaiah.

The descriptive phrase "a rock was cut out, but not by human hands" sounds like Isaiah's constituents looking back to Abraham and Sarah, "the rock from which you were cut out" (Dan 2:34 NIV; cf. Isa 51:1–2). And just as Isaiah said Jacob would crush the mountains "like chaff," so, too, the rock in the vision crushed the four-part composite image into pieces that blew away "like chaff" (Isa 41:15–16; cf. Dan 2:35). In this way, readers of Daniel who know the prophecies of Isaiah hear a secret message of hope not disclosed to Nebuchadnezzar and the wizards and sages of his court.[9]

---

[8] See Wendy L. Widder, "The Court Stories of Joseph (Gen 41) and Daniel (Dan 2) in Canonical Context: A Theological Paradigm for God's Work among the Nations," *OTE* 27, no. 3 (2014): 1112–14 [1112–28]. And for other studies that detect as many as eighteen similarities between Genesis 41 and Daniel 2, see *OTUOT*, 619, n. 3.

[9] See *OTUOT*, 620–22.

The vision in Daniel 2 relegated the rule of Babylon to the golden head of a statue. Predictably, the next episode in Daniel 3 begins with a giant image completely made of gold as though Babylonian rule would last forever.[10] When Shadrach, Meshach, and Abednego refused to pay homage to the image, they were thrown into the raging furnace (see Ancient Connections 6.2). Nebuchadnezzar saw another figure who looked like "a son of the gods" walking around in the furnace with the trio (3:25). The extra figure in the furnace acts like a magnet for various interpretations. Sometimes this gets translated as "the Son of God" (KJV), and it often gets drawn into discussions of "Christophanies" (preincarnate appearances of Christ). Unlike a similar Hebrew phrase that could signify "son of the gods" or "Son of God" depending on context, in Aramaic it only signifies "son of the gods."[11] Care needs to be taken not to trivialize the coming of the Son of God by suggesting he makes many short visits to earth. The Scriptures indicate that the incarnation of God in the Messiah is an unprecedented event.

ANCIENT CONNECTIONS 6.2: BOWING BEFORE A KING

Plutarch (46–119 CE) explains the need to bow before the Persian king Artaxerxes (464–424 BCE).

> Out of all the excellent laws we possess, we take most pride in honouring the king and prostrating ourselves before him as the image of the god who rules the universe.[a] So, if you approve our customs and will make obeisance to him, you may see and speak to the king. But if you do not accept this, you will need to use other intermediaries to communicate with him; because it is against our customs for the king to grant an audience to a man who refuses to pay him obeisance. (Plutarch, *Themistocles* 274–75, in *PE*, 534)

[a] Since the Persian king was never considered a god, this was Plutarch's comment to Greeks who regarded such behavior as appropriate (*PE*, 539, n. 2).

The story of the humbling of Nebuchadnezzar in Daniel 4 bears some resemblance to the seven-year mental breakdown of King Nabonidus, the father of Belshazzar (see table I.3 in the introduction), recorded in an Aramaic writing found among the Dead

---

[10] Though a different image, Herodotus (I, 183) speaks of a twenty-two-ton enthroned golden cult-statue of Bel-Marduk in Babylon (*PE*, 249).

[11] See Widder, *Daniel*, 75.

Sea Scrolls (4Q242/4QPrNab). The similarities have sparked much debate regarding a possible relationship. But the "Prayer of Nabonidus" is quite fragmentary, with some of the similarities being merely possible ways to reconstruct the text. Collins warns against overstating conclusions based on elements reconstructed in the "Prayer of Nabonidus" from Daniel 4.[12] Though the ancient tradition is challenging to read, readers need to consider the evidence that sparks debates. Notice how the gaps in the "Prayer of Nabonidus" require caution when comparing it to Daniel 4.

> . . . words of p[ra]yer of Nabonidus, king of [Ba]bylon, [the Great] King, [when he was stricken] with a pernicious inflammation by the decree of G[o]d, in [the municipality of] Temin.
>
> "I was stricken for seven years, and ever since [. . .] I became comparable [. . .], and . . . my offense—he forgave it. A diviner, who was himself a Jew fro[. . .], provided an interpretation, and wrote . . . to render honor greatness to the name of G[. . .]: 'You were stricken with a pernicious inflammation [. . .] you continued for seven years to pray [. . .] gods of silver and gold [. . .], wood and stone . . . clay, because [. . .]ion that t[. . .] (true) divinities.'" (*COS* 1.89:286)[13]

The extraordinary element of the biblical account of Nebuchadnezzar is that 4:1–18 and 34–37 were presented in first person. Daniel interprets the mighty tree that was chopped down in the vision as a mental breakdown of Nebuchadnezzar. The vision shares many similarities with Ezekiel's scenario of the Assyrian Empire as a mighty tree chopped down (cf. Ezek 31:1–18). As soon as Daniel finished warning the king, the narrative jump cuts twelve months ahead to Nebuchadnezzar's arrogance: "Is this not Babylon the Great *that I have built* to be a royal residence *by my vast power and for my majestic glory?*" (Dan 4:30, emphasis added).

The juxtaposition of the dire warning and the arrogant boasting offers a dramatic setup to the king's mental derangement. Until he repents.

No one in Scripture gives voice to the sovereign power of the Most High better than the ruthless tyrant Nebuchadnezzar. The irony of hearing this message from the humbled ruler is itself part of the message of Daniel.

> But at the end of those days, I, Nebuchadnezzar, looked up to heaven, and my sanity returned to me. Then I praised the Most High and honored and glorified him who lives forever: For his dominion is an everlasting dominion, and

---

[12] See John J. Collins, *Daniel*, Hermeneia (Minneapolis: Fortress, 1993), 218.

[13] The reconstructions are replaced by ellipses in the prayer itself, and parenthetical supplements by the editors are not included.

his kingdom is from generation to generation. All the inhabitants of the earth are counted as nothing, and *he does what he wants* with the army of heaven and the inhabitants of the earth. *There is no one who can block his hand* or say to him, "What have you done?" (vv. 34–35, emphasis added)

Widder explains the purpose of the humbling of Nebuchadnezzar: "It is important because of who Nebuchadnezzar was." He captured Jerusalem, burned the temple, and took God's people into captivity. "In humbling *this* king, the God of Israel demonstrated his sovereignty over *all* kings and kingdoms."[14] That is why it is critical to let readers hear King Nebuchadnezzar's acknowledgment of God's sovereignty in his own words.

Daniel 5 follows with the folly of Belshazzar's feast. Drunken guests mishandled the articles of the temple of Jerusalem. A manifestation of a hand writing on the wall doomed the ruler that very night.

An important observation is missing in the narrative of Daniel 5. The divine interventions appearing elsewhere repeatedly brought Nebuchadnezzar and Darius to praise the Most High (2:47; 4:2, 34–35, 37; 6:26–27). Not so with Belshazzar. He was killed the same night, without praising the God of Israel, ending the Neo-Babylonian Empire and establishing the rule of Darius the Mede. The difficulty with identifying Darius is discussed in table 6.1 earlier.

Daniel 6 features satirical ridicule and humor at the expense of the royal court of Babylon, though in a more lighthearted manner than the Esther story. Daniel 6 and Esther are the only scriptural references to the irrevocable laws of the Medes and Persians. The account in Esther shows how the leaders got around the obstacle by simply making new contradictory rulings (3:10; 8:8; cf. 1:19; 8:3, 5). In Daniel the irrevocable law of the Medes and Persians trapped the hapless, impotent king (6:8, 12, 15). The story delights readers with the king's sleepless night worrying about Daniel with the lions and then ironically feeding Daniel's opponents to the ravenous lions.

The vision of Daniel 7 features surrealistic imagery. "Surrealistic" means it is something like reality, but different. Visionary scenarios often use "like" or "as" to describe visionary elements on the analogy of reality. In this vision Daniel saw a creature "like" a lion with eagle wings and feet "like" a human being (Dan 7:4). The next two creatures were "like" a bear and "like" a leopard with four heads (vv. 5, 6).[15] These

---

[14] Wendy L. Widder, "Letting Nebuchadnezzar Speak: The Purpose of the First-Person Narrative in Daniel 4," *OTE* 32, no. 1 (2019): 211 [197–214].

[15] The Aramaic preposition of simile "like, as" is spelled the same and functions much like the Hebrew preposition of simile "like, as" (see "*k*," *HALOT* 2:1896). On Ezekiel's excessive

all set up the terrifying fourth wild animal that was "different" from the previous wild animals (v. 7). The fourth wild animal began with ten horns until three were uprooted by a little horn speaking arrogant words against the Most High (v. 25; cf. vv. 8, 11). The vision reaches its climax when the one "like" a human being came on the clouds (v. 13). It is interesting to think through the imagery of the revelatory visions in Daniel in light of the artwork of ancient Babylon, such as the fantastic creatures emblazoned on the Ishtar Gate (see figure 6.1).

Figure 6.1: Walking Dragon beside Ishtar Gate in Ancient Babylon‡

Sketch by Gary Edward Schnittjer

‡ The walls beside the massive Ishtar Gate of ancient Babylon feature brightly colored glazed bricks with golden-yellow lions, bulls, and walking dragons against a deep blue background. The gate was built c. 575 BCE during the rule of Nebuchadnezzar II. The sketch is based on part of the gate on display in the Metropolitan Museum of Art in New York City.

The four creatures in the vision of Daniel 7 seem to correlate to the four parts of the composite image of the vision in Daniel 2. The book of Daniel identifies these four parts as kingdoms or empires but does not name them. The traditional correlation is called the "Roman view" and sees the four empires as Babylon, Media-Persia, Greece, and Rome. In recent years many evangelical scholars have become convinced

use of the preposition of simile "like, as," in his many scenarios and allegories, see *OTUOT*, 348–49, esp. 349, n. 89.

that the evidence better fits the "Greek view," with the four nations as Babylon, Media, Persia, and Greece (table 6.3).[16] Evangelical scholars of both views regard the visions as predictive and coming from Daniel (see discussion of date on pages 158–61). Also, both views regard the ultimate fulfillment of these visions as coming in the work of Jesus the Messiah. The celestial delegate's identification of the goat as Greece in Daniel 8 strengthens the case for the Greek view. The present study favors the Greek view and sees the arrogant little horn as referring to Antiochus IV Epiphanes who (in)famously desecrated the Second Temple in Jerusalem in the 160s BCE. This view helps explain the ten horns and then a little horn since Antiochus can be counted as the eleventh ruler in the Seleucid kingdom going back to Alexander the Great as the first ruler.[17] Still, both views will be listed in the tables. Caution should be taken with interpretation of these visions because even after hearing the interpretations Daniel was troubled and confused (7:28; 8:27; 12:8).

Table 6.3: The Kingdoms of the Visions of Daniel 2 and 7

Daniel 2	Daniel 7	Greek view	(Traditional) Roman view
Head of gold	Lion	Babylon	Babylon
Chest and arms of silver	Bear	Media	Media-Persia
Belly and thighs of bronze	Leopard	Persia	Greece
Legs of iron and feet of clay	Terrifying wild animal	Greece	Rome

The celestial attendant explained to Daniel that the vision of the one like a human being symbolized the people of the Most High. Compare the vision and its explanation to consider the identity of the one like a human being (emphases added).

I looked in my night visions, and there, with the clouds in the heavens <u>someone like a human being</u> came. . . . **To him was given authority**, honour and **kingship**; all peoples, nations and languages were to revere him. *His authority is an authority that lasts permanently*, that won't pass away, his kingship one that won't be destroyed. (7:13a, 14 FT)

---

[16] For explanation of the Greek view, see Widder, *Daniel*, 52–54, 158–61; John H. Walton, "The Four Kingdoms of Daniel," *JETS* 29, no. 1 (1986): 25–36.

[17] See Widder, *Daniel*, 162.

The kingship, the authority and the greatness of the kingships under the entire heavens **will be given to** <u>the people of the sacred one</u> on high. *Its kingship will be a kingship lasting permanently.* All authorities will revere and bow down to it." (7:27 FT; cf. v. 18)

Bold signifies the parallels between the dominion and the kingdom that was given to the one like a human being in verse 14. That helps identify this figure as representing (or symbolizing) the people of the Most High who were given the kingdom and dominion in verses 18 and 27.

Readers familiar with the New Testament may recognize the language of "with the clouds in the heavens someone like a human being came" (FT) in verse 13 as a description of the Messiah's identity (see Matt 24:30; Mark 13:26; Luke 21:27). The italicized phrases in verses 14 and 27 show how the Messiah exceeds the collective of the people of the Most High. The Messiah is uniquely identified with the Most High. It is the Messiah who will rule over an everlasting kingdom. It is important to keep in mind the overlap between the individual and the collective within the biblical outlook.[18] The Messiah represents the people who inherit the blessing of the Messiah.[19]

For the present purposes, attention to Daniel 8 is limited to the way the vision's creatures and the empires they represent correspond to the creatures and the empires of the visions of Daniel 2 and 7 (see discussion of Daniel 7 above). Whereas the earlier visions did not name the empires to which they correlated, Dan 8:20–21 designated the ram and the goat as Media-Persia and Greece respectively. Compare table 6.3 with table 6.4.

Daniel 9 opens with Daniel studying the scroll of Jeremiah and wondering if the seventy years of the devastation had been fulfilled (Jer 25:11–12; 29:10).[20] Daniel responded by making a collective confession of sin. The prayer overflows with quotations and allusions to earlier Scriptures. The most important allusions stem from collective confession of sin based on Lev 26:40 and affirmation of Yahweh's faithfulness to his covenant quoted from Deut 7:9 (cf. Dan 9:4–5).[21] Daniel prayed these Scriptures hoping to trigger Yahweh's covenantal mercies. Though Jeremiah's seventy

---

[18] See Gary Edward Schnittjer, "Say You, Say Ye: Individual and Collective Identity and Responsibility in Torah," *Center for Hebraic Thought*, March 9, 2022, https://hebraicthought.org/individual-collective-identity-responsibility-torah/.

[19] Cf. "you" plural in Isa 55:3; Acts 13:34.

[20] On the seventy years in Scripture, see Gary Edward Schnittjer, "Individual versus Collective Retribution in the Chronicler's Ideology of Exile," *JBTS* 4, no. 1 (2019): 126–28 [113–32].

[21] See *OTUOT*, 622–24.

Table 6.4: The Kingdoms of the Vision of Daniel 8

Daniel 8	Greek view	(Traditional) Roman view
Ram with two horns	Media-Persia	Media-Persia
Goat with one then four horns	Greece	Greece

years prompted Daniel's prayer, Daniel's use of the Torah shows how Yahweh's sovereign will among the empires fit together with his covenantal promises to the Hebrew ancestors.

In response to Daniel's prayer, a celestial delegate named Gabriel was dispatched to declare that the seventy years is actually seventy weeks of years for the holy city in three segments (seven weeks + sixty-two weeks + one week). After the first seven weeks from when word went out, the messiah (v. 25) could be seen as Cyrus, who was elsewhere called *Yahweh's messiah* (Isa 45:1 AT).[22] Between the sixty-two weeks and the last week the messiah, or the anointed one, would be cut off (Dan 9:26).

The Hebrew word for messiah means "anointed one" (the Greek word is "Christ," *christos*).[23] The first messiah in the Bible is Aaron, who was anointed as high priest in Leviticus 8. The anointing of David three times also associates messiahship with Davidic rulers (see 2 Sam 22:51//Ps 18:50; figure 3.2 in chapter 3). The term *messiah* can refer to God's chosen ones, like priests and kings, as well as to Jesus of Nazareth as the Messiah, the Son of God. This naturally leads to contested interpretations of the identity of the messiah cut off in Dan 9:26. Some evangelical interpreters espouse the visions of Daniel as predictive (see discussion of date earlier in the chapter) and follow the Greek view of the visions of Daniel (see table 6.3). They identify the messiah who is cut off as Onias III, the last legitimate high priest of Jerusalem killed in 171 BCE, or they think it refers to another unidentified person in the era when Antiochus IV Epiphanes troubled Jerusalem in the 160s BCE.[24] This messiah who is cut off functions as an expectational pattern of Jesus of Nazareth.[25]

---

[22] See Widder, *Daniel*, 203. For six competing views, see Andrew E. Steinmann, *Daniel*, CC (St. Louis: Concordia, 2008), 469–70.

[23] See "*mashiyah*," *HALOT* 1:645.

[24] Widder sees the messiah of Dan 9:26 as Onias III (*Daniel*, 203). House espouses the Greek view but thinks the seventy weeks are not clear enough to identify the messiah who was cut off. See Paul House, *Daniel*, TOTC (Downers Grove, IL: IVP Academic, 2018), 161.

[25] On typological patterns, see *OTUOT*, 902.

Evangelical interpreters who follow the Roman view only identify the messiah who is cut off as Jesus.[26]

The set of battles in the vision in Daniel 10–12 have been subjected to many competing interpretations. The large number of details have been aligned with various historical circumstances. Many evangelical interpretations see the initial historical fulfillments as typological patterns that are fulfilled by Jesus the Messiah.

The vision includes the king of the north, who many interpreters identify with the Seleucid ruler Antiochus IV Epiphanes (175–164 BCE; see figure 6.2), taking possession of the beautiful land—the land of promise. The climactic scenes come when the king's forces occupied and profaned the temple. They were responsible for setting up "the abomination that causes desolation" (11:31 NIV; cf. 9:27). The Hebrew root *shmm* of the phrase "that causes desolation" may have been a parody of the god Baal Shamem ("Lord of the Heavens")—the Syrian equivalent of Olympian Zeus (figure 6.2)—that was set up in the temple of Jerusalem in 167 BCE.[27] The sacrifices to this idol in the temple may have included pigs.[28]

Antiochus's regime tried to Hellenize the people of Judah (on Hellenization see the introduction). They encouraged people to stop practicing circumcision and to worship false gods.[29] They made it a capital offense to read the Torah or to obey the Torah.[30] Daniel 11:33–35 seems to speak to this terrible situation later narrated in a writing known as 1 Maccabees (see footnotes 28–30). These similarities are what drive much of the controversy about dating the book of Daniel—whether it predicts these events or presents history in the form of a vision (see discussion of date at the beginning of this chapter).

In this context of oppression, those who are wise in the vision instruct many, but some are killed (11:33). To make matters worse, many join the company of the wise insincerely (v. 34). Those who fall (die) in these struggles need to wait for the appointed time (v. 35). This sets up the hope for resurrection (12:2–3). The teaching on resurrection will be taken up in the section on Biblical Connections. For the moment it is enough to observe that the terrible events in the days of Antiochus are part of the framework of the coming of the Messiah from Nazareth.[31]

---

[26] See Steinmann, *Daniel*, 448, 472–74.

[27] See John Goldingay, *Daniel*, rev. ed. WBC (Grand Rapids: Zondervan Academic, 2019), 424, 540.

[28] See 1 Macc 1:47, 59; 2 Macc 6:2, 4.

[29] See 1 Macc 1:45–48.

[30] See 1 Macc 1:57.

[31] See Widder, *Daniel*, 237.

Figure 6.2: Ancient Seleucid Silver Coin in the
Image of Antiochus IV Epiphanes‡

Sketch by Gary Edward Schnittjer

‡ The front of the coin (sliver tetradrachm) depicts Antiochus IV. The back of the coin shows the enthroned god Zeus along with the following inscription in Greek: "Belonging to king Antiochus. God made manifest (*epiphanous*), bringer of victory."

Biblical Connections

The most explicit teaching on resurrection within Israel's Scriptures appears in Daniel 12. It is based on earlier revelation in Isaiah. Notice the way Daniel's visions build on the imagery of "awake" as resurrection in Isa 26:19 to refer to death as "sleep" in Dan 12:2. Yet, the significant advance of revelation in Daniel's vision is to expand resurrection beyond the blessed to include raising rebels to judgment and contempt (emphases added).[32]

> Your dead <u>will live</u>; their bodies will rise. <u>Awake</u> and sing, you who dwell in <u>the dust</u>! For you will be covered with the morning dew, and the earth will bring out the departed spirits. (Isa 26:19)

> And they will go out and look at the dead bodies of those who have rebelled against me. For their worm will not die and the fire that burns them will not be satisfied, and they **will be contemptible** to all flesh. (66:24 AT)

> Many who sleep in <u>the dust</u> of the earth will <u>awake</u>, some to eternal <u>life</u>, and some to disgrace and eternal **contempt**. (Dan 12:2, emphases added)

---

[32] The discussion in this section is based on *OTUOT*, 624–28.

Interpreters debate whether Dan 12:2 looks ahead to all people rising—called *general resurrection*—or if the text simply expands resurrection by adding some who arise to judgment. Whichever way Dan 12:2 should be interpreted, the New Testament builds on this and teaches general resurrection of all people to life or to death (John 5:29; Acts 24:15; Rev 20:4–5, 12–13).

When Dan 12:3 refers to "those who are wise" (NIV) it includes the wise ones who suffered and died in 11:33, 35. Daniel 12:3 uses the imagery of the Suffering Servant of Isaiah 52–53 since he is also one who acted wisely. The Suffering Servant made many righteous in a legal sense by his sacrifice (Isa 53:11). The wise ones who rise again in Daniel's vision lead others to righteousness by their wisdom (Dan 12:3). They shine like stars in the sense that they will teach others by their wisdom (emphases signifying parallels and similarities added).

> See, my servant <u>will act wisely</u>; he will be raised and lifted up and highly exalted. (Isa 52:13 NIV)

> Out of the suffering of his soul he shall see *light*, he shall be satisfied, by his knowledge my righteous servant **shall make many righteous**, and their iniquities he shall bear. (53:11 AT)

> <u>Those who are wise</u> *will shine like the brightness* of the heavens, and those **who lead many to righteousness,** *like the stars* for ever and ever. (Dan 12:3 NIV)

In sum, Daniel's vision builds on the teachings of resurrection and the Suffering Servant in Isaiah's prophecy.

Gospel Connections

Jesus connected imagery in the visions of Daniel to expectations from the psalms of David. In this way Messiah's teaching about himself provides a guide for his followers to interpret Israel's Scriptures in light of the gospel.

In a public teaching session within the temple courts, Jesus put the messianic expectations of biblical scholars of his own day to a test. He asked those listening why the scholars says the Messiah is the son of David (Mark 12:35). He quotes Ps 110:1, which presents the problem.

> [Jesus said:] "David himself says by the Holy Spirit: The Lord declared to my Lord, '**Sit at my right hand** until I put your enemies under your feet.'

David himself calls him 'Lord.' How then can he be his son?" (Mark 12:36–37a, emphasis added)

The crowd enjoyed Jesus's questioning of the difficulties of the scholarly interpretation. He emphasized that according to David himself the Messiah was both the son of David and yet greater than David (see italics).

In a private teaching session to his followers on the Mount of Olives, Jesus uses imagery from the vision of Daniel 7 to speak of his coming. He tells them that people would see "the son of a human coming in the clouds" (Mark 13:26 AT, emphasis added).

Readers have an advantage over eyewitnesses in this case because they know both the public and private teachings of Jesus. This prepares readers to hear the remarkable answer Jesus gave when he is on trial before the high priest. The high priest asks directly, "Are you the Messiah, the Son of the Blessed One?" (14:61b). Notice the way Jesus the Messiah answers by inserting an allusion to Ps 110:1 from his public speech into the middle of an allusion to Dan 7:13 from his private teaching (allusions emphasized).[33]

> Jesus said, "I am. You will see the son of a human **sitting at the right hand** [Ps 110:1, bold] of the strong one and coming on the clouds of heaven [Dan 7:13, underlining]." (14:62 AT)

The use of Daniel's vision interwoven with the psalm of David demonstrates how to interpret Israel's Scriptures. The Scriptures bear witness to the gospel of Messiah.

Life Connections

It is worth remembering the basics amid the many spectacular revelations in the Daniel story. Daniel reveals and interprets visions of the king that confounded the royal wizards and sages. He lives through a night trapped with hungry lions. He sees extraordinary visions of the coming salvation of God.

Yet, the ordinary acts of devotion should not be missed. Daniel prayed regularly (6:10), and he studied Scripture (9:2). Daniel must have studied Scripture often, because his prayer is filled with Scripture (vv. 4–19).

---

[33] See Mark L. Strauss, *Mark*, Zondervan Exegetical Commentary on the New Testament (Grand Rapids: Zondervan, 2014), 656–57.

Daniel's commitment to Scripture reading and prayer provide us with an opportunity to consider ourselves. Would our enemies need to conspire against us based on how much we pray? If charged with being devout Christians, is there enough evidence to convict us? Do our studies of the Scriptures overflow into our prayer life? These are products of a lifelong commitment to the basics.

It is not exciting or glamorous. But it is good and right. Pray. Study Scripture.

Interactive Questions

How does the date of the authorship of Daniel relate to whether or not the visions are predictive? What does the evidence suggest?

What are the reasons for regarding the broad structure of Daniel as 1–6 and 7–12? What about 1, 2–7, 8–12? How do these different views of the structure affect the interpretation of Daniel?

What are the interpretive benefits of recognizing the similarities and differences between the dream interpretation stories in Genesis 41 and Daniel 2?

What can be learned about human pride and the sovereignty of the Most High by comparing the accounts of Nebuchadnezzar and Belshazzar in Daniel 4 and 5?

Why are visions often presented in a surrealistic manner?

What is the theological significance of the visions of the four-part composite statue in Daniel 2 and the four wild animals in Daniel 7?

What evidence in Daniel 7 points to the one like a human symbolizing the collective people of the Most High? What evidence in Daniel 7 points to the one like the son of a human as the Son of God?

What evidence in Daniel cautions against overconfidence in interpreting the specific details of the visions?

What are at least three specific ways scriptural study affected Daniel's prayer in chapter 9?

What is the meaning and significance of the abomination that causes desolation in Dan 11:31?

What does Dan 12:2–3 add to the biblical doctrine of the resurrection that had not been revealed previously?

What is the significance of Messiah's use of the imagery of one like the son of a human coming on the clouds?

Study Resources

House, Paul R. *Daniel.* TOTC. Downers Grove, IL: IVP Academic, 2018.

Longman, Tremper, III. *How to Read Daniel.* Downers Grove, IL: IVP Academic, 2020.

Steinmann, Andrew E. *Daniel.* CC. St. Louis: Concordia, 2008.

Widder, Wendy L. *Daniel.* SGBC. Grand Rapids: Zondervan, 2016.

———. *Daniel.* Zondervan Exegetical Commentary on the Old Testament. Grand Rapids: Zondervan Academic, forthcoming.

7

Esther

Outline

Esther requests an edict for Jews to protect themselves (8)

Jews defend themselves, and Haman's sons are impaled (9:1–19)

Purim instituted (9:20–32)

Mordecai elevated (10)

Author, Date, and Message

The author of Esther is unknown.

The Persian king Ahasuerus (also known by his Greek name Xerxes) ruled 486–465 BCE. Esther's time as consort (queen) of Ahasuerus began in his seventh year (479) shortly after his famous failed invasion of Greece (Esth 2:16).[1] The opening verse presupposes a later perspective of authorship by looking back: "The following events happened in the days of Ahasuerus. (I am referring to *that Ahasuerus who* used to rule over 127 provinces extending all the way from India to Ethiopia)" (1:1 NET, emphasis added). The phrase "that Ahasuerus who . . ." may seek to disambiguate Xerxes I (486–465) from Xerxes II (424). If so, the authorship of Esther would be after 424, which fits with observations scholars have made about the similarity of the Hebrew of Esther and Chronicles (see chapter 9 for its date of c. 400). The absence of any Greek suggests Esther was written before the rise of the Greek Empire in 330.[2]

Three versions of Esther have survived. Protestant English Bibles are translated from the Hebrew version. The Septuagintal version was translated from a slightly different Hebrew version along with six imaginative Expansions dating from 114 or 78 BCE (based on persons listed in Additions to Esth 11:1).[3] The Alpha version is a Greek translation of a Hebrew parent text much like the Hebrew version of Esther with the six Expansions of the Septuagintal version added on.[4] Though the following discussion takes note of the Septuagintal version, this chapter is based on

---

[1] See Anthony Tomasino, "Esther," *Zondervan Illustrated Bible Backgrounds Commentary* (Grand Rapids: Zondervan, 2009), 3:471.

[2] On the similarity of the Hebrew of Esther and Chronicles as well as the absence of Greek, see Carey A. Moore, "Esther, Book of," *ABD* 2:641.

[3] See Moore, "Esther, Book of." Moore says 114 BCE is more likely.

[4] See Karen H. Jobes, *The Alpha-Text of Esther: Its Character and Relationship to the Masoretic Text* (Atlanta: Scholars Press, 1996), 220; Emanuel Tov, *Textual Criticism of the Hebrew Bible*, 4th ed. (Minneapolis: Fortress, 2022), 227. The use of "Expansions" (versus "Additions") follows Tov.

the authoritative Hebrew version of Esther appearing in the English Bible. Thus, when this chapter says Esther, the Esther narrative, and the like, it refers to the Hebrew version.

The keys to the message of the satirical Esther story are the absence of any reference to God or to the Torah, the lack of covenantal devotion of Esther and Mordecai, and a set of striking coincidences. The view taken here is that the author intentionally omits God. The book emphasizes lack of covenantal behavior in the leading Jewish characters. The author foregrounds circumstances that invite readers to decide if they are coincidental or if correct theology needs to be supplied from elsewhere in the Bible.

What is the clue to see more than coincidence? The Festival of Purim celebrates the deliverance of the Jews in Esther. Purim is named for the Akkadian word for "lots" (*pur*) that work like dice (9:24, 26).[5] The name of the festival, "Purim," invites readers to see more than a coincidental casting of lots and other mere coincidences. One of the proverbs captures the sense: "The lot is cast in the fold of the coat, *but every ruling it makes is from Yahweh*" (Prov 16:33 FT, emphasis added).

By design the theology of Esther is do-it-yourself (DIY). Without theology supplied from elsewhere the Esther story seems like a series of striking coincidences that just happened to protect the Jews from anti-Semitic genocide. But biblical readers protest. These things did not just happen. Elsewhere, scriptural narrators and characters attribute acts of deliverance to God's providence. The following interpretive overview suggests that resources for theological interpretation of Esther include the foreign royal court stories of Joseph and Daniel.

In Esther, unlike Genesis, the narrator does not whisper, "Yahweh was with Esther and her people." In Esther, unlike Daniel, the characters do not attribute anything to God, because they do not acknowledge him and they do not call upon him. That raises the question of the Esther story: Will God be faithful to deliver his people if they do not obey the covenant or call upon him?

In sum, what is the DIY message of Esther? The casting of lots (*purim*) only seems to be chance to those who do not know any better. Yahweh is with his people and will deliver them even when they do not deserve it. He does this because he is faithful to what he has said. Readers supply this message by comparing the Esther story with its counterparts in the Bible.

---

[5] See "*pūru* B," *CAD* 12:528–29 [2.b].

Interpretive Overview

After a brief summary emphasizing key plot points, the present purpose is to evaluate the genre of Esther and how to read it in biblical context. These are keys to a correct interpretation of Esther.

The Esther narrative tells of the deliverance of the Jews from genocide by an unlikely heroine from the harem of King Ahasuerus. Hadassah, who went by the name Esther, won the king's favor and became queen from among many who had been taken into the harem. The anti-Semitic plot of Haman, a royal official, to kill all Jews stemmed from the Jew Mordecai's refusal to pay honor to Haman after the king had promoted him. The text does not explain Mordecai's motive for refusing the honor due Haman (3:2). Elsewhere in Scripture there is no problem with showing honor to Gentiles, as in the case of Abraham bowing before the Hittites, and many others (Gen 23:7; cf., e.g., 33:3; 42:6; 43:26). Mordecai was not being asked to bow before an image or gods as in the case of Daniel's associates (Dan 3:12). But Mordecai's apparently selfish act put the entire Jewish people at risk.

To save the Jews, Mordecai persuaded his niece Esther to speak to the king. He said, "If you keep silent at this time, relief and deliverance will come to the Jewish people from another place, but you and your father's family will be destroyed. Who knows, perhaps you have come to your royal position *for such a time as this*" (Esth 4:14, emphasis added). When Mordecai said Esther may be destroyed, some wonder if he threatened to expose her identity as a Jew to coerce her into speaking with the king. If so, Mordecai may have realized that his own refusal to give honor where honor is due may cost Jews their lives.[6] The narrative style leaves much unsaid, so readers debate the motives for what the characters say and do.

God is never mentioned. Mordecai and Esther do not call upon Yahweh for help. This fits with their strategy to hide Esther's Jewish identity by her noncovenantal name and noncovenantal behaviors (see later discussion, especially table 7.1).

The Esther narrative offers clues that should prevent readers from demonizing Esther. Readings from women's studies' perspectives tend to condemn Esther for being more interested in her own beauty than in saving her people.[7] Yet Esther

---

[6] The suggestions for Mordecai's disrespect of Haman and potential threat of Esther come from Karen H. Jobes, *Esther*, NIVAC (Grand Rapids: Zondervan, 1999), 20. This is against Phillips, who says the language differs in Esth 3:2, but she fails to note that the same term for "bow down/honor" (*shthvh*) appears in Gen 23:7; 33:3; 42:6; etc. See Elaine Phillips, "Esther," EBC, rev. ed. (Grand Rapids: Zondervan, 2010), 623.

[7] See Angeline M. G. Song, "Not Just a Bimbo: A Reading of Esther by a Singaporean

"was taken" (grammatically passive) into the harem (2:8). Angeline Song suggests that Esther may be "outwardly pragmatic" to survive and cultivate allies in a hostile environment.[8] A close reading of the text shows that Esther's conformity to male expectations "disguise her intentions" in her defiant action to save her people. The evidence suggests that "Esther will utilize seduction in order to get her way."[9] Yet Esther does more than satisfy the king's sensual appetite. Song stresses that "she lifted up his loyalty" (vv. 9, 17 AT).[10] These are the kinds of clues readers can investigate to see how God used Esther to deliver his people.

Esther boldly accuses Haman of his anti-Semitic genocidal conspiracy before the king. When the king returns from getting some air in his anger, he finds Haman has accosted Esther (7:8). Though Haman was begging for mercy, he had transgressed a firm boundary. No one may approach a woman of the palace (see Ancient Connections 7.1). The enraged king has Haman impaled on the same seventy-five-foot pole Haman had set up to impale Mordecai. The king also grants Jews the right to defend themselves against haters who try to murder them according to Haman's edict. The story ends by explaining the Feast of Purim to celebrate deliverance from destruction.

ANCIENT CONNECTIONS 7.1: RULES PROTECTING WOMEN OF THE PALACE

Ancient women of the palace were strictly off-limits to all but the king. The ancient Assyrian ruler Tiglath-pileser I (1114–1076 BCE) established harsh punishments for encroaching on the women of the palace.

> If a woman of the palace sings or quarrels with another of her rank, and one of the royal eunuchs, courtiers, or servants stands listening, he will be beaten one hundred times (and) one of his ears will be cut off. . . . If a courtier wishes to speak with a woman of the palace, he may not approach closer to her than seven paces. (*ARI* 2:43)

Immigrant in Aotearoa New Zealand," in *Sea of Readings: The Bible in the South Pacific*, ed. Jione Havea (Atlanta: SBL Press, 2018), 134 [131–45].

[8] See Song, "Not Just a Bimbo," 134–35.

[9] See Laura Quick and Ellena Lyell, "Clothing, Conformity, and Power: Garment Imagery in the Book of Esther," *VT* 72, no. 3 (2022): 483–84, 491, citations from 484 and 483 respectively [474–94].

[10] See Song, "Not Just a Bimbo," 137–38.

Plutarch (46–119 CE) says of the palace women of the Persian ruler Artaxerxes, son of Ahasuerus (464 BCE):

> The barbarians [Persians] are terribly jealous, especially about anything unchaste, so that not merely someone approaching and touching a royal concubine, but even when somebody, during a journey, overtakes or crosses the path of the carriages in which they are transported, he is punished with death. (Plutarch, *Artoxerxes* 27.1, in *PE*, 595)

Standard discussions of the genre of Esther pivot on whether it is fictional or historical. Arguments for Esther as fiction build on the dramatic literary style, while arguments for history start with the Feast of Purim. They say it would be strange to design a feast around something that did not happen.[11] It is easy to agree that the Feast of Purim points to the historical basis of Esther. It also helps that a tablet discovered in Persepolis speaks of a person named Marduka who served as an upper-level accountant associated with Susa during the latter years of Darius and the early years of Xerxes. Since the names Marduka and Marduku were common, it is also possible that Mordecai was one of the other four persons so named on other Elamite tablets discovered in Persepolis (on Persepolis see discussion at figure I.12 in the introduction).[12]

The supposed contrast between historical account and ideological drama—a story with an agenda—distorts the issue. The problem with the debate is straight-forward. First, pitting ideology against history fails because every historical account is ideological.

Second, real events can be presented through literary drama.[13] Aristotle, a near-contemporary of the author of Esther, affirms the artistic presentation of real events in *Poetics* (c. 335 BCE).[14] The false binaries of either historical or ideological and either historical or artistic both fail because they are not realistic. David Firth makes a compelling case that this story of "historical events" is meant to "entertain."[15] Taking

---

[11] See David G. Firth, "The Third Quest for the Historical Mordecai and the Genre of the Book of Esther," *OTE* 16, no. 2 (2003): 233–43; David G. Firth, *The Message of Esther* (Downers Grove, IL: InterVarsity, 2010), 21–25.

[12] See Edwin M. Yamauchi, *Persia and the Bible* (Grand Rapids: Baker, 1990), 235.

[13] Similarly, see Jobes, *Esther*, 31–32.

[14] See the quotation of Aristotle on this issue in the discussion of narrative shaping in the introduction.

[15] See Firth, *Esther*, 24.

a both/and approach makes sense of the evidence in this historical and ideological-artistic narrative.

The more pressing matter is identifying the function of the satirical, ironic qualities of the Esther story. The book is shot through with mocking presentations of the bumbling, hapless royalty of the Persian court.[16] The royal court admitted that Queen Vashti made them look like fools in the opening scene (1:17–18). But the book is not like distasteful late-night comedy.

The Esther story is a classy satirical narrative. Its genre may be compared to Charlie Chaplin's *The Great Dictator*, which uses classical music played by a symphonic orchestra under some of its scenes. A scene in the middle of the film epitomizes Chaplin's ridicule of Adolf Hitler's lust for power by killing civilian undesirables during World War II. Chaplin, who played a power-hungry, tyrannical European dictator in Hitler's image, does a ballet-like lover's dance with a floating globe-balloon while symphonic strings play Wagner's *Lohengrin* prelude (figure 7.1). The classy satire makes the Nazi dictator look like a fool.

Figure 7.1: Charlie Chaplin Mocks the Nazis in *The Great Dictator*‡

Sketch by Gary Edward Schnittjer

‡ Filming began in September 1939 when the Nazis were invading Poland. It was released in 1940 before the United States entered World War II. Hitler is reported to have viewed it twice while staying in a mansion he had seized in Bavaria.

---

[16] On Esther as a comedy, see Adele Berlin, *Esther*, JPSBC (Philadelphia: Jewish Publication Society, 2001), 16–22.

The genre of Esther is not only classy satire, but it is also family friendly in how it handles delicate subjects such as sex and violence. Perhaps the family-friendly framing of Esther has made it susceptible to reading against the sense of the text—that is, as though Mordecai and Esther acted uprightly and in accord with the covenant.[17] This begins to get at the intended function of the Esther story as Purim instruction.

Both the hiddenness of God and the lack of commitment to covenantal standards come out clearly when Esther is compared to other biblical royal-court narratives. Daniel and Esther each differ from the Joseph story in Genesis after which they are both modeled. The similarities explained elsewhere (see table 7.2 later in this chapter) are necessary to highlight differences.[18] Daniel is frequently more Joseph-like than Joseph himself. Esther and Mordecai explicitly and implicitly have dissimilarities when compared to Joseph, which makes them very unlike Daniel, especially in his devout lifestyle to God. Consider each row of comparisons in table 7.1.

Readers of Genesis may conclude that Yahweh was with Joseph because he honored God in situations such as refusing to have relations with Mrs. Potiphar. He refused the temptress, asking, "How could I do this immense evil, and how could I sin against God?" (Gen 39:9). Or, when Daniel was taken into the royal court, he refused to eat the king's provisions and was well known for daily praying to his God (Dan 1:8; 6:5, 10–11). The noncovenantal lifestyle of Esther separates her from Joseph and Daniel. Deliverance in the Esther narrative comes without any of the virtues of Joseph or Daniel.[19]

The major outcome of comparing Esther and Daniel to the Joseph story after which they are modeled relates to the noncovenantal lifestyle of Mordecai and Esther. Deliverance of God's people is not earned by human obedience. This helps draw the correct conclusion about Joseph and Daniel also. They did not earn deliverance by righteous actions. Salvation belongs to Yahweh by his grace.

The noncovenantal lifestyle of Mordecai and Esther has opened them to harsh criticism. Pierce suggests the Esther story may serve as a warning against assimilation into the empire's secular culture.[20] Esther's marriage to an uncircum-

---

[17] Similarly, see Jobes, *Esther*, 113.

[18] Comparisons between Joseph, Daniel, and Esther are developed from *OTUOT*, 614. For a comparison that fails to adequately handle the Joseph connection, see Matthew Michael, "Daniel at the Beauty Pageant and Esther in the Lion's Den: Literary Intertextuality and Shared Motifs between the Books of Daniel and Esther," *OTE* 29, no. 1 (2016): 116–32.

[19] For a similar evaluation of Esther developed independently, see Jobes, *Esther*, 20.

[20] See Ronald W. Pierce, "The Politics of Esther and Mordechai: Courage or Compromise?" *BBR* 2 (1992): 75–89.

Table 7.1: Differences between Three Biblical Royal Foreign Court Stories

Joseph	Daniel	Esther
Passively given a new name (Zaphenath-paneah) (Gen 41:45)	Passively given a new name (Belshazzar) (Dan 1:7)	Hadassah takes a new name Esther apparently after Ishtar,[a] the Mesopotamian goddess of love and war (Esth 2:7); Mordecai is named after the god Marduk[b]
Known as a Hebrew (39:14, 17; 41:12)	Known as a devout Jew (6:5, 16)	Actively hides her ancestry (2:10, 20)
No prayer recorded	Prays and studies Scripture (2:20–23; 6:10; 9:2–3)	Fasts but no prayer recorded (4:16)
Married a Gentile (41:45)	Possibly made a eunuch; marital status not specified (1:3)	Intimate consort of an uncircumcised Gentile, then a concubine (queen) in the royal harem (2:16–17)
Predates dietary restrictions (cf. 43:34)	Refuses the king's food (1:8)	Eats the royal food (2:9)
Gives credit to God (39:9; 41:25, 28, 32, 51–52; 45:5–9; 50:20, 24–25)	Gives credit to God (2:28, 37, 45; 4:24; 5:18, 24; 6:22)	Does not acknowledge God
Narrator explicitly refers to God's providential care (39:2, 21, 23)	Narrator explicitly refers to God's providential care (1:9, 17)	Narrator excludes references to God
Foreigners acknowledge the God of Joseph (39:3; 41:39)	Foreigners acknowledge the God of Daniel (2:47; 3:28; 4:34–35; 6:26–27)	Foreigners do not acknowledge the God of Esther or Mordecai

[a] See "ʾester," *HALOT* 1:76.

[b] See "mordochay," *HALOT* 1:632.

cised king fits the profile of an apostasy marriage (Exod 34:16; Deut 7:3–4). This provides something of a worst-case scenario. Could God use people who systematically hide their covenantal identity and even participate in apostasy marriage? That is exactly the point of the parallels with the Joseph story. It is one thing to be passively caught up in evil schemes and be used by God as Joseph was. But what about Mordecai and Esther, who actively cultivated noncovenant lifestyles (Esth 2:10, 20)? The Esther story shows the deliverance of the Jews facilitated by just such lead characters.

The bold approach of the Hebrew Esther story ruffled feathers from the beginning. The Septuagintal version "fixed" many of the "problems" by adding six new fictionalized Expansions in which God directly intervenes with visions and Mordecai and Esther pray.[21] Septuagintal Esther mentions God over fifty times. Since it seems as though Mordecai had brought the trouble on the Jews by his unwillingness to honor royalty, the Septuagintal version of Esther affirms that his actions were not based on pride. The Septuagintal version does well to highlight many of the things that readers have always found uncomfortable. They are things the author of Hebrew Esther intended (see an example in Ancient Connections 7.2).[22]

The Septuagintal version also seems to have been motivated by some of the same anxieties as the male royal Persian court, who worries about what will happen to the patriarchal establishment if Vashti gets away with disobeying the king (1:17–18). The Septuagintal version gets rid of this problem by making Esther more "feminine" and less strong, even fainting at one point (cf. Additions to Esth 15:3, 7, 15). By contrast, the Hebrew version presents Esther as strong and with authority.[23]

---

[21] The differences between Hebrew Esther and Septuagintal Esther correspond with the two most important text critical guidelines to determine the more original text. The principle of the *shorter* text acknowledges that later scribes were more likely to add than delete text. The principle of the *more difficult* text recognizes that later scribes were more likely to smooth out grammatical and ideological issues. Both of these guidelines affirm the originality of Hebrew Esther. It is nearly impossible to imagine later scribes removing prayers and references to God. Thank you to Carmen Joy Imes for this observation.

[22] An English translation of Greek (Septuagint) Esther is available in the NRSVue at BibleGateway.com. Greek Esther 14 (quoted in Ancient Connections 7.2) is part of Addition C inserted at the beginning of Greek Esther 5.

[23] See Brittany N. Melton, "Conspicuous Females and an Inconspicuous God: The Distinctive Characterization of Women and God in the *Megilloth*," in *Reading Lamentations Intertextuality*, ed. Heath A. Thomas and Brittany N. Melton (New York: T&T Clark, 2021), 196, 202 [193–203].

ANCIENT CONNECTIONS 7.2: SEPTUAGINTAL VERSION "FIXES" ESTHER

The following is an excerpt from Esther's prayer in the fictionalized Expansion inserted into the Septuagintal version after Mordecai challenges Esther to appeal to the king. Notice the underlined language, which is similar to the confessions of collective sin by Daniel, Ezra, and Nehemiah (cf. Dan 9:5; Ezra 9:6; Neh 1:6). The bold phrases seek to repair Esther's noncovenantal character by making it seem as if her actions are sacrificial and for the greater good.

> She [Esther] prayed to the Lord God of Israel . . . And now we have sinned before you, and you have delivered us into the hands of our enemies. . . . But save us by your hand and help me, who am alone and have no helper but you, O Lord. You have knowledge of all things, and **you know that I hate** the splendor of the lawless and **abhor the bed of the uncircumcised** and of any alien. **You know my necessity**, that I abhor the sign of my proud position. . . . And your servant has not eaten at Haman's table, and I have not honored the king's feast or drunk the wine of libations [offerings]. **Your servant has had no joy since the day that I was brought here** until now, except in you, O Lord God of Abraham. (Additions to Esth 14:3a, 6, 14–16a, 17–18 NRSVue [Addition C in Greek Esther 5], emphasis added)

In sum, the Esther narrative calls for a DIY approach for its message. It is not simply the absence of references to God by the narrator. The protagonists' noncovenantal lifestyles push readers to trust in Yahweh's providential faithfulness to his word even when his people do not deserve it.

Biblical Connections

The four biblical stories of Hebrews in foreign royal courts (Moses, Esther, Daniel, and Nehemiah) after Genesis each echo the story of Joseph in the ancient Egyptian royal court in different ways. Connections between the Joseph and Esther stories are not formal quotations but similar themes, settings, and scenarios (see table 7.2).

Table 7.2: Similarities between the Joseph and Esther Stories‡

Genesis	Esther
Joseph resists doing the will of Mrs. Potiphar "day after day" (39:10).	Mordecai resists submitting to Haman "day after day" (3:4).
[Joseph to his brothers:] "God sent me ahead of you to establish you as a remnant within the land and to keep you alive by a great deliverance" (45:7).	[Mordecai to Esther:] "If you keep silent at this time, relief and deliverance will come to the Jewish people from another place. . . . Who knows, perhaps you have come to your royal position for such a time as this" (4:14).
Pharaoh honors Joseph by royal garments and heralds (41:41–43).	Ahasuerus honors Mordecai by royal garments and heralds (6:8–9).
[Judah to Joseph:] "I could not bear to see the grief that would overwhelm my father" (44:34b).	[Esther to Ahasuerus:] "For how could I bear to see the disaster that would come on my people?" (8:6a)
Joseph elevated as second to Pharaoh (41:41).	Mordecai elevated as second to Ahasuerus (10:3).

‡ Table based on Schnittjer, *Torah Story*, 2nd ed., 158, emphasis added (see intro., n. 10).

The parallels between the Joseph and Esther stories invite readers of the latter to supply what is not there. In Genesis, Joseph and the narrator both explain away coincidence as the providential interventions of God (Gen 39:2–3, 5, 21–23; 45:5–9). At the close of Genesis, Joseph uses words that could serve as the underlying theology that readers need to bring to Esther: "You planned evil against me; *God planned it for good to bring about the present result—the survival of many people*" (50:20, emphasis added). The Esther narrative encourages readers to look past circumstances to detect the providence of God.

Gospel Connections

Many Christians have a difficult time learning that assurance of salvation has little to do with strength of faith and everything to do with the object of faith. Esther pushes further.

The Esther narrative invites readers to evaluate God's faithfulness to his covenantal people even when they hide their identity and do not call upon him. Paul proclaims to the congregants at Rome the basis of assurance as God's power demonstrated in the love of the Messiah. God's chosen ones can depend on him in the face of anyone, anywhere, even at the worst times. "Who is the one who condemns? Christ Jesus is the one who died, but even more, has been raised; he also is at the right hand of God and intercedes for us" (Rom 8:34).

Life Connections

The Esther narrative provides readers an opportunity to interpret their own circumstances when there is no narrator whispering, as there is in Genesis that Yahweh is with his chosen ones even in the worst of circumstances (Gen 39:2–3, 5, 21–23). There is nothing wrong with interpreting life's circumstances while we loudly sing hymns in a worship gathering. But the Esther story invites readers to consider Yahweh's faithfulness at times of unspeakable evil when he seems absent.

Interactive Questions

Why did the author intentionally omit any mention of God?

What factors contribute to evaluating Esther as historical narrative?

What is the problem with drawing a contrast between history and ideology or history and literary art?

Why is it necessary to identify the kind of satire pervasive in the Esther story?

How are the Esther and Daniel stories different from the Joseph story on which they are both modeled?

Why is it important to recognize the similarities and differences between the Joseph and Esther stories?

Why is it important to recognize the noncovenantal lifestyle of Mordecai and Esther?

What about the Esther story bothered ancient interpreters enough for them to "fix" it in the Septuagintal version?

How does Esther help readers interpret difficult circumstances?

Study Resources

Berlin, Adele. *Esther*. JPSBC. Philadelphia: Jewish Publication Society, 2001.

Firth, David G. *The Message of Esther*. Downers Grove, IL: InterVarsity, 2010.

Jobes, Karen H. *Esther*. NIVAC. Grand Rapids: Zondervan, 1999.

Phillips, Elaine. "Esther." EBC, 569–674. Rev. ed. Grand Rapids: Zondervan, 2010.

8

Ezra-Nehemiah

Outline

Rebuilding the temple (Ezra 1–6)
  Sheshbazzar and company return with the temple vessels (1)
  List of returning exiles (2)
  Laying the foundation of the Second Temple (3)
  Negotiating opposition against rebuilding the temple (4)
  Completing the Second Temple (5–6)
Return of the Torah and the need for repentance and purity (7–10)
  Ezra returns (7–8)
  Ezra's prayer for repentance (9)
  Judah repents via mass divorce from apostasy marriages (10)
Rebuilding the walls of Jerusalem (Nehemiah 1–6)
  Nehemiah's prayer of repentance for the walls of Jerusalem (1)
  Nehemiah's return (2)
  Panoramic list of those rebuilding the city walls (3)
  Rebuilding the walls in the face of opposition (4)
  Economic reforms among the returned exiles (5)
  Walls are finished amid sustained opposition (6:1–7:4)

Law and covenant and ongoing need for repentance and mercy (7–13)

Nehemiah considers a census and reviews the old list of returned exiles (akin to Ezra 2) (7:5–73)

Reading Scripture and celebrating tabernacles (8)

Levitical prayer (9)

Solemn oath of restoration assembly (10)

Lists of restoration assembly (11:1–12:26)

Dedication of the walls (12:27–13:3)

Nehemiah enacts a series of reforms in his second term (13:4–31)[1]

Author, Date, and Message

The author of Ezra-Nehemiah is unknown. The nature of the authorship of Ezra-Nehemiah requires detailed discussion.

The present study accepts the view that Ezra-Nehemiah is one book that was broken into two scrolls—Ezra and Nehemiah—much like Samuel, Kings, and Chronicles. Until about the 1970s the dominant view was that the Chronicler (the author of Chronicles) wrote Ezra-Nehemiah. Part of this view is based on the nearly identical versions of the edict of Cyrus, king of Persia, appearing in the last verses of Chronicles and the first verses of Ezra-Nehemiah (2 Chr 36:22–23//Ezra 1:1–4). However, Sara Japhet compiled convincing evidence that demonstrates Ezra-Nehemiah is a separate book by a separate author than Chronicles.[2]

The authorship of Ezra-Nehemiah is unique within the Bible. The vast majority of Ezra-Nehemiah is made up of literary artifacts or sources—edicts, administrative texts, lists, letters, memoirs, and so on.

The author did not so much tell the story as show the story. The author chose to show the story by the historical literary artifacts themselves. Out of 685 verses, one scholar counts 618 verses of literary artifacts and 67 verses of narration, while another counts 599 and 86.[3] The broad point here does not require sorting out these differences. It is enough to note that the author of Ezra-Nehemiah did very little narrating.

---

[1] Outline adapted from Gary Edward Schnittjer, *Ezra-Nehemiah*, BOTCHB (Grand Rapids: Baker Academic, forthcoming).

[2] See Sara Japhet, "The Supposed Common Authorship of Chronicles and Ezra-Nehemiah Investigated Anew," *VT* 18 (1968): 330–71.

[3] See James C. VanderKam, "Ezra-Nehemiah or Ezra and Nehemiah?," in *Priests, Prophets and Scribes: Essays on the Formation and Heritage of Second Temple Judaism in Honour of Joseph Blenkinsopp*, ed. Eugene Ulrich et al., JSOTSup 149 (Sheffield, UK: JSOT Press, 1992), 63–64 [55–75]; Andrew E. Steinmann, *Ezra and Nehemiah*, CC (St. Louis: Concordia, 2010), 64–65.

The author and intended readership were bilingual, switching from Hebrew to Aramaic and back more than once. And, because the author used first-person letters as well as the first-person memoirs of Ezra and the first-person memoirs of Nehemiah, the narrative frequently shifts from third person to first person and back. All these factors are put together in table 8.1, a list of literary artifacts, shifts from first-person to third-person perspective and vice versa, and shifts between Hebrew and Aramaic.

Table 8.1: Editorial Shifts in Ezra-Nehemiah[‡]

Perspective	Historical Literary Artifacts	Language
Ezra 1:1–4, first person 1:5–4:10, third person	Ezra 1:2–4, edict of Cyrus 1:9–11, inventory of temple vessels returned 2:1–3:1a, list of returning exiles with attached segue (538 BCE)	Hebrew (Ezra 1:1–4:7)
4:11–22, first person 5:1–5, third person[a] 5:7b–17, first person 6:1–5, third person 6:6–12, first person 6:13–7:11, third person	4:7–22, letters to and from Artaxerxes regarding sedition via Jerusalem temple building (before 445) 5:6–17, letter to Darius warning of sedition via Jerusalem temple building (520) 6:3–5, edict of Cyrus 6:6–12, letter from Darius authorizing Jerusalem temple construction (520)	Aramaic (4:8–6:18)
	7:1b–5, telescoped genealogy of Ezra	Hebrew (6:19–7:11)
7:12–26, first person	7:12–26, letter from Artaxerxes authorizing Ezra (458)	Aramaic (7:12–26)
7:27–8:34, first person[b]	7:28–8:34; 9:1–15, first-person account of Ezra 8:1–14, list of returning exiles with Ezra (458) 8:18b–20, embedded list of Levites 8:26–27, embedded list of gifts	Hebrew (7:27–Neh 13:31)

Continued

8:35–36, third person		Hebrew (continued)
9:1–15, first person[b]		
10:1–44, third person	10:18–44, list of those who divorced foreign wives	
Neh 1:1a, third person		
1:1b–2:20, first person[c]	Neh 1:1b–2:20; 4:1–7:5; 12:27–43; 13:4–31, first-person account of Nehemiah	
3:1–32, third person	3:1–32, annotated list of persons repairing walls of Jerusalem	
4:1–5:13, first person[c]		
5:14–19, first person[c]		
6:1–7:5, first person[c]	6:6–7, embedded letter from Sanballat to Nehemiah	
7:6–12:26, third person	7:6–8:1a, list of returning exiles with attached segue (538)	
	8:4, 7; 9:4–5a, embedded lists of leaders and Levites participating in Scripture reading and prayer	
	9:5b–37, retrospective prayer	
	10:1–29, 30–39, list and oath	
	11:3–12:26, series of lists: inhabitants of Jerusalem (11:3–19); inhabitants of Judah (11:20–24); idealized list of villages of Judah (11:25–30); cities of Benjamin (11:31–36); priests and Levites who returned with Zerubbabel and Joshua (12:1–9); genealogy from Joshua to Jaddua (12:10–11); first and second generation of returning priests (12:12–21); Levites from the days of Eliashib to Jaddua (12:22–24); gatekeepers (12:25–26)	

12:27–43, first person[c]	12:32b–36, 41–42, embedded lists of participants in celebration of wall
12:44–13:3, third person	
13:4–31, first person[c]	

‡ Table adapted from Schnittjer, *Ezra-Nehemiah*, (forthcoming).

[a] Except Ezra 5:4, which is in first person, though 5:3 is in third person.

[b] First-person accounts of Ezra include Ezra 7:27–8:34; 9:1–15. These passages together are often referred to as *Ezra's memoirs*.

[c] First-person accounts of Nehemiah include Neh 1:1b–2:20; 4:1–7:5; 12:27–43; 13:4–31. These passages together are often referred to as *Nehemiah's memoirs*. Nehemiah's memoirs are all from his first term as governor of Jerusalem in 445 BCE, except 5:14–19; 13:4–31, which are set in his second term in c. 430–426 BCE.

Ezra-Nehemiah may seem bumpy and jumbly compared to the literary graces of Genesis, Ruth, and John. But it would be a mistake to conclude Ezra-Nehemiah is messy and artless. The author brilliantly brings readers face-to-face with the historical artifacts themselves. This is a different kind of art.

Reading Ezra-Nehemiah is not like going to a Broadway show. It is more like getting a backstage tour including the orchestra pit, trap doors, and changing rooms. This requires that readers bring the correct expectations to this story comprised of historical sources.

The literary artifacts themselves go back to the edict of Cyrus in 539 BCE and continue off and on for about 112 years in the main story to c. 430–426 BCE, and then another roughly 100 years to c. 330 in the lists of Nehemiah 11–12. But when were they compiled?

The list of priests in Neh 12:11–12 goes down to Jaddua, who may have been the one known by that name at the time Alexander the Great took over many lands of the ancient Near East. Referring to Darius as the Persian in 12:22 may be to distinguish him as Darius II (423–404 BCE) or III (336–333 BCE) versus Darius I (522–486 BCE). Referring to kings as "the Persian" at all, including Cyrus in Ezra 1:1, seems to suggest a post–Persian Empire setting.[4]

---

[4] As observed by Herbert Edward Ryle, *The Books of Ezra and Nehemiah*, Cambridge Bible for Schools and Colleges (Cambridge: Cambridge University Press, 1893), xxiv.

Ezra-Nehemiah narrates the first century-plus of the (failed) restoration for a readership at the beginning of a new era of the Greek Empire (333–323 BCE) or at the beginning of the Ptolemaic rule over Judah (323–198 BCE). Thus, the main events of the returns of Zerubbabel (a descendant from the Davidic line), and Joshua the high priest (538 BCE), Ezra the priest (458 BCE), and Nehemiah the civil leader and layperson (445 BCE) were between one and two centuries in the past from the perspective of the first readership of Ezra-Nehemiah in its present form. The beginning of a new version of the empire offered an opportunity to look back across the restoration and make much-needed adjustments.

The message of Ezra-Nehemiah has two sides. The story begins with Yahweh faithfully accomplishing what he had promised through Jeremiah (cf. Jer 25:11–12). Yahweh enacts the new exodus from exile as promised in Isaiah 40–55. There is no blood and there are no frogs or gnats like the first exodus. But God's direct interventions appear across the entire narrative, working through the edicts, letters, and administrative decisions of the Persian kings.[5]

The story ends with the bitter failure of the restoration assembly (returned exiles). The restoration fails because the returned exiles are addicted to covenant-breaking. They are exactly like their ancestors who were taken into exile. It is as if they never left.

Interpretive Overview

This interpretive overview will briefly observe the challenging issue of chronology, then consider selected story lines in the four parts of the book (see outline, page 193).

Observing the chronological structure of Ezra-Nehemiah can help readers expect big gaps from one episode to the next. As noted earlier, of the approximately 200-year span of the stories and lists in Ezra-Nehemiah, only a little more than a century is covered in the story from the edict of Cyrus (539 BCE) to Nehemiah's second term as governor of Jerusalem (430–426 BCE). And of these approximately 112 years, the narrative only treats about twenty-three years, leaving gaps of about eighty-nine years (figure 8.1).[6]

---

[5] See Ezra 1:1, 5; 5:2, 5; 6:14; 7:6, 9, 27; 8:31; Neh 2:8; 4:15, 20; 6:12, 16; 9:33; 12:43.

[6] On the dates here, see Gary N. Knoppers, "Periodization in Ancient Israelite Historiography: Three Case Studies," in *Periodisierung und Epochenbewusstsein im Alten Testament und in seinem Umfeld*, ed. Josef Wiesehöfer and Thomas Krüger (Stuttgart: Franz Steiner Verlag, 2012), 133, 134, esp. nn. 40, 41 [121–37]. Knoppers uses the approximate dates 428–426 BCE (133, n. 40) to allow some time for the problems of Neh 13:4–31 to arise after Nehemiah returned to Artaxerxes in 433 BCE, which supposes that the twelve years of 13:6

Figure 8.1: Narrated Events between Gaps in Ezra-Nehemiah‡

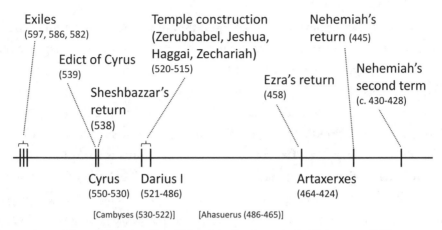

‡ Figure adapted from Schnittjer, *Ezra-Nehemiah*, (forthcoming). All dates are BCE.

Without taking note of the chronology, a reader may miss the gaps. Immediately after narrating the Passover in 515 BCE at the completion of the rebuilding of the temple (Ezra 6:19–22), the story continues, "*After these events,* during the reign of King Artaxerxes of Persia, Ezra . . ." (7:1, emphasis added). But notice the fifty-seven-year gap between Ezra 6:22 and 7:1 (see figure 8.1). Left out is that the generation who rebuilt the temple and the next two generations lived and died in their ancestors' homeland, to which they had returned. That is, there is no direct connection between building the temple in Ezra 1–6 and Ezra's return to Jerusalem nearly sixty years later. The author connected these events from different times by placing them in a continuous narrative. In this way Ezra-Nehemiah shows the work of God and the rebellion of the restoration assembly across the first century and a decade of the Second Temple community.

According to Japhet, the narrative shape of Ezra-Nehemiah revolves around two pairs of principal leaders: Zerubbabel and Joshua in Ezra 1–6 and Ezra and Nehemiah in Ezra 7–Nehemiah 13.[7] This is fine as far as it goes. Yet, the important temporary leadership of several others needs to be acknowledged even though it reduces the

---

refers to his first governorship on location in Jerusalem. Yet elsewhere Knoppers says 430 BCE is the approximate end of the second mission (134, n. 41), which apparently supposes that the twelve years of 13:6 refers to time in the royal court after a shorter first governorship of Jerusalem on location. The language of Neh 13:6 allows for either option.

[7] See Sara Japhet, *From the Rivers of Babylon to the Highlands of Judah: Collected Studies of the Restoration Period* (Winona Lake, IN: Eisenbrauns, 2012), 416–31, esp. 420–22; cf. 245–67; Knoppers, "Periodization," 132–37.

symmetry: Sheshbazzar (Ezra 1:8), Haggai and Zechariah (5:1; 6:14), Shecaniah (10:2), and Eliashib (Neh 3:1; cf. 13:28).

In summary of this point, keeping in mind the chronological situation of the isolated events narrated together in Ezra-Nehemiah as well as key leaders can help make sense of the theological interpretation of the events by the author.

Ezra 1–6 tells of the early returns and the obstacles that made it take many years to rebuild the temple in Jerusalem. Ezra 1:1 begins with Yahweh stirring the spirit of Cyrus. The term "stirred" in verse 1 (NRSVue) likely comes from Isa 45:13, where Yahweh stirred up one to set free exiles and rebuild—Cyrus is named in 45:1.[8] The imagery of divine stirring of a ruler is an ancient conventional way of describing the impetus behind a major building project (see Ancient Connections 8.1). The narrator builds on this convention by connecting it to a deeper cause—namely, the word of Yahweh through the prophet Jeremiah (Ezra 1:1).[9] The connection to the prophetic word, apparently the seventy weeks of Jer 25:11–12 (cf. 29:10), makes the entire story of Ezra-Nehemiah an act of Yahweh's faithfulness to his word.

ANCIENT CONNECTIONS 8.1: GOD STIRRING A RULER'S HEART TO REBUILD

Nebuchadnezzar II, king of Babylon, finished rebuilding two ziggurats (Mesopotamian pyramids) started by his predecessor. The one in Borshippa spoke of Marduk *stirring his heart* to rebuild it. This corresponds in a broad sense to Yahweh the God of Israel *stirring the spirit* of Cyrus, king of Persia, to write an edict to encourage the rebuilding of the temple in Jerusalem (Ezra 1:1//2 Chr 36:22 NRSVue).[a] Nebuchadnezzar said:

> My great lord Marduk *stirred my heart to rebuild it* [E-ur-(me)-imin-anki (House that Controls the Seven *Me*'s [Decrees] of Heaven and Underworld), the ziggurat of Borsippa]. I did not alter its location and I did not move its foundation platform. In a favourable month, on a propitious day, I repaired the brickwork of its sanctum and the baked

---

[8] NIV and other translations add Cyrus, though he is not named in Isa 45:13 (see NET note).

[9] The evidence suggests a direct relationship between Ezra 1:1–3 and 2 Chr 36:22–23. However, the direction of dependence is not clear. See *OTUOT*, 839–41.

brick of its mantle, I re-erected what of it had collapsed and placed my inscriptions in the (places where I had) repaired its ruins. I set my hand to rebuilding it and finishing it (to) the top. I made it anew as it had been of old and finished it (to) the top as in bygone times.[b]

[a] The italicized Akkadian and Hebrew phrases ("stirred the heart/spirit") are related semantically, not linguistically. The Akkadian verb *stir* (*dekû*) is used elsewhere of Marduk, prompting a building project (*CAD* 3:128 [6.c]), and the Akkadian noun *heart* (*libbu*) is often used with the sense of "mind," "intention," or the like (*CAD* 9:169–70). Thank you to Nancy Erickson for help with this Akkadian phrase.

[b] From "Two-column Foundation Cylinders of E-ur-me-imin-anki," in George, "A Stele of Nebuchadnezzar II," 169 [153–69] (see introduction, Ancient Connections I.5).

The edict of Cyrus itself seems to provide the outline that the author used to structure Ezra 1–6. Cyrus called upon the people of Yahweh to "go up" to Jerusalem and to "rebuild" the house of God (1:3 NRSVue). Ezra 1–3 focuses on the initial return to Jerusalem, and 4–6 narrates the building of the Second Temple. The major theme of the entire section is Yahweh's faithfulness to fulfill his word.

The narrator again uses the term "stirred" in 1:5 (NRSVue) to speak of God moving the hearts of the people to return to Jerusalem. The use of "stirred" here likely alludes to Hag 1:14, which says Yahweh stirred up the spirit of Zerubbabel, Joshua, and the people to begin working on the house of God. Thus, the references to Yahweh stirring Cyrus and the returning exiles in Ezra 1:1, 5 connect these actions and show the return from exile as fulfillment of Isa 45:13; Jer 25:11–12; and Hag 1:14.

The long list of returning exiles in Ezra 2 demonstrates the author's concern for literal fulfillment. The people who returned to their ancestors' homeland were descendants of those taken into exile. The list includes genealogical notes to verify family identities and to affirm the priestly prerogative to serve in the rebuilt temple. The oldest returning exiles had been citizens of the Davidic kingdom when they were children. They had seen Solomon's temple before it was destroyed. When they saw the foundations of the Second Temple in 537 BCE they wept loudly (3:12). Readers are not sure of the cause of their weeping—sadness for the destruction of Solomon's temple, dejection at the meagerness of the foundations of the Second Temple, or joy for the rebuilding. This apparently intentional ambiguity helps focus on a range of emotions. In any case, their loud weeping joined the shouts of joy of the younger returning exiles, and the loud noise was "heard far away" (v. 13). This sets up the closing celebration for the rebuilt walls of Jerusalem ninety-two years later in 445 BCE that could be "heard far away" (Neh 12:43).

The initial start in 537 BCE is interrupted by enemies of the Yahwistic Judeans (Ezra 4:4–5), and the returned exiles do not get back to work until the days of the prophets Haggai and Zechariah about twenty years later (5:1). The author seems to lack written sources of this season of trouble. But because it is historical, not fictional, the author could not imaginatively fill in the backstory. So the author borrowed literary artifacts from the future trouble of Jerusalem. Notice the resumptive repetition by repeating "the reign of King Darius of Persia" in Ezra 4:5 and 4:24 (on resumptive repetition, see introduction). In between the author inserts troubles from the days of the Persian kings Xerxes and Artaxerxes (see figure 8.1). The author's dischronological use of previews of later troubles within Ezra 4 creates continuity with the bitter opposition faced by the restoration assembly across all of Ezra-Nehemiah.

The restart and completion of the rebuilding of the temple comes from the recovery of an archival copy of the edict of Cyrus that Darius's scribes found housed in Ecbatana in 520 BCE (6:2; see figure I.12 in introduction). Darius made the search in response to a letter with charges of sedition brought against the returned exiles (5:6–17). Based on the recovered edict of Cyrus, Darius writes a letter giving the empire's financial and political support to finishing the temple in Jerusalem as well as threatening terrible harm to any who interfered (6:6–12). The support of Zerubbabel and Joshua by Darius, Haggai, and Zechariah helped finish the Second Temple by 515 BCE (vv. 14–15).

Ezra's return to Jerusalem from Babylon many decades later in Ezra 7–8 is filled with anxieties about predators attacking the civilian travelers, who were loaded down with many tons of gold, silver, and other valuables. But for all the fear of attacks, nothing happened. Ezra and those who returned with him sought God's favor and gave credit to him for the safe travels (8:21, 31). Anxieties about attacks that never came against the returned captives is a recurring theme in Ezra-Nehemiah.

After Ezra arrived in Jerusalem, the next scene is the sensational mass divorce in Ezra 9–10. It is a collective attempt to get right with God. Much confusion surrounds the reason Israel needed to take such drastic measures.

The dominant view sees Ezra as a bad guy with bad theology who used his position of leadership to do bad things.[10] These interpreters regard Ezra as a hater—racist and sexist—driven by a fanatical commitment to religious separatism. This view sees the mass divorce as grounded in racial and ethnic ideology with no regard for the women and children who were victims of the divorces. These distortions are based in part on basic misunderstandings of 9:1–2. The present approach takes the opposite

---

[10] For references, see *OTUOT*, 655, n. 50. The discussion here is based on 655–64.

minority approach—namely, that the problem facing the restoration assembly is unfaithfulness to God that led to apostasy marriages.

The problem with the dominant view starts with translations like the ESV and NRSVue, which read Ezra 9:1 against the sense of the Hebrew text. They do this by suppressing the preposition of analogy, "like" or "as" (*k-*).[11] The leaders of Jerusalem did *not* tell Ezra that the leaders and the people had married Canaanites. That hardly makes sense because many centuries earlier the nations of Canaan, Ammon, and Moab had lost their identity and assimilated into other cultures. The leaders accuse the priests and the people of marrying people who do detestable things *like* the Canaanites did. Compare the ESV without the preposition and the NIV with it (emphases added).

> [Preposition omitted:] "The people of Israel and the priests and the Levites have not separated themselves from the peoples of the lands with their abominations, *from* the Canaanites, the Hittites, the Perizzites, the Jebusites, the Ammonites, the Moabites, the Egyptians, and the Amorites." (9:1b ESV)

> "The people of Israel, including the priests and the Levites, have not kept themselves separate from the neighboring peoples with their detestable practices, *like* those of the Canaanites, Hittites, Perizzites, Jebusites, Ammonites, Moabites, Egyptians and Amorites." (9:1b NIV)

Notice how the ESV and NRSVue make the problem seem racial. But the issue had nothing at all to do with race, ethnicity, or biological relations. The NIV and CSB are more accurate here by translating the preposition "like" that is in the Hebrew text. The rebellion of the returned exiles is marrying outside the covenant to spouses who practice detestable things against God's covenantal will.[12] The symptom of apostasy marriages points to the underlying problem of not trusting Yahweh.

The dominant set of views regards the phrase in Ezra 9:2, "the holy seed has become mixed with the surrounding peoples" as a racial or ethnic issue. This view reads a modern, racially charged sense onto this phrase. But starting with how Ezra-Nehemiah uses this language offers a different view. Nehemiah 9:2 begins, "*The seed* of Israel" (AT, emphasis added) and continues, "separated themselves from all foreigners, and they stood and confessed their sins" (CSB). The seed of Israel in

---

[11] See GKC §118s.

[12] "Detestable practices" include, for example, eating ritually impure animals (Deut 14:3), blemished sacrifices (17:1), cross-dressing (22:5), giving the wages of a prostitute to the temple (23:18), dishonest measures in commerce (25:16), and secret idolatry (27:15). See "*to'abah*," II.2.c *HALOT* 2:1703b.

Neh 9:2 includes within it others "from the surrounding peoples" who had turned to the Torah of God (Neh 10:28).[13] In Ezra-Nehemiah others from outside the restoration assembly were always welcome to join if they repent and turn to the God of Israel (see Gospel Connections, page 212). Notice the way the returning exiles make room for those who could not demonstrate ancestry from the preexilic Judeans (Ezra 2:59–60).

In sum, the evidence shows that Ezra was not seeking racial or ethnic purity.[14] The crippling problem of the restoration assembly in Ezra 9:1–2 is unfaithfulness to God that leads to apostasy marriages.

Readers need to take care not to think of the narrative in Ezra 9–10 as a model to be followed. Within the Ezra-Nehemiah narrative the mass divorce signals the beginning of the bad ending of the book. Elsewhere in Scripture, Paul and Sosthenes suggest—not command—that people who become Christians may decide not to divorce in order to bring the gospel to their unconverted spouse (1 Cor 7:12–14). Paul and Timothy warn the same congregation against instituting "mismatched" marriages with unbelievers (2 Cor 6:14 NRSVue).

In Ezra-Nehemiah the apostasy marriages and mass divorce should be regarded as symptoms of deeper issues—lack of trust in God and a desire to get right with him. The dramatic mass divorce in Ezra 9–10 is impressive. It shows the collective commitment of a people who desperately wanted to get right with God.

But it did not work. Twelve years later, in 445 BCE, the people stage another mass divorce as part of their preparations to make a solemn oath (Neh 9:2). Nehemiah 13:1–3 presents another account of a mass divorce. The opening phrase "At that time" in 13:1 makes it difficult to know if this is an additional mass divorce or if it refers to either Ezra 9–10 or Neh 9:2. In any case, twelve years after the mass divorce in Neh 9:2, Jerusalem is again overrun with apostasy marriages (13:23–27).

The apostasy marriages went beyond the laity and included the Levites and the priests (Ezra 9:1; 10:18–24; Neh 13:28–29). The first person on the list of those who participated in the mass divorce is the family of Joshua the high priest, who returned with Zerubbabel (Ezra 10:18). This means that arranging for apostasy marriages for one's children began immediately with the first returning exiles. The high priest led

---

[13] Nehemiah 9–10 occurs all on the same day: the twenty-fourth day of the seventh month in 445 BCE (Neh 9:1).

[14] See Life Connections, page 213, for Ezra's prowess as a good scriptural exegete.

the way. In this way the failure of the restoration matches the failure of Israel in the days of the judges and the fall of Solomon from early in his rule (see chapters 2 and 4). Likewise, the rebellion of the restoration assembly goes back to the earliest returning exiles and persists across the generations of the faltering restoration.

Nehemiah 1–6 tells of the return of King Artaxerxes's cupbearer, Nehemiah, to rebuild the walls of Jerusalem in 445 BCE (see figure 8.1). A cupbearer was one of the king's highly trusted courtiers, and the position gave Nehemiah an advantage over other rival provincial governors in the region of Judah (see figure 8.2). Nehemiah never looks better than when readers first meet him. He fasts and prays Scripture-soaked prayers, begging for God's mercy (Neh 1:4–11).

The remarkable feat of bringing together affluent and poor, worship personnel and laity to rebuild the walls of Jerusalem in fifty-two days speaks well of Nehemiah's leadership (6:15). Civilians, standing with a weapon in one hand and tools in the other, who rebuilt the walls are in great danger from the bitter enemies of the restoration assembly (4:15–20). As elsewhere in Ezra-Nehemiah, after all the anxiety nothing happens. But the threat is real (see Ancient Connections 8.2). The leaders and people pray and give credit to God (4:9, 14, 20).

Figure 8.2: Attendant Bringing a Covered Drink‡

Sketch by Gary Edward Schnittjer

‡ Sketch of relief on stairway to Darius the Great's palace in Persepolis (see figure I.12). The attendant wears Median clothing including a long tunic over thick trousers. He carries a dagger and brings a covered goblet into the king's banquet. Carrying a weapon signifies the importance of this role. Cupbearers, like Nehemiah (Neh 1:11; 2:1), were high courtiers trusted by the king (C. U. Wolf, "Cupbearer," *IDB* 1:749).

ANCIENT CONNECTIONS 8.2: DESTRUCTION OF THE TEMPLE OF GOD AT ELEPHANTINE

A competing temple to the God of Israel stood on the island of Elephantine on the Nile in Egypt from sometime before 525 to 410 BCE, when it was destroyed. The locals who destroyed this temple are not part of the threat against Jerusalem in Nehemiah's day. But this shows that the Judeans rebuilding the walls of Jerusalem needed to be on guard against their enemies, who had threatened violence against them. The following letter was sent in 407 from those in the aftermath of the temple of Elephantine's destruction to Bagavahya, the governor of Judah, who served after Nehemiah.

> In the month of Tammuz, year 14 of Darius the king,[a] when Arsames left and went to the king, the priests of Khnub the god who (are) in Elephantine the fortress . . . saying: "The Temple of YHW[b] the God which is in Elephantine the fortress let them remove from there." Afterwards, that Vidranga, the wicked, a letter sent . . . saying: "The Temple which is in Elephantine the fortress let them demolish." Afterwards, Nafaina led the Egyptians with other troops. They came to the fortress of Elephantine with their implements, broke into that Temple, [and] demolished it to the ground. (COS 3.51:126)

[a] Darius II (423–405 BCE).

[b] YWH is a different form of Yahweh, the proper name of Israel's God.

Nestled among the episodes of constructing the wall is the account of social reforms in Nehemiah 5. In spite of Nehemiah's important reforms to help those in financial trouble, the account casts Nehemiah himself in a bad light in at least two ways.

First, Nehemiah confessed his part in making predatory loans to the poorest Judeans, some of whom were driven to sell their children into slavery (5:10; cf. vv. 1–5). Selling daughters into slavery is especially bitter because they could not be bought back (v. 5).[15] It is remarkable that Nehemiah would oppress the neediest Judeans since as a top courtier he is among the most affluent people in Judah, if not

---

[15] See OTUOT, 126.

the empire. Twelve years after Nehemiah reformed his ways and stopped oppressing the poor, he read his journal (in what we call 5:1–13) and reflected on it (in what we call 5:14–19). This reflection reveals the extent of Nehemiah's wealth. He decided not to take a salary but is still able to host lavish dinner parties for 150 or more people every night (cf. vv. 17–18). This forces the question: If Nehemiah was so wealthy, why would he seek more wealth by oppressing the poorest Judeans with predatory loans?

Second, there seem to be two basic times to place the two-part episode in Neh 5:1–6, 7–13, and both make Nehemiah look bad. If Neh 5:1–13 is placed in its chronological sequence, then Nehemiah's predatory loans almost certainly were made while he lived in the Persian castle in Susa. The walls were built in less than two months, and the extreme protracted poverty crisis in 5:1–5 seems like it occurred over a long period. In this scenario, the report of Jerusalem Nehemiah got from Hanani in 1:2 may have been learned while traveling to Judah on Nehemiah's behalf to handle his predatory loans to the poor. If Nehemiah did not make predatory loans until he went to Jerusalem in 445 BCE, then the crisis in 5:1–5 likely occurred sometime later during his first term as governor of Jerusalem but is placed within the wall-building narrative to show that all was not well between the well-to-do and the poor who worked side by side on the wall. That is, while Nehemiah was overseeing the wall building and serving as governor, he was also earning extra income by pressing predatory loans on the neediest Judeans. Either scenario leaves a bad taste in readers' mouths. Though it is easy to see that Nehemiah meant it when he promised to reform his ways in verse 10, it is hard to stomach his self-congratulatory prayer in verse 19.[16]

Readers need to take care to interpret biblical narratives in context. Ezra–Nehemiah narrates the failure of the restoration.[17] This means readers should be wary of holding up the mass divorce in Ezra 9–10 (see earlier) or Nehemiah (5:10, cf. vv. 1–5) as models of how to act.

Nehemiah 7–13 presents a variety of exciting elements but ends badly. Nehemiah 7 portrays Nehemiah reading over the list of initial returning exiles ninety-two years earlier (Ezra 2//Nehemiah 7). The ending of the list in Ezra 2 segues into a Festival of Tabernacles in 537 BCE, just as the same list in Nehemiah 7 ends by segueing

---

[16] For a detailed study of Nehemiah's one-line prayers, see Gary Edward Schnittjer, "The Bad Ending of Ezra-Nehemiah," *BSac* 173 (2016): 49–55 [32–56].

[17] See Schnittjer, 45–46, 56.

into a Tabernacles celebration in 445. In this way the author establishes the striking continuity of the work of God across the restoration.

Nehemiah 8–10 presents eleven days of collective Scripture study, starting before and running through the eight-day Tabernacles celebration after finishing the wall.[18] It was not Ezra's idea or the Levites' or the leaders'. The people initiate and actively listen to Ezra's Torah reading. Of the fourteen uses of "the people" in 8:1–16, nine say "all the people."[19] The renewal in Nehemiah 8–10 places heavy emphasis on collective study, collective confession, and collective commitment that starts with the people themselves.

The people's remarkable collective study of Scripture leads to three concrete outcomes. One, they make personal tabernacles from branches, enacting a kind of living parable during the Tabernacles celebration (Neh 8:16; cf. Lev 23:40). Two, the Levites lead the people in a Scripture-soaked retrospective prayer of confession. Nehemiah 9 is the longest retrospective prayer in the Christian Bible.[20] The high point of the prayer is when the restoration assembly redefines their identity based on their slavery (vassalage) to the empire rather than exile (see Biblical Connections in chapter 4). Three, the restoration assembly makes an unprecedented solemn oath in writing in Nehemiah 10 (see Biblical Connections, page 212).

Rebuilding the walls of Jerusalem in Nehemiah 1–6 and the collective Scripture study and renewal in 8–10 offer much encouragement to readers. But Ezra-Nehemiah does not end with the celebration parade around the new walls of Jerusalem in 12:27–43.

Nehemiah's second term as governor is twelve years after the remarkable solemn oath of the people in Nehemiah 10 (see figure 8.1). His second term is described in Neh 5:14–19 and 13:4–31. It is almost as though Nehemiah used the written solemn oath as a checklist, and he discovered that the restoration assembly had failed to live up to every part of it (table 8.2).

---

[18] See *OTUOT*, 675. Note: Neh 8:1–8 (first day of the seventh month), 8:13 (day 2), 8:18 (days 15–22), 9:3 (day 24).

[19] See Neh 8:1, 3, 5 [3x], 6, 7 [2x], 9 [3x], 11, 12, 16. See *OTUOT*, 668; Tamara Cohn Eskenazi, *In an Age of Prose: A Literary Approach to Ezra-Nehemiah* (Atlanta: Scholars Press, 1988), 97.

[20] For a comparison of Nehemiah 9 and the other retrospective prayers in Scripture, see *OTUOT*, 161.

Table 8.2: Systematic Failure of the Restoration
Assembly to Live Up to the Solemn Oath

Promises	Failures
10:32-33; 39b (support the temple); 10:35-39 (give tithes and firstfruits to support worship personnel)	13:4-9 (archenemy Tobiah quartered in temple area); 13:10-14 (not supporting the Levites)
10:31 (honor Sabbath by not merchandising)	13:15-22 (Sabbath-breaking including merchandising)
10:30 (abstain from apostasy marriages)	13:23-27 (apostasy marriages by the laity); 13:28-29 (apostasy marriage by the house of the high priest)
10:34 (wood contribution)	13:31 (neglect of the wood contribution)

The ending of Ezra-Nehemiah emphasizes the complete failure of the restoration to the same degree that the beginning shows Yahweh's faithfulness to his word. The exclamation point comes with Nehemiah's discovery of the high priest Eliashib's grandson in an apostasy marriage with the daughter of an archenemy of the restoration, Sanballat the Horonite (see Ancient Connections 8.3). Readers remember that Eliashib was the very first one listed in helping to rebuild the wall (Neh 3:1). Now his own family's apostasy marriage closes the story line. It is fitting, but not in a good way.

The first in the list of apostasy marriages in Ezra 10:18 is the family of Joshua the high priest, who co-led the first return to Judah. The last exhibit of apostasy marriages in Neh 13:28 is in the family of Eliashib the high priest. If Ezra-Nehemiah is about leadership, it includes the high priests who lead the way in apostasy marriages.

The narrative ends with Nehemiah alone in Jerusalem trying to stop the people from breaking the covenant (vv. 4–31).[21] Jerusalem is in full rebellion once again. Nehemiah has enemy things thrown out of the temple; he tried to persuade and threatens Sabbath breakers; and he subsequently pummels, tears out the beards of, and chases away those in apostasy marriages. Long gone were collective efforts to get right with God like the mass divorces, corporate Torah reading and prayer,

---

[21] See Schnittjer, "Bad Ending," 41–46, 55–56.

ANCIENT CONNECTIONS 8.3: LETTER TO THE HIGH PRIEST OF JERUSALEM

When a competing temple of God on the island of Elephantine in Egypt was destroyed in 410 BCE, the local Jewish leaders sent a letter that was not answered to the high priest in Jerusalem. The high priest was Johanan, grandson on his father's side of Eliashib the high priest, who helped build the walls of Jerusalem (Neh 3:1), and the son-in-law of Sanballat the Horonite (13:28–29), a mortal enemy of Nehemiah and the people of Judah (2:19; 4:7; 6:1, 5).

> Moreover, before this, at the time that this evil was done to us [destroying the temple at Elephantine], a letter we sent (to) our lord, and to Jehohanan the High Priest and his colleagues the priests who are in Jerusalem, and to Avastana the brother of Anani and the nobles of the Jews. A letter they did not send us. (*COS* 3.51:128)

and the restoration assembly's solemn oath. The exile did not fix Israel. Watching Nehemiah travel solo around Jerusalem makes it seem as though the exile did not change anything.

It is as though exile never happened. God would need to restore Israel another way.

Biblical Connections

The solemn oath of the restoration assembly in Nehemiah 10 is the high point of the restoration assembly's collective attempts to get right with God. It is also one of the most remarkable interpretations of the Torah in the Bible. Two things make it remarkable.[22]

First, the solemn oath is in first person. Absolute prohibitions and admonitions of the Torah typically declare, "You shall not . . ." or "You shall . . ." Similarly, case laws say, "If . . . , you shall/shall not . . ." In the Torah, these are intermixed between *you* singular and *you* plural to emphasize individual and collective responsibility.[23] Case laws can also appear in third person: "If a person . . ." In the Torah, laws are a set of obligations and standards placed on the people. Not so in Nehemiah 10.

---

[22] See *OTUOT*, 676–82.
[23] See Schnittjer, "Say You, Say Ye," *Center for Hebraic Thought* (see chap. 6, n. 18).

No one places the obligations on the restoration assembly. They take legal obligations upon themselves. They said, "*We shall not* give our daughters . . . or take their daughters . . . *We shall not* buy from them on the Sabbath . . . *We shall* forgo in the seventh year . . . *We shall not* neglect the house of our God" (Neh 10:30–39 AT, emphasis added).

Second, and even more remarkable, all of the legal standards the restoration assembly promised not to do or to do are *above* the standards required in Torah.

- It is not only Israel who promises not to arrange apostasy marriages for their sons and daughters with others (v. 30; Exod 34:16; Deut 7:3), but even the outsiders who had just joined them that day (Neh 10:28; cf. 9:2) promise not to seek marriage matches outside the restoration assembly they had just entered.
- They agree not only to abstain from working on the Sabbath (Exod 20:8–11//Deut 5:12–15) but also not to purchase goods on the Sabbath (Neh 10:31).
- They go beyond the onetime half-shekel contribution of ancient Israel to build the tabernacle (Exod 30:11–16) and commit to an annual third-shekel temple contribution or tax (Neh 10:32–33).
- They go beyond having the worship personnel at the temple manage the fuel needed to keep the sacrificial fires perpetually burning (Lev 6:12–13) by committing themselves to a rotation among the laity to provide wood for the altar (Neh 10:34).
- They go further than committing to bring their tithes to the place of worship every third year during pilgrimage festivals (Deut 14:22–29; 26:12) and institute regional locations for the annual collection of firstfruits and tithes by the Levites (Neh 10:35–39).

The solemn oath of the restoration assembly is unprecedented and unique.[24] They promise to go above and beyond mere Torah obedience. It is easy to quickly move to their utter failure at keeping any of these promises upon Nehemiah's return twelve years later (13:4–31; cf. table 8.2). But after observing that this promise ends in failure, it is worth returning to Nehemiah 10 to consider the remarkable commitment of the restoration assembly.

---

[24] Perhaps the willing communal life of the earliest days of the church in Acts come close, though it is not based on a collective oath (cf., e.g., Acts 2:44–47; 4:32–37).

The solemn oath is their own idea. They even write their names on it (10:1–29). Scoffing at their failure is fine but inadequate. The solemn oath invites readers to acknowledge the unusual zeal and commitment of the restoration assembly.

Gospel Connections

Like the Torah and Prophets, Ezra-Nehemiah shows how outsiders who repent are always welcome. The first Passover included instructions for circumcised residing foreigners to participate like any citizen of Israel (Exod 12:48). Likewise the prophets see a place in the temple for foreigners and eunuchs who turn to Yahweh (Isa 56:1–8). Ezekiel goes so far as to nearly erase the distinction between residing foreigners and Israel. He foretells of a time when residing foreigners shall inherit land like anyone else in Israel (Ezek 47:22–23). The Passover celebration after rebuilding the temple in the days of Zerubbabel and Joshua echoes the very first Passover in Egypt by welcoming outsiders to join them. "And they ate, namely, the sons of Israel, the ones who returned from exile, *and all the ones who separated themselves from the ritual obstructions of the nations of the land to them, to seek Yahweh the God of Israel*" (Ezra 6:21 AT, emphasis added).

The restoration assembly of Ezra-Nehemiah came together collectively for mass divorces more than once (Ezra 10; Neh 9:2; 13:1–3). These sensational acts of seeking to get right with God should not eclipse their posture toward others of the peoples of the lands who turned to the God of Israel. Seventy years after rebuilding the temple, the restoration assembly welcomed others who repented and turned to God to join them in a solemn oath.

> The rest of the people, the priests, the Levites, the gatekeepers, the singers, the temple servants, and *all those who have separated themselves from the peoples of the lands to the Torah of God*, their wives, their sons, their daughters, all who know enough to understand, join with their fellows, their nobles, and enter into a curse and an oath to walk in the Torah of God . . . (Neh 10:28–29a AT, emphasis added)

This evidence shows the importance of repentance as the gateway into a new identity with the people of God. The New Testament expands this emphasis. The Messiah called his followers to share the gospel and make disciples among the nations, and this becomes a core part of the Christian identity and mission (Matt 28:19–20). But this does not erase the distinction between Israel and the other peoples.

Throughout Romans Paul wrestles with the identity of Jews and Gentiles. They are the same in terms of sin (Rom 3:9). This naturally led to the dramatic conclusion that they are the same when it comes to grace. "For the Scripture says, Everyone who believes on him will not be put to shame, since there is no distinction between Jew and Greek, because the same Lord of all richly blesses all who call on him. *For everyone who calls on the name of the Lord will be saved*" (10:11–13, emphasis added).

The gospel opens the way for anyone who repents. Repentance leads those who were once outside the covenant into the assembly of God's people.

Life Connections

Ezra was known as an expert Torah scholar by the pagan civil ruler king Artaxerxes (Ezra 7:12, 21). The narrator also takes a high view of Ezra as skilled with the Torah (v. 6). What does it take to be good at Scripture study?

The narrator breaks down Ezra's skill into three sequential steps: commitment, action, and instruction.

> For Ezra *prepared his heart to study* the Torah of Yahweh, *to obey* it, and *to teach* Israel its decrees and judgments (v. 10 AT, emphasis added)

All three steps go together. It starts with a commitment to seek scriptural teaching: "preparing one's heart to study" (AT). But expertise in scriptural study can never be about knowledge itself. Expert study leads to "obeying" (AT) what it says. Study and submission of one's will to obey Scripture come before teaching others. At the same time, handling the Scriptures well needs to go beyond our own selves. Study and obedience should lead to teaching.

If we evaluate our own Scripture skills, do we have all three parts? Do we actively seek to study Scripture? When we study Scripture does it move us to action? As we become equipped, where might God be leading us to teach? How would it look in our own lives to be skilled with Scripture?

Interactive Questions

What is unique about the use of literary artifacts within Ezra-Nehemiah?

What is the purpose of the literary artifacts in Ezra-Nehemiah?

What is the message of Ezra-Nehemiah as it pertains to God? What is the message as it pertains to the restoration assembly?

What are two chronological aspects of Ezra-Nehemiah, and how do they relate to properly interpreting the story?

What is different about the way God intervened in the exodus from Egypt and the way he intervened on behalf of the restoration?

What is the role of the edict of Cyrus in Ezra 1–6?

What are the problems with the ethnic interpretation of the wrongful marriages in Ezra 9:1–2? What biblical evidence supports the apostasy marriage view?

What does Nehemiah's confession in Neh 5:10 say about him positively? Negatively?

What did the people accomplish by eleven days of collective Scripture study in Nehemiah 8?

In what ways does Neh 13:4–31 point to the failure of the restoration?

What are two remarkable features of the solemn oath in Nehemiah 10? Why are they remarkable?

What evidence shows that others were welcome to join the restoration assembly?

What can we learn from Ezra 7:10 about the right way to study Scripture?

Study Resources

Eskenazi, Tamara Cohn. *In an Age of Prose: A Literary Approach to Ezra-Nehemiah.* Atlanta: Scholars Press, 1988.

Harrington, Hannah K. *The Books of Ezra and Nehemiah.* NICOT. Grand Rapids: Eerdmans, 2022.

Schnittjer, Gary Edward. "The Bad Ending of Ezra-Nehemiah." *BSac* 173 (2016): 32–56.

———. *Ezra-Nehemiah.* BOTCHB. Grand Rapids: Baker Academic, forthcoming.

———. "Ezra-Nehemiah." In *Old Testament Use of Old Testament*, 630–92. Grand Rapids: Zondervan Academic, 2021.

Williamson, Hugh G. M. *Ezra, Nehemiah.* WBC. Waco, TX: Word Books, 1985.

9

Chronicles

Outline

Universal origin of ancestry of all Israel as a context for the Davidic kingdom (1 Chronicles 1–9)

David establishes Jerusalem as home of the ark and future home of the temple (10–29)

Solomon builds the temple for the worship of Yahweh (2 Chronicles 1–9)

The temple in the hands of the Davidic kings until its destruction and the captivity of Israel (10–36)[1]

Author, Date, and Message

The author of Chronicles is unknown. In this study the author will be called the Chronicler.[2]

---

[1] Outline adapted from *OTUOT*, 706.

[2] The approach here regards Chronicles and Ezra-Nehemiah as separate books by separate authors. See the second footnote in chapter 8.

Chronicles could have been written in its received form no earlier than the latest descendant of David listed in the line of Zerubbabel. But the difference between 1 Chr 3:21 in the Hebrew and the Septuagint is very difficult. The Hebrew version lists six and the Septuagintal version ten generations from Zerubbabel. If the common scholarly standard of approximately twenty years per generation starts from Zerubbabel's last known appearance in 520 BCE,[3] it leads to c. 400 for the Hebrew version of 3:21 and c. 320 for the Septuagintal version of 3:21. A detailed comparison of the evidence related to this textual difficulty has been presented elsewhere.[4] The evidence suggests the Hebrew is more likely original. Thus, the present study regards Chronicles as written no earlier than c. 400 BCE.

Before moving on, figure 9.1 presents 3:19–24 in a graphic format to show the six generations from Zerubbabel and to illustrate one way to summarize biblical genealogies in study and teaching.[5] Graphic diagrams can help when studying the theologically loaded genealogies in 1 Chronicles 1–9. Please open to 3:19–24 and compare it to figure 9.1 to see some of the challenges that come with reading and studying genealogies.

Figure 9.1: Descendants of Zerubbabel in 1 Chronicles 3:19–24

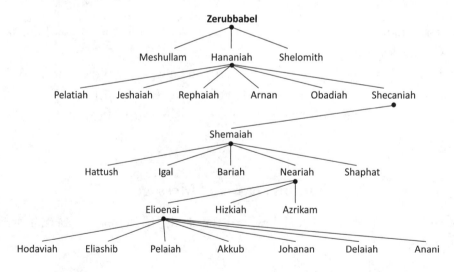

---

[3] See Ezra 5:2; Hag 1:12; 2:2, 21; Zech 4:9.

[4] See *OTUOT*, 840, n. 303.

[5] This genealogy diagramming style is suggested by Bryan Murawski, *Preaching Difficult Texts of the Old Testament* (Peabody, MA: Hendrickson Academic, 2021), 28. For alternate styles, see 20, 26.

The date of Chronicles provides important background to understand its message. After all, the serial story of the Torah that continues through the Deuteronomistic narrative (Genesis to Kings) already goes from the creation of the heavens and earth to the fall of Jerusalem and the exile. Why would the Chronicler need to retell that story?

Since Chronicles dates no earlier than c. 400 BCE, it presupposes the failure of the restoration as narrated in Ezra-Nehemiah and as preached against in Malachi. The discouraged Yahwistic Judeans of the failed restoration badly needed the Chronicler's new version of the old story to upgrade their identity. They needed to understand what it means to join David and Solomon by worshipping in the temple at the very place where Abraham almost sacrificed Isaac and where fire fell from heaven after David repented.

Chronicles uses genealogies beginning with Adam to situate Israel and the Davidic line, as well as the priests and Levites, in relation to humanity as a whole. The genealogies are followed by David, Solomon, and the Davidic kings with a narrow focus on their commitment to worship at the temple in Jerusalem. Chronicles ends with readers situated between the exile and Cyrus's edict that invites a return to Jerusalem to rebuild Yahweh's temple (2 Chr 36:22–23).

The Chronicler shows that throughout the Davidic kingdom times of backsliding often preceded times of renewal. Neglect of the symbols of worship, such as the temple, the ark, Jerusalem, as well as idolatry all point toward a failure to serve Yahweh. The turning points from backslidden rebellion to renewal often begin with worship and service of Yahweh. Figure 9.2 presents the most important times of renewal in Chronicles.

Figure 9.2: Recurring Renewals in Chronicles‡

‡ See 1 Chr 13:1–8; 15:25–16:3; 2 Chronicles 29–31; 33:12–13; 36:22–23. Figure adapted from *OTUOT*, 701.

The message of Chronicles is that Yahweh calls his whole people to worship him in the place he has chosen for the temple in Jerusalem. David shows what it means to worship by repentance and devoting himself to the praise of Yahweh's name. David is a model for worship as God's people await fulfillment of the Davidic promise. The call to worship applies to well-known and to ordinary persons alike, as the long lists of genealogies in the opening chapters demonstrate.

Interpretive Overview

This interpretive overview is not designed to summarize all the details of Chronicles. It introduces the dominant themes of the Chronicler's interpretive agenda, how to interpret synoptic contexts, and major interpretive elements in each of the four sections of the book (see outline, page 215).

Interpreters of all stripes agree on the dominant themes that drive the Chronicler's narrative interpretation (see table 9.1). Each of the themes require brief comment.

Table 9.1: Dominant Themes in Chronicles[‡]

David-Solomon

All Israel

Temple-worship-priests-Levites-Jerusalem

Retribution

Scriptural instruction

[‡] Adapted from *OTUOT*, 703.

These themes are determined based on how Chronicles reuses earlier Scriptures in its own presentation of the story. About half of Chronicles comes from Samuel and Kings, and much of the new material in Chronicles focuses on temple worship.

The centerpiece of Chronicles is a new version of the David and Solomon stories introduced by genealogies and concluded by the Davidic kingdom in Jerusalem. Dramatic differences include omitting David's sin with Bathsheba and omitting Solomon's downfall. Many interpreters exaggerate the supposed idealization of David and Solomon in Chronicles.[6] This misses the point. David sins (1 Chronicles 21), Bathsheba and Tamar are listed (3:5, 9), and Solomon's wisdom and accomplishments are diminished (Chronicles omits almost all of 1 Kgs 3:16–4:34). The Chronicler does not revise David's and Solomon's stories to idealize them but to emphasize their part in establishing worship in Jerusalem. This shifts the focus from private to public aspects of David and Solomon as well as much additional attention to their preparations for and building of the temple. David and Solomon embodied messianic hope by prioritizing all of life as worship of Yahweh.

---

[6] For a study showing that viewing David and Solomon as idealized requires suppressing the biblical evidence, see Sara Japhet, *The Ideology of the Book of Chronicles and Its Place in Biblical Thought* (Winona Lake, IN: Eisenbrauns, 2009), 368–81. Note: the 2009 edition is paginated differently than the 1989 edition.

Chronicles constantly emphasizes all Israel. The phrase "all Israel" is often added. The author of Kings treats both the northern kingdom of Israel and the southern kingdom of Judah. Conversely, the Chronicler only treats the Davidic kings in Jerusalem as ruling over all Israel. When the northern tribes breaks off and form a rival kingdom, the Chronicler treats them like other foreign nations.

Chronicles everywhere focuses on temple worship in Jerusalem, with lots of added attention to the Levites. This is a key to upgrading the identity of the discouraged readership of the failed restoration and calling them to renewal.

The section of Chronicles on the Davidic kingdom (2 Chronicles 10–36) adds much detail to emphasize retribution not included in Kings. Though retribution usually refers to punishing those who deserve judgment, it can also refer to rewarding the righteous. The Chronicler adds righteous acts to show why a king lived long, and he adds negative consequences to reveal what happens to wicked kings. But it is important not to overemphasize this interpretive tendency. The Chronicler treats five kings (one in four, or 25 percent) in a more complex manner as well as introducing dynamic portrayals of many of the kings' relationships to Yahweh (see later discussion). These tendencies do not fit with a simplistic retributive reading.

Lastly, Chronicles includes more allusions to earlier Scriptures than any book of the Christian Bible by a wide margin. Chronicles not only represents large sections of Samuel and Kings in a new way, but the Chronicler also recycles these materials in ways that strengthen Deuteronomistic emphases.[7] In addition, the Chronicler makes heavy use of the Torah and targeted use of the Prophets and Psalms in re-presenting the rise and fall of the Davidic kingdom.

The term *synoptic* means "to see together" and is used to describe two or more biblical texts that narrate the same events from different perspectives.[8] The Chronicler counts on readers knowing the old story in Samuel and Kings well as he surprises them frequently with dramatic variations. Modern interpreters tend to use a modern approach to compare Chronicles to Samuel and Kings when they ask such questions as these: What is the same? What is deleted? What is added? What was rearranged? Why? This modern approach has much merit.

The present chapter is based on an ancient approach to synoptic narratives developed by Aristotle, a Greek near contemporary of the Chronicler, in his *Poetics* (c. 335

---

[7] On the Deuteronomistic narrative (Joshua-Judges-Samuel-Kings), see the introduction.

[8] For a list of synoptic narratives in the Old Testament, see Gary Edward Schnittjer, "Kadesh Infidelities of Deuteronomy 1 and Its Synoptic Implications," *JETS* 63, no. 1 (2020): 96, n. 2 and table 1 [95–120].

BCE).[9] Three of Aristotle's observations regarding synoptic narratives can strengthen interpretation of them (table 9.2).

Table 9.2: Ancient Observations on Synoptic Narrative from Aristotle's *Poetics*

Selectivity. Authors decide what part of the plot to narrate (1456a, 6–9).

Arrangement. Authors decide how to organize the sequence of events including dischronological sequence (e.g., previews and flashbacks), jump cuts, and the like (1459a, 32–34).

Voicing. Authors decide on actions versus embedded speeches versus narrative comments (1460a, 7–8). Aristotle points out that even one different word can shift the implications of the entire context (1458b, 18–21).

Nine whole chapters of genealogies open Chronicles. Nine. Even the form of 1 Chronicles 1–9 itself says something to readers. It does more than emphasize theological themes since that could be accomplished with short genealogies. It is something like a monument.[10] Wealthy persons could set up monuments to memorialize someone beloved, like Jacob did for Rachel (Gen 35:20), or to memorialize themselves like Saul and Absalom did (1 Sam 15:12; 2 Sam 18:18). The massive genealogies memorialize ordinary folk alongside the celebrated preexilic dead. In this way the Chronicler shows his discouraged readership that when they worship at the temple, they join David, Solomon, and the ordinary folk memorialized in the opening of Chronicles.

Every part of the genealogies in 1 Chronicles 1–9 is specially designed to contribute to the leading theological themes of Chronicles. This is true both in broad perspective and up close working with the details.

The first chapter of Chronicles presents an abridged set of genealogies from Genesis that is simultaneously faithful to Genesis and promotes the theological vision of Chronicles. The way Genesis first presents genealogical branches then the main stem is a clue for one strategy used in Chronicles. The main stem of the genealogies of 1 Chronicles 1 connects Adam to the twelve sons of the Hebrew ancestor Israel in 2:1–2, which then anticipates twelve genealogies representing all Israel in 1 Chronicles 2–9. More than anything else the genealogies of Genesis in 1 Chronicles 1 connect

---

[9] The discussion here is abbreviated from Schnittjer, "Kadesh Infidelities," 104. See Aristotle, *Poetics* (see intro., n. 14).

[10] These observations are based on David Janzen, "A Monument and a Name: The Primary Purpose of the Chronicles' Genealogies," *JSOT* 43, no. 1 (2018): 64–66 [45–66].

Adam to David in a mere one chapter and fifteen verses. This places the temple work of David and Solomon within the framework of the human race. Consider the way 1 Chronicles 1 is Genesis-shaped (see figure 9.3).

Figure 9.3: Genesis-Shaped Genealogies of 1 Chronicles 1[‡]

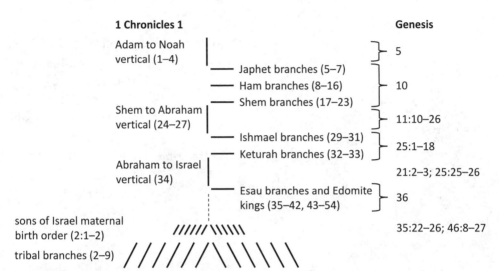

‡ Figure adapted from *OTUOT*, 723.

One way to look at the overall structure of 1 Chronicles 2–9 is geographically (see figure 9.4). Like Genesis, Numbers, and Judges, the Chronicler fronts the tribe of Judah, David's tribe.[11] Why? The purpose of putting David's tribe first (and spending three chapters on Judah's genealogies) owes much to David's commitment to prioritize Levitical worship (1 Chronicles 23–26) as well as to build a temple for Yahweh. The Chronicler then goes south through Simeon and northward through the Transjordan tribes—Reuben, Gad, and the half-tribe of Manasseh. The treatment of the Transjordan tribes ends with their unfaithfulness against God and their exile by Tiglath-pileser III (5:25–26; cf. table I.5). Next is Levi with the priests and Levites. Levi occupies the central place in the genealogies because the Levites were central to the Chronicler's vision of worship in Israel. After the tribes of the former northern kingdom of Israel comes Benjamin. The importance of Judah and Benjamin at the opening and closing of the lists suggests their role as home to all Yahwistic Israel. There are no "ten lost tribes" in Chronicles. When the northern kingdom breaks away

---

[11] See Gen 46:28; Num 2:3; 7:12; Judg 1:1–2; 20:18.

from the one true Davidic kingdom of all Israel, Yahweh seekers from every tribe migrate into the regions of Judah and Benjamin, the new home of all Israel (2 Chr 11:3, 13, 16; 15:9).[12]

Figure 9.4: Geographical Sequence of the Tribal Genealogies in 1 Chronicles 2–9‡

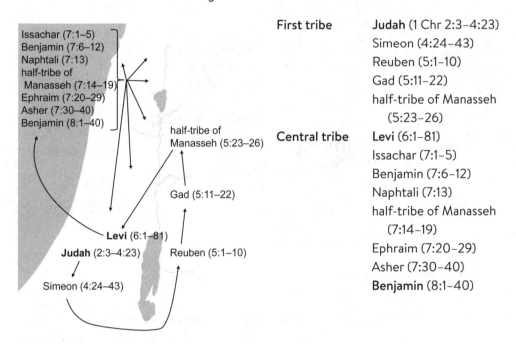

‡ Adapted from *OTUOT*, 707.

The opening of 1 Chronicles 9 looks back to the exile and first return to the land (vv. 1–2). Thus, when the book closes with the edict of Cyrus, readers learn before the story itself begins that there was some kind of response to the edict. Ending with the edict of Cyrus is not primarily to get people to return to the land—they had already returned. Instead, it is to remind the people that the temple is a fulfillment of Yahweh's word through the prophets. Starting with the return helps readers look back at the entire story from a restoration perspective.

The narrative proper of Chronicles begins with the death of Saul (10:1–4). This is necessary because Chronicles treats all the kings of Israel from Saul to Zedekiah. The story of Saul's apostasy and death also provides a setting of covenantal decline

---

[12] See *OTUOT*, 776–77.

against which to present the renewal toward the temple under David and Solomon (see figure 9.2).[13]

The presentation of David and Solomon in 1 Chronicles 11–2 Chronicles 9 differs dramatically from the older version in Samuel and Kings. The present discussion highlights leading examples in which the Chronicler emphasizes worship, the election of David, and the selection of a place for Yahweh's name to dwell as promised in the place legislation of Deuteronomy 12.

In Samuel, David did not begin to get the ark of the covenant (2 Sam 6:1–11) until after he defeated the Philistines (5:17–25). Chronicles reverses this, with David and all Israel getting the ark (1 Chr 13:5–14) before David defeats the Philistines (14:8–17). This rearrangement shows David's prioritization of the ark much in line with the commitment voiced in Ps 132:2–5—a psalm that the Chronicler may have had in mind since he quoted it elsewhere (2 Chr 6:41–42).[14]

The Chronicler inserts a psalm remix into 1 Chr 16:8–36, which deals with the celebration that occurred when David and all Israel brings the ark into Jerusalem (see Life Connections, page 235). Psalms sometimes refers to the ark as God's "strength" (Ps 78:61; 132:8). In any case, notice how the Chronicler replaces the last word of Ps 96:6 in his psalm medley with "place," apparently based on Deut 12:5, 11, 14, which promises Yahweh will one day choose a place for his name to dwell.

> Splendor and majesty are before him; strength and beauty are in his sanctuary. (Ps 96:6)

> Splendor and majesty are before him; **strength** and joy are in his **place**. (1 Chr 16:27, emphasis added)

Saying "strength . . . [is] in his place" is a poetic way to refer to the ark in the temple. The Chronicler's edited psalm in his edited narrative bring together the divine election of a place for worship and the divine election of the Davidic king.

The Chronicler's version of the Davidic promise includes a subtle shift in pronouns from "your" to "my," with major effects for the house of David. It begins when Yahweh takes David's son as his own: "I will be his father, and he will be my son" (2 Sam 7:14a//1 Chr 17:13a). By taking David's son as Yahweh's own son, David's house becomes Yahweh's house. This naturally leads to the change of pronouns (emphasis added).

---

[13] For a detailed treatment of the death of Saul in Chronicles, see *OTUOT*, 728–31.

[14] See Gary N. Knoppers, *I Chronicles 10–29*, AB (New York: Doubleday, 2004), 590–91.

"**Your** house and **your** kingdom will endure forever before me; your throne will be established forever." (2 Sam 7:16 NIV)

I will set him over **my** house and **my** kingdom forever; his throne will be established forever. (1 Chr 17:14 NIV)

In Chronicles, David spells out the implications of Yahweh's adoption of Solomon in terms of a connection between the ancient blessing of Judah in Gen 49:8–12 and Solomon as the ruler of the kingdom of Yahweh over Israel.

Yahweh, the God of Israel, chose me from my entire ancestral house to be king over Israel forever. **For he chose Judah** as a leader, and in the line of Judah my father's family, and from my father's family he was pleased to make me king over all Israel. From among all my sons—for Yahweh has given me many—**he chose my son Solomon to sit upon the throne of the kingdom of Yahweh over Israel.** (1 Chr 28:4–5 AT, emphasis added; cf. 29:23)

The election of David is a natural outcome of ancient expectations set in motion in the days of the Hebrew ancestors. Just as David refers to Judah as "leader" in 1 Chr 28:4, so too in 5:2 the Chronicler says, "Judah was the strongest among his brothers and a **leader** came from him" (AT, emphasis added).

In private to Solomon and in public before all Israel, David shares his interpretation of why Yahweh would not let him build the temple. Ironically, in David's efforts to gain the rest needed to build the temple by defeating his enemies (Deut 12:10), he disqualified himself from being allowed to build a temple for God. As David said, he had "shed so much blood" that his son of peace would need to build the temple (1 Chr 22:8; 28:3). Since it takes a warring king to secure rest and a peaceful king to build a house for Yahweh, building a temple for God necessarily is a multigenerational project.[15]

Based on securing "rest" for Jerusalem, David shifts the responsibilities of the Levites (23:25–26). In the Torah the Levites need to carry the ark and transport the tabernacle in Israel's travels. Establishing a permanent place of rest in Jerusalem means that the Levites are out of a job. David reassigns the Levites to lead Israel in worship (vv. 25–30).

David's reassignment of the Levites appears within the largest block of new materials in Chronicles, not in Samuel or Kings (1 Chronicles 22–28 and most of 29). This massive insertion appears directly after David purchased the threshing floor—the future home of the temple.

---

[15] See Schnittjer, "Your House Is My House," (see intro., n. 3).

When David sinned with the census, he bought the threshing floor of Ornan just above Jerusalem to make a sacrifice of repentance.[16] David's humble sacrifice epitomizes proper worship. Just as fire came out of the holy of holies to consume the sacrifice at the dedication of the tabernacle, so too fire fell from heaven to consume David's sacrifice on the threshing floor (Lev 9:24; 1 Chr 21:26). This sets up the high point in Chronicles when Solomon finishes building the temple.

One of the events the Chronicler uses twice is when the glory fills the temple (2 Chr 5:14; 7:1).[17] This event echoes the glory filling the tabernacle when it is finished in Exod 40:34. In the second version of this event, the Chronicler speaks of fire falling from heaven, just as it did when David made his sacrifice. This triggers a response of worship by all Israel.

> When Solomon finished praying, fire came down from heaven and consumed the burnt offering and the sacrifices, and the glory of Yahweh filled the temple. The priests could not enter the temple of Yahweh because the glory of Yahweh filled the temple of Yahweh. When all Israel saw fire coming down and the glory of Yahweh upon the temple, *they knelt down with their faces toward the ground, and they bowed down and praised Yahweh*, saying, "For he is good and his covenantal loyalty endures forever." (2 Chr 7:1–3 AT, emphasis added)

These two moments when fire falls from heaven at the very same place that Yahweh has chosen for his name to dwell—the threshing floor where the temple was built—show what worship should be. Worship includes humble repentance like David's offering and humble praising of Yahweh like all Israel's submission. In these ways the Chronicler shows his readership how they need to respond in worship at the very same place as David, Solomon, and all Israel.

The revelation of Yahweh to Solomon includes Yahweh's explanation of rightful response to sin that guides the story of the Davidic kingdom in 2 Chronicles 10–36. Yahweh says, "If my people, who are called by my name, *will humble themselves* and pray and seek my face and turn from their wicked ways, then I will hear from heaven, and I will forgive their sin and will heal their land" (7:14 NIV, emphasis added). The key Hebrew verb *will humble themselves* in its reflexive stem connects proper worship in Chronicles with the exilic response according to the Torah: "If then their

---

[16] The Jebusite owner of the threshing floor is called Araunah in 2 Sam 24:16 and Ornan in 1 Chr 21:15.

[17] On cloning events in Chronicles, see *OTUOT*, 712, 891.

uncircumcised heart *humbles itself,* and then they pay for their iniquity, then I will remember my covenant" (Lev 26:41b–42a AT, emphasis added). The Chronicler's presentation of the Davidic kingdom uses this key term *will humble themselves* to show repentant turning points from rebellion toward worship of Yahweh (see later discussion).

Many interpreters have rightly noted that the presentation of individual kings in 2 Chronicles 10–36 emphasizes retribution. The Chronicler goes to great lengths to spell out both obedience that triggers blessing and judgment that follows disobedience. But this should not be pressed too far. As noted earlier, five out of twenty kings were treated in a complex manner that does not easily fit with a simplistic view of mechanical retribution. Close attention is needed to sort through the Chronicler's complex treatments of Rehoboam (2 Chr 12:1–16), Jehoshaphat (18:1–19:3), Ahaziah (22:1–9), Amaziah (25:1–26:2), and Hezekiah (32:24–26, 31).[18] The Chronicler does not take a cookie-cutter approach to the messy details of the rebellious kings of Judah.

Kings presents individual kings in a static manner relative to their standing before God. They are good (did right in the eyes of Yahweh) or evil (did evil in the eyes of Yahweh).[19] Though Chronicles follows Kings in many cases, for other kings the Chronicler works at a more granular level and presents the kings in dynamic ways going from good to evil or vice versa. This dynamic treatment of kings overlaps with but is a broader idea than the complex treatment of five of the kings mentioned in the previous paragraph. Table 9.3 displays the dynamic treatment of the kings of 2 Chronicles 10–36 in a comparative manner.

Chronicles includes three new chapters about Hezekiah not in Kings, highlighting his commitment to renew worship after the long rebellion of Ahaz (2 Chronicles 29–31; see figure 9.2; on Ahaz's rebellion see chapter 4). The centerpiece of Hezekiah's renewal is an invitational Passover ceremony that included remnants of the northern tribes after the northern kingdom of Israel fell (30:1, 10–12; see Ancient Connections 9.1). The entire Passover narrative is built on an extended echo effect of 2 Chr 7:14— to show in practice what it means to obey 2 Chr 7:14 (quoted earlier). Table 9.4 (page 228) is designed as a reading guide to help focus on the worship-shaped presentation of Hezekiah's Passover.

---

[18] See *OTUOT*, 778–80, 785–86, 793–94, 798–801, 816–18.

[19] The only exception in Kings is Solomon, who went from good to bad in 1 Kgs 10:26 (see chapter 4).

Table 9.3: Dynamic Presentation of Selected Kings in Chronicles[‡]

	Evaluation in Chronicles	Static Evaluation in Kings
Rehoboam[a]	Good, then bad (2 Chr 12:1–2)	Bad (1 Kgs 14:22)
Abijam	Judah relied on Yahweh (13:18)	Bad (15:3)
Asa	Good, then bad (16:1–2, 7)	Good (15:11)
Jehoshaphat[a]	Good, then bad (18:1–2; 19:2–3)	Good (22:43)
Jehoram/ Joram	Bad (21:6)	Bad (2 Kgs 8:18)
Ahaziah[a]	Bad (22:4)	Bad (8:27)
Queen Athaliah	Bad (22:3)	N/A
Joash/Jehoash	Good, then bad (24:17–18)	Good (12:2)
Amaziah[a]	Good, then bad (25:14)	Good (14:3)
Azariah/Uzziah	Good, then bad (26:16)	Good (15:3)
Jotham	Good (27:2)	Good (15:34)
Ahaz	Bad (28:1)	Bad (16:2)
Hezekiah[a]	Good, then bad, then good (32:25–26)	Good (18:3)[b]
Manasseh	Bad, then good (33:12–13)	Bad (21:2)
Amon	Bad (33:22)	Bad (21:20)
Josiah	Very good but bad ending (35:22)	Good (22:2)
Jehoahaz	N/A	Bad (23:32)
Jehoiakim	Bad (36:5)	Bad (23:37)
Jehoiachin	Bad (36:9)	Bad (24:9)
Zedekiah	Bad (36:12)	Bad (24:19)

[‡] On evaluations in Chronicles, see *OTUOT*, 716, and citations there.

[a] The Chronicler treats these five kings in a complex manner. See *OTUOT*, 703–4.

[b] The ending of the Hezekiah story, as noted by Isaiah but not by a narrative evaluation (2 Kgs 20:16–18), may be an exception (see chapter 4). Thank you to the blind peer reviewer for this observation.

Table 9.4: Extended Echo Effect of 2 Chr 7:14 in Hezekiah's Passover[‡]

	2 Chr 7:14	Hezekiah's Passover (2 Chronicles 30)
Human worship	Humble themselves	Humble themselves (30:11)
	Pray	Pray (30:18)
	Seek	Seeks (30:19)
	Turn	Returns (30:6, 9)
Yahweh's restoration	Will hear	Hears (30:20)
	Will forgive	Pardons (30:18)
	Will heal	Heals (30:20)

[‡]Table adapted from *OTUOT*, 814. All terms are based on the same Hebrew roots except "seek" and "forgive" or "pardon," which are based on synonyms.

Two elements of Hezekiah's Passover and prayer should not be missed. First, many who participated in the Passover were ritually impure and knowingly violated the standards (30:17–19). This pushes the issue of violating standards of worship far beyond the shift of the Passover date to the second month as sanctioned in the Torah (v. 2; cf. Num 9:6–14). Second, worship based on humble repentance takes priority over ritual pollution as indicated by Yahweh's forgiveness. This advancement of revelation anticipates God's redemptive mercy emphasized in the New Testament.

The Chronicler's presentation of Manasseh folds the entire cycle from rebellion to renewal into a single lifetime—compared to a multigenerational cycle in the cases elsewhere in Chronicles (see figure 9.2). The repentance of Manasseh would be a big surprise to readers. This notoriously wicked ruler had been blamed for the exile for nearly 200 years (Jer 15:4; see 2 Kgs 23:26–27; 24:3–4). This may explain why the Chronicler gives his most extensive citation of his written source including a description of its contents (2 Chr 33:18–19). The lengthy source citation can help sooth sharp readerly reactions from the surprising narrative.

The reader who does not remember the depth of Manasseh's rebellion would do well to reread 2 Kgs 21:1–18, which gives no hint of anything other than spectacular rebellion. The Chronicler selects a different part of the plot that is not treated in the earlier account (see table 9.2). Manasseh is taken into Babylonian captivity in a Zedekiah-like manner (2 Chr 33:11; cf. 2 Kgs 25:7). While imprisoned Manasseh "humbled himself" and offered a 2 Chr 7:14–shaped prayer to Yahweh (2 Chr 33:12). God restored Manasseh to Jerusalem, where he went on to do acts of worship renewal (see figure 9.2).

ANCIENT CONNECTIONS 9.1: PASSOVER LETTER

Elephantine is an island in ancient Egypt with a Jewish population that at one time had their own temple, including when this letter was written in 419 BCE. The letter is reminiscent of the letters of Hezekiah, inviting the remnant tribes of the former northern kingdom of Israel to join Judah in celebrating Passover in Jerusalem (2 Chr 30:1, 10–12).

> [To] my [brethren Yedo]niah and his colleagues the [J]ewish gar[rison], your brother Hanan[iah]. The welfare of my brother may God[a] [seek at all times]. Now, this year, the fifth year of King Darius,[b] word was sent from the king to Arsa[mes saying, *"Authorize a festival of unleavened bread for the* Jew]ish [garrison]." So do you count fou[rteen days of the month of Nisan and] ob[serve *the passover*], and from the 15th to the 21st day of [Nisan observe the festival of unleavened bread].[c] Be (ritually) clean and take heed. [Do n]o work [on the 15th or the 21st day, no]r drink [beer, nor eat] anything [in] which the[re is] leaven [from the 14th at] sundown until the 21st of Nis[an. Br]ing into your closets [anything leavened that you may have on hand] and seal it up between those date[s. *By order of King Darius.*
>
> To] my brethren Yedoniah and the Jewish garrison, your brother Hanani[ah]. (*ANET*, 491, emphasis original).

[a] It is unclear if this plural-looking form should be "God" like Hebrew or "gods" if a pagan scribe composed the letter (*COS* 3:117, n. 7).

[b] Darius II (423–405 BCE).

[c] On the Passover and unleavened bread, see Lev 23:5–8.

Manasseh's remarkable change of heart while in Babylonian captivity models the ideal response for readers of Chronicles. And, more importantly, if even wicked Manasseh, who was blamed for exile, could humble himself and get right with Yahweh, there is hope for anyone.

The Chronicler reshapes the account of Josiah in significant ways, including several substantial expansions.[20] No king presented in Kings devoted himself more fully to Torah and to the effort to bring Judah back to Yahweh's covenant than Josiah, as

---

[20] See *OTUOT*, 822–31, esp. synoptic comparison tables, 823, 829.

the author made explicit (2 Kgs 23:25). The account of Josiah's death in Kings is jarring (v. 29). Chronicles enhances Josiah's already stellar record (2 Chr 34:1–35:19). Except for one thing.

Josiah ignores a message from God through King Necho when the Egyptian king is on his way to a battle in northwest Mesopotamia (35:21). The Chronicler uses extended echo effect (see introduction) to present Josiah's death in an Ahab-like manner. Ahab was a former king of Israel unmatched in wickedness (cf. 1 Kgs 16:30–33). Notice the imagery of Ahab piled onto the Chronicler's story of Josiah's death immediately after he rejects God's word through Necho (bold signifies verbal parallels with the Ahab account and underlining signifies similarities with the Ahab account).

> But Necho sent messengers to him, saying, "What quarrel is there, king of Judah, between you and me? It is not you I am attacking at this time, but the house with which I am at war. God has told me to hurry; so stop opposing God, who is with me, or he will destroy you."
>
> Josiah, however, would not turn away from him, but **disguised himself** [on Ahab cf. 2 Chr 18:29//1 Kgs 22:30] to engage him in battle. He would not listen to what Necho had said at God's command but went to fight him on the plain of Megiddo.
>
> <u>Archers shot King Josiah</u>, and he told his officers, "<u>Take me away</u>; **I am badly** **wounded**." So they took him out of **his chariot**, put him in **his other chariot** and brought him to Jerusalem, where **he died** [on Ahab, cf. 2 Chr 18:33–34//1 Kgs 22:34–35]. (2 Chr 35:21–24a NIV)

The readership of Chronicles familiar with the old version of wicked Ahab and faithful Josiah in Kings would be shocked. The Chronicler needs to emphasize the Ahab-like death of Josiah. This shows that everyone is subject to the judgment of God, even Josiah.

What the Chronicler did with the worst and best kings needs to be compared. No one, including the very worst king Manasseh, is beyond hope. If Manasseh could humble himself and be forgiven, there is hope for all who humble themselves. No one, including the most faithful covenantal reformer Josiah, can oppose the word of God and get away with it. These striking presentations of the worst and best kings should sober readers regarding the importance of humble worship of Yahweh.[21]

Despite God's patience with rebellious Judah, he eventually sends them into exile

---

[21] See *OTUOT*, 830–31.

by the Babylonians (2 Chr 36:17–20). Then the Chronicler interprets Scripture by the Scriptures to explain the basis of Jeremiah's seventy years.

The Chronicler uses the expectation of repayment for missed Sabbath years for the land in Leviticus 26 to calculate what Israel owes. The need to give the land rest is part of the running personification of the land in Leviticus—not nauseating the land with rebellion (Lev 18:25, 28), circumcising the trees in the land to consecrate it (19:23 KJV), and giving the land Sabbath rest (25:2–4).[22] Since Israel never honored the instruction to give the land Sabbath rest every seventh year, Yahweh takes all the Sabbath years at one time. In the Chronicler's approach, this means Israel had been in rebellion for 490 years. If this is then divided by the missed Sabbath years every seven years, this equals seventy years of exile: 490 ÷ 7 = 70. Notice the way the Chronicler interprets these two Scriptures together to explain the exile (emphases added).[23]

> "But I will scatter you among the nations. . . . Then the **land** will make up for **its Sabbath** years during the time it lies **desolate**, while you are in the land of your enemies." (Lev 26:33–34a)

> This whole <u>land</u> will become a <u>desolate</u> ruin, and these nations will serve the king of Babylon for <u>seventy years</u>. (Jer 25:11)

> This happened to fulfill the word of Yahweh through Jeremiah, until the <u>land</u> had made up for **its sabbaths** all the days of its **desolation** it rested until <u>seventy years</u> were fulfilled. (2 Chr 36:21 AT)

Chronicles ends with Yahweh stirring the spirit of Cyrus king of Persia to call the people of Yahweh to return to their ancestors' homeland and rebuild the temple (see Ancient Connections 8.1 in the chapter on Ezra-Nehemiah). The discovery of the Cyrus Cylinder focused on Babylon affirms Cyrus's policy of allowing and encouraging his subjects to renew traditional worship of their ancestors (see Ancient Connections 9.2). The Chronicler famously cut off the edict of Cyrus in midsentence with "let them go up" (v. 23 AT). In this way the Chronicler provides a fitting closing invitation to serve Yahweh and worship him: "Whoever is among you of all his [Yahweh's] people, may Yahweh their God be with them. *Let them go up*" (v. 23b AT, emphasis added).

---

[22] See Schnittjer, *Torah Story*, 2nd ed., 298–99 (see intro., n. 10). For an extension of the idea of land and humans in solidarity in Genesis and Job, see Matthew Lynch, *Portraying Violence in the Hebrew Bible: A Literary and Cultural Study* (Cambridge: Cambridge University Press, 2020), 42–45.

[23] See Gary Edward Schnittjer, "Individual versus Collective Retribution in the Chronicler's Ideology of Exile," *JBTS* 4, no. 1 (2019): 125–26; cf. 127–29 [113–32].

ANCIENT CONNECTIONS 9.2: CYRUS CYLINDER

The Cyrus Cylinder dates from when Persia took over the empire formerly ruled by Babylon. It demonstrates that Cyrus promoted conquered nations' return to their homelands and restoration of their worship centers. It focuses on restoring Babylon and has some parallels with the edict of Cyrus to the people of Judah at the closing of Chronicles.

I, Cyrus, king of the universe, mighty king, king of Babylon, king of Sumer and Akkad, king of the four quarters, son of Cambyses, great king, king of Anshan, grandson of Cyrus, great king, king of Anshan, descendant of Teispes, great king, king of Anshan, eternal seed of kingship, whose reign was loved by Bel and Nabu and whose kingship they wanted to please their hearts—**when I had entered Babylon peacefully, I set up, with acclamation and rejoicing, the seat of lordship in the palace of the ruler. Marduk, the great lord, [. . .] me the great heart, [. . .] of Babylon, daily I cared for his worship.** My numerous troops marched peacefully through Babylon. I did not allow any troublemaker to arise in the whole land of Sumer and Akkad. The city of Babylon and all its cult-centres I maintained in well-being. The inhabitants of Babylon, [who] against the will [of the gods . . .] a yoke unsuitable for them, I allowed them to find rest from their exhaustion, their servitude I relieved. Marduk, the great lord, rejoiced at my [good] deeds. Me, Cyrus, the king, who worships him, and Cambyses, my very own son, as well as all my troops he blessed mercifully. In well-being we [walk] happily before him. [At his] great [command] all the kings, who sit on thrones, from all parts of the world, from the Upper Sea to the Lower Sea, who dwell [in distant regions], all the kings of Amurru, who dwell in tents, brought their heavy tribute to me and kissed my feet in Babylon. From [. . .], Ashur and Susa, Agade, Eshnunna, Zamban, Meturnu and Der as far as the territory of Gutium, the cities on the other side of the Tigris, whose dwelling-places had [of o]ld fallen into ruin—**the gods who dwelt there I returned to their home and let them move into an eternal dwelling. All their people I collected and brought them back to their homes.** (lines 20–32, in *PE*, 71–72, emphasis added)

Biblical Connections

Jesus draws on Chronicles and other biblical texts in at least two of his fictional narrative riddles commonly called *parables*.

Jesus borrows parts of the account of the good Samarians in his riddle of the good Samaritan. Here "Samarians" refers to the people of the capital city of Samaria in the days of the competing Hebrew kingdoms: Israel in the north and Judah in the south. Meanwhile, "Samaritans" refers to the religious sectarians of Messiah's day who rejected the temple of Jerusalem because in the Samaritan version of the Torah, the tenth commandment demands worship of God at Mount Gerizim in the northern hill country of Israel. The people of the kingdom of Judah were often bitter rivals of the Samarians of the northern kingdom of Israel, much like the Jews despised the Samaritans in the days of the Messiah.

After taking a large number of Judeans captive in the days of King Ahaz of Jerusalem (see table I.5 in the introduction), a Samarian prophet convinces the people to release the Judeans. The Samarians submit to the prophet, provide for the captive Judeans, and send them to Jericho. In the Messiah's riddle to the Torah expert, notice how he uses the actions of the good Samarians as a narrative template of the good Samaritan (underlining signifies shared language in the Septuagint and Luke, and bold signifies similar themes).

> Then the men who were designated by name took charge of the captives and provided clothes for their naked ones from the plunder. They clothed them, gave them sandals, food and drink, **dressed their** wounds, and **provided donkeys** for all the feeble. The Israelites brought them to Jericho, the City of Palms, among their brothers. Then they returned to Samaria. (2 Chr 28:15)

> Jesus took up the question and said, "A man was going down from Jerusalem to Jericho and fell into the hands of robbers. They stripped him, beat him up, and fled, leaving him half dead. . . . But a Samaritan on his journey came up to him, and when he saw the man, he had compassion. He went over to him and **bandaged** his wounds, pouring on olive oil and wine. Then he **put him on his own animal**, brought him to an inn, and took care of him." (Luke 10:30, 33–34)

The obedience of the good Samarians puts King Ahaz in a bad light because he sought help from Tiglath-pileser III (see chapter 4). Meanwhile, Jesus uses the riddle of the good Samaritan to urge the Torah scholar to expand his view of neighbors who need to be loved—based on the command to love your neighbor—to include even bitter rivals like the Samaritans.[24]

When Jesus confronts his opponents in the temple courts, he tells the riddle of the wicked vine growers against the leaders mishandling their ministry to Israel, known as a vineyard in various places like Isa 5:1–10. Notice how Jesus loosely follows the Chronicler's condemnation of Judah in his riddle (emphases added).

> Yahweh, the God of their ancestors, *persistently sent word by his messengers again and again,* because he had pity on his people and on his dwelling place. *But they mocked God's messengers, despising his words, and ridiculing his prophets until the wrath of Yahweh was aroused against his people and there was no remedy.* (2 Chr 36:15–16 AT)

> At harvest time he [the vineyard owner] sent a servant to the farmers to collect some of the fruit of the vineyard from them. *But they took him, beat him, and sent him away empty-handed. . . . Then he sent another, and they killed that one. He also sent many others; some they beat, and others they killed.* He still had one to send, a beloved son. Finally he sent him to them. . . . So they seized him, killed him, and threw him out of the vineyard. *What then will the owner of the vineyard do? He will come and kill the farmers and give the vineyard to others.* (Mark 12:2–3, 5–6a, 8–9)[25]

Jesus uses the long history of Israel rejecting Yahweh's messengers, but he adds a new ending. At last the owner of the vineyard sends his son. But they kill him also. There is much irony in the narrator explaining that the religious scholars respond to the riddle by seeking to have Jesus arrested (12:12).

Gospel Connections

One of several places that the Chronicler builds the new version of the story of the Davidic kingdom on deep biblical context is the location of the temple. The Chronicler adds two details about its location that do not appear in the parallel passage in Kings or anywhere else in the Bible.

---

[24] For a more detailed discussion of the good Samarians of 2 Chronicles 28 and the good Samaritan of Luke 10, see *OTUOT*, 807–8. On the command to love your neighbor, see Gary Edward Schnittjer, "Going Vertical with Love Thy Neighbor: Exegetical Use of Scripture in Leviticus 19.18b," *JSOT* 47, no. 1 (2022): 114–42.

[25] Cf. parallels in Matt 21:33–46; Luke 20:9–19.

Solomon began to build the temple of Yahweh in Jerusalem *on Mount Moriah* where Yahweh had appeared to his father David, *at the place designated by David on the threshing floor of Ornan the Jebusite.* (2 Chr 3:1 AT, emphasis added)

In the first layer of context, readers of Chronicles are invited to realize that when they go to the temple to worship, they go to the threshing floor where David repented of his sin with the census (1 Chr 21:24–26). In the deeper context, readers of Chronicles realize the temple is built upon Mount Moriah, the very place Abraham nearly sacrificed his son Isaac (Gen 22:2).

Readers of the New Testament realize that Messiah was crucified a short distance from Mount Moriah at the Skull, Golgotha (Mark 15:22). God provided a ram in the place of Isaac. The Messiah had no substitute. He himself is the substitute for sinners. As Paul said, "He did not even spare his own Son but offered him up for us all" (Rom 8:32).

Life Connections

One of the leading goals of the Chronicler's new version of an old story is to call God's people to worship. Just as the genealogies begin with a universal framework by starting with Adam, so too the call to worship is universal in scope. We can consider how this connects with our lives.

The Chronicler reworks excerpts from three psalms and places them in 1 Chronicles 16 to celebrate David and all Israel bringing the ark into Jerusalem.[26] The psalm medley opens with excerpts of Psalm 105 focused on Yahweh's election of Israel. The Chronicler's remixed psalm celebrates the covenant with Abraham and the land of promise granted to Israel (1 Chr 16:16–18//Ps 105:9–11).

Nothing could seem more focused on Yahweh's election of Israel than this psalm in this setting, as David and the people bring the ark into Jerusalem for the first time. At this very point the Chronicler makes one of his boldest moves by splicing in a universal call to worship from Psalm 96 with its worldwide scope. In this way the Chronicler anticipates Paul's emphasis on Abraham as the father of many nations by faith (Rom 4:16–17). Notice how the international call to worship Yahweh in Psalm 96 connects to the covenantal framework of Israel.[27]

---

[26] See 1 Chr 16:8–22//Ps 105:1–15; 1 Chr 16:23–33//Ps 96:1b–10, 11–13; 1 Chr 16:34–36//Ps 106:1, 47–48.

[27] See *OTUOT*, 739–40.

[From Ps 105] Remember his covenant forever. . . . the covenant he made with Abraham, swore to Isaac, and confirmed to Jacob as a decree, and to Israel as a permanent covenant: "I will give the land of Canaan to you as your inherited portion." . . . [From Ps 96] Recount his spendour <u>among the nations</u>, among all the people his extraordinary deeds. . . . <u>Kin-groups of the peoples, give Yahweh, give Yahweh</u> spendour and vigour. Give Yahweh the splendour due his name, <u>take up an offering and come before him. Bow low</u> to Yahweh in his sacred glory. . . . They should say among the nations, "Yahweh has become king." (1 Chr 16:15a, 16–18 CSB, 24, 28–29, 31b FT, emphases added)

The Chronicler's psalm medley calls all people to worship the God of Israel in three ways that need to characterize our worship. (1) All people are to give Yahweh glory. (2) Everyone is to bring an offering. Too many people miss this second element of worship, but the Chronicler's psalm remix follows the Torah's repeated emphasis of not coming before Yahweh empty-handed (Exod 23:15; 34:20; Deut 16:16–17). (3) Everyone is to bow in submission before Yahweh.

Do these three things characterize our worship—giving Yahweh glory, bringing an offering when we come before him, and humbling ourselves before him?

The Chronicler's new version of an old story of worship has much to offer God's people who live in the hinterlands of the empire awaiting the fulfillment of his promises to David.

Interactive Questions

What evidence suggests the earliest date for the authorship of Chronicles?

How does the failure of the restoration as seen in Ezra-Nehemiah and Malachi help make sense of the purpose of Chronicles?

How do the recurring renewals in Chronicles relate to its message?

What connects the dominant themes in Chronicles?

What evidence suggests the Chronicler was not trying to idealize David and Solomon?

How do Aristotle's observations on synoptic narratives guide responsible interpretation of Chronicles?

What is the significance of comparing 1 Chronicles 1–9 to a memorial?

What is the implication of beginning the genealogies of Chronicles with Adam?

What is the significance of the placement of Judah, Levi, and Benjamin in the sequence of tribes in 1 Chronicles 2–9?

How does 1 Chr 16:27 interpret the significance of the ark coming into Jerusalem (v. 1) in light of earlier Scriptures?

What are the implications of the shift in pronouns in 1 Chr 17:14?

Why and how did the ark coming to rest in Jerusalem change the role of the Levites?

How do the two times fire falls from heaven in Chronicles connect to earlier Scripture, and what is the significance of this connection?

How and why does 2 Chr 7:14 provide a key to interpreting the accounts of the Davidic kings in 2 Chronicles 10–36?

How do the five kings Chronicles treats in a complex manner help readers properly handle the Chronicler's emphasis on retribution?

Compare and contrast with biblical evidence one of the kings that Kings treats in a static manner with the same king treated in a dynamic manner in Chronicles.

What are the implications of the Chronicler's reshaping of Hezekiah's Passover in light of 2 Chr 7:14?

What does a comparison of Manasseh and Josiah in Chronicles teach readers?

What is the significance of Jeremiah's seventy years in 2 Chronicles 36?

How did Jesus use Chronicles for one of his parables?

What is the effect of observing that the threshing floor of Ornan is Mount Moriah?

What are the universal implications of the psalm medley in 1 Chronicles 16?

Study Resources

Endres, John C., William R. Millar, and John Barclay Burns, eds. *Chronicles and Its Synoptic Parallels in Samuel, Kings, and Related Biblical Texts*. Collegeville, MN: Liturgical Press, 1998.

Japhet, Sara. *I & II Chronicles*. Old Testament Library. Louisville: WJK, 1993.

Klein, Ralph W. *1 Chronicles*. Hermeneia. Minneapolis: Fortress, 2006.

———. *2 Chronicles*. Hermeneia. Minneapolis: Fortress, 2012.

Schnittjer, Gary Edward. "Individual versus Collective Retribution in the Chronicler's Ideology of Exile." *JBTS* 4, no. 1 (2019): 113–32.

———. "Chronicles." In *Old Testament Use of Old Testament*, 693–846. Grand Rapids: Zondervan Academic, 2021.

———. "Your House Is My House: Exegetical Intersection within the Davidic Promise." *BSac* (forthcoming).

ACKNOWLEDGMENTS

I express my gratitude to the Lord for the strength and opportunity to write this book. Thank you to Cairn University and the School of Divinity for their generous support. They provided me with a reduced teaching schedule in spring 2022 which helped me to finish this project. Granting me a distinguished professorship beginning in the summer of 2022 has freed up much time to manage this project through the editorial process. I am grateful for their funding critical feedback on the manuscript from an Old Testament scholar. I am also thankful for their sponsoring research assistants and covering the costs of annual academic conferences as well as a book budget. The university president, provost, and dean of the School of Divinity have offered substantial support for scholarship that benefits students.

I offer gratitude to the staff of the library at Cairn University. They frequently secured obscure yet needed research for this project. They are professional, prompt, and cheerful.

I am grateful to several Old Testament scholars who took the time to read and critique draft chapters of this project. Thank you to: Brian Luther for feedback on the chapters on Judges and Samuel; Bryan Murawski for feedback on the chapters on Judges, Samuel, Esther, and Ezra-Nehemiah; Wendy Widder for feedback on the chapter on Daniel; and Matthew Lynch for feedback to the chapters on Ezra-Nehemiah and Chronicles.

Special thanks to Carmen Joy Imes for critical feedback on the entire book amid her full schedule of teaching and research. Carmen pushed back on many matters of interpretation and weak arguments as well as pointing out a large number of stylistic issues. I am especially grateful for her challenges of interpretations that forced me back to the scriptures. Carmen worked through the sidebars, interactive questions, and study resources pointing out problems and missing elements as well as areas that needed improvement. Carmen offered suggestions regarding tables and figures that did not visualize their points as clearly as they should (including Figures I.9, 2.1, 3.1, 4.1, 4.3, 4.5 to which I made substantive changes based on her feedback). All of Carmen's suggestions kept in view the goal of helping student readers. This book is much improved due to Carmen's investment.

I express my gratitude to the substantive issues raised by the blind peer reviewer. Many areas were strengthened by the critiques to the draft manuscript.

Thank you to Katy Davis for alerting me to a sculptural relief in Ashurbanipal's palace, and a related study, that helped clarify the evidence in Ancient Connections 4.2.

I am grateful to Nancy Erickson for her help with several Akkadian translations and investigations of the semantic and syntactical sense of tricky cuneiform phrases.

Thank you to Barbara Arnold for looking up every Bible reference to check for errors. She also made a number of grammatical and interpretive suggestions. Barbara's investment in uncovering errors and problems is a gift to readers.

Thank you to John Goldingay for permission to quote several verses from *The First Testament* and to anglicize the spelling of some proper names.

Thanks to Bill Krewson for providing a high-definition image of the silver tetradrachm featuring Antiochus Epiphanes IV from his collection. Thank you to Kevin McFadden for answering my questions about and helping me with the coin's inscription.

Many thanks go to my fellow editor Mark Strauss for his collaboration in getting this series of textbooks off the ground and for much wise counsel along the way. I have benefited from Mark's feedback, questions, and suggestions on the entire manuscript. Mark especially detected modifications that would help students.

I am grateful to Madison Trammel for thinking through how to approach this series in a way that would benefit students. Madison also helped Mark and me work through several complications. I appreciate the professionalism of those at B&H Academic and their commitment to getting the project right. Thank you to Michael McEwen, Renée Chavez, Marissa Wold, and the team of editors, interior designers, marketers, and others for their investment in making this book work well for students.

I am grateful to my wife, Cheri. I continue to reap the benefits of her putting me through my graduate studies without which this project would have been impossible. Cheri protects time set aside for research. I am especially thankful for her proofreading of this project that identified many issues that no one else saw. For all of this and more, I say thank you.

It is a great pleasure to dedicate this book to Varun and Jess.

INDEX OF TABLES, FIGURES, AND
ANCIENT CONNECTIONS

Tables

Ancient Connections

SUBJECT INDEX

AUTHOR INDEX

SCRIPTURE AND ANCIENT
LITERATURE INDEX

Ancient Sources